The Sugar Season

The Sugar Season

A YEAR IN THE LIFE
OF MAPLE SYRUP—
AND ONE FAMILY'S QUEST
FOR THE SWEETEST HARVEST

Douglas Whynott

DA CAPO PRESS

A Member of the Perseus Books Group

Editorial production by *Marra*thon Production Services.
www.marrathon.net

Book design by Jane Raese
Set in 10-point Linoletter

Library of Congress Cataloging-in-Publication Data
is available for this book.
ISBN 978-0-306-82204-9 (hardcover)
ISBN 978-0-306-82205-6 (e-book)

Published by Da Capo Press
A Member of the Perseus Books Group
www.dacapopress.com

Da Capo Press books are available at special discounts for
bulk purchases in the U.S. by corporations, institutions, and
other organizations. For more information, please contact the
Special Markets Department at the Perseus Books Group,
2300 Chestnut Street, Suite 200, Philadelphia, PA 19103,
or call (800) 810-4145, ext. 5000, or e-mail
special.markets@perseusbooks.com.

10 9 8 7 6 5 4 3 2 1

FOR JAY NEUGEBOREN

CONTENTS

Am I not a sugar maple man, then? Boil down the sweet sap which the spring causes to flow within you. Stop not at syrup—go on to sugar, though you present the world with but a single crystal.

—Henry David Thoreau

It is certain that every farmer having one hundred acres of sugar maple land, in a state of ordinary American improvement (that is, one third covered with judicious reserves of wood and timber, and two thirds cleared for the culture of grass and grain), can make one thousand pounds of sugar with only his necessary farming and kitchen utensils, if his family consists of a man, a woman and a child of ten years, including himself.

—Coxe Turner, 1794, from Helen and Scott Nearing,
The Maple Sugar Book

THE EXTENT OF THE SHOCK
IS EQUIVALENT TO THE RATE
OF THE FLOW

THOUGH IT WAS JANUARY and well ahead of the time when sap normally runs in the maple trees in New Hampshire and Vermont, the weather was warm and the trees were beginning to stir. When I was in Boston during that last week of January in 2012 the temperature was 54°. Students were wearing T-shirts on the Boston Common, and a friend told me that when she had some trees cut in her yard, the sap was running. I knew I had to get over to Bascom's to see if it was running there.

Some meteorologists were saying there had been three Novembers, starting with the one in November, followed by two more in December and January. The fall of 2011 in the northeastern United States had been one of the warmest in in history, and January was the tenth consecutive month with above-normal temperatures. There were surprising temperature readings throughout the North, such as in

Minot, North Dakota, where the temperature got up to 61°
on January 5.

The question, of course, was whether February would be
a fourth November. This seemed possible on February 1,
when a heat wave passed through the Northeast and temperatures got into the sixties. The cause was two opposing
weather fronts, one spinning clockwise to the west and a
Bermuda front off the coast spinning counterclockwise,
working together like paddle wheels to pull up a current of
warm air from the south. The heat brought on a thaw and
awakened maple trees, causing the earliest sap flow that all
the maple syrup producers I talked to had ever experienced.
Those who tapped their trees early enough got their first
maple syrup crop of the 2012 sugar season.

I went to Bascom's Maple Farm on February 1. I drove up
a hill called Sugar House Road, passing by a row of ancient
maple trees that line that road next to a hay field, next to
lines of tubing in the woods and the house that Ken Bascom
built and that Bruce Bascom grew up in. I came to a stop in
the parking lot in front of the sugarhouse. Bascom's was a
quiet place now, and nothing like it would be in a few
weeks—or maybe sooner—when steam would be blasting up
through the roof in a column four feet wide and the scent of
maple would fill the air.

Anyone going to that place experiences the soul-stirring
views. Bascom's stands near the top of a landform called
Mount Kingsbury, in Acworth, New Hampshire. They are
1400 feet above sea level, not all that high up compared to
other mountains, but the perch is quite high relative to the
surrounding landscape. The Connecticut River, four miles to
the west, is 200 feet above sea level, and so from Mount

Kingsbury and where Bascom's stands are views of fifty miles, halfway across Vermont to the Green Mountains, to some of the ski slopes and as far as Mount Greylock in Massachusetts. Someone who worked for Bruce Bascom said that Bruce had never left this mountain, which was both true and untrue. Bruce left it many times, but you could say his heart never left it, and he had set out after college to save this farm and had once said to me, "Why should I go anywhere when I can be here?" He also said, "I have seen a lot of sugarhouses, and I think this one is the best."

Sugarhouses are located in some of the most beautiful places. They sit by groves of maple trees, sugar orchards some people call them or, more commonly, sugarbushes. Maples are among the most magnificent trees on earth, in a plant form long known as the giver of life. We know this ever so truly now, in that trees extract carbon from the air and produce oxygen. I, for one, love to go into the forest and breathe the cool oxygenated air. Maple trees process carbon during photosynthesis, making carbohydrates that they later convert to sugar when the warm weather comes and the sap begins to flow. The wood of the sugar maple, also called rock maple, is extremely hard and produces those striations called bird's eye maple and tiger maple. During the time when the sap runs, the maple tree produces gas internally, which pressurizes the tree and aids in the sap flow—the maple is one of those rare trees that have air inside. And maple trees produce that soft green light in the summer season. Of course they most famously blaze spectacularly in the fall. Sugarhouses are there, by these places, by these trees. Sugarhouses help define those landscapes and the cultures built around them.

In the minds of most people, those who know something about maple syrup and its production, a sugarhouse is a cottage-sized building with a smokestack for a wood fire and a cupola or some other sort of opening for venting steam. The sugarhouse sits alongside a road, maybe an unpaved country road. There is a woodpile outside and maybe buckets hanging on trees nearby. Possibly there is a horse, maybe a draft horse used to pull a wagon and gather maple sap. Snow covers the ground, a fire is burning, and the sugarhouse door is open. There is syrup ready to be sampled.

I have wondered if there is the equivalent of the sugarhouse in any other form of agriculture. Apple orchards have their farm stands, and I know of some orchards where farm stands have grown into stores or where, in the fall, many people come to pick apples. But any other agricultures with the architectures of sugarhouses? Everyone who makes maple syrup has some form of sugarhouse. Bruce Bascom said that within an hour's drive of his place in southwestern New Hampshire there are a thousand sugarhouses. He claims there are 20,000 maple sugarmakers in the United States, so if you subtract those who make syrup on a small scale in their kitchens or in backyards, there may be 15,000 sugarhouses in the United States. And many more in Canada, where much more syrup is made.

The image of the sugarhouse, smokestack, and steam is iconic, but sugarhouses are as varied as the imaginations of their owners. Some are swaybacked and mossy old sheds handed down through the generations. Some are as smartly carpentered as new barns. Others are plumber's dreams of pipes and steam. Some are restaurants and sugarhouses in one, where people go for pancakes and to watch the syrup

being made. Some are small personal museums with collec-
tions of buckets, shoulder yokes, and sugar molds. Bruce told
me of one in Quebec with a piano, a dining room, and chef,
and quarters for workers during the sugar season.

And there is this sugarhouse, the one at Bascom's. Some
people have said this one actually isn't a sugarhouse, that it's
an industrial plant. Bruce always refers to the place as a
sugarhouse. He wouldn't say he was going to be in the office
on any particular day—he would be at the sugarhouse. The
Bascom sugarhouse is 170 feet long and 100 feet wide, and it
is these dimensions, and maybe the buttoned-down look of
the place, that puts doubt in people's minds as to whether
this place is in fact a sugarhouse.

When I stopped in front of Bascom's on February 1, I went
in the main entrance to the building, through the door below
the sign with the large maple leaf. I saw Doris LeVasseur,
who takes calls and, if necessary, speaks over the intercom
that can be heard in this building and the warehouses behind it. Usually her messages are for Bruce. I passed by
Doris and down a hallway with a row of offices for two financial managers, an office manager, an operations manager
and, at the end, the office Bruce Bascom works from. He
wasn't there. His office is cluttered with papers and reports
and many bottles and jugs of maple syrup of diverse origin
as well as samples of maple sugar in powdered form. The
blinds in Bruce's office are always shuttered, with just
enough open so he can look at the parking lot and down the
hill. I went through the door beyond his office, grabbed a
hairnet from a container, and walked into the room, a very
large room where there was a small bottling plant and also
an evaporator, medium in size but souped up in technology.

The evaporator was silent and still, which meant they weren't making syrup on February 1.

There are two floors in the Bascom sugarhouse, and I headed up to the second floor to the store. Bruce claims that from this store more equipment is sold for making maple syrup than from any other retail space in the United States. I have no way of verifying that, but I do know that on weekends and especially as the sugar season approaches, this place is as busy as a toy store before Christmas.

Bruce was standing behind the counter. Though he spends most of his time in the office, Bruce fills in at the store when needed or when he wants to talk and visit with sugarmakers. Bruce's wife, Liz Bascom, was at the register. Bruce had on his usual dress—khaki trousers with frayed cuffs, a worn plaid jacket, and a hat with Bascom Maple Farms on the front. He dressed down in the store and made a point to not show wealth because he didn't want his customers thinking that he made too much money. Bruce wanted to buy a new truck—and could have, would have paid cash for one—but he just couldn't seem to do it. He would say his father never spent money on consumer goods, only on farm improvements, and he could get a lot more miles out of that Toyota sedan he drove, that one with the New Hampshire license plate that read, "Maple." When he was in the store dealing with customers, he usually had an amused expression on his face. Bruce was having a good time there. Sixty-one years old, with a ring of white hair and a bald pate, Bruce reminded me of Ben Franklin. He was an artisan thinker.

I asked him what he thought of this warm weather. "I can't predict the season," he said. "There's no snow so far, but just because the ground is clear doesn't mean we won't get three feet of snow in March." Most people wouldn't want three feet of snow in March, but that wasn't the case for the people in the store—and for Bruce. Snow in March meant a longer sap run.

He said he had been to an agricultural fair in Barre, Vermont, that he talked to others like himself who bought maple syrup in very large quantities.

"Everybody is long," Bruce said. This meant a surplus supply, following the big maple syrup crop of the cold winter and spring of 2011. The 2011 crop had been fifty percent more than in 2010, a winter on the warmer side.

A pressing question for Bruce beyond the weather was how the crop of 2012, yet to come, would play into the price of maple syrup on the bulk market. Maple syrup is sold by the pound on the bulk market, rather than by the gallon (there are eleven pounds to a gallon). Bruce bought millions of pounds every year. For him, a nickel on the price per pound for a million pounds of syrup would mean a $50,000 difference. "Too much syrup could be a disaster," Bruce said. "Too little and the price could move up." Bruce felt strongly that the price should not move up.

From the reception area down below, Doris called Bruce's name over the intercom. There was a call for him, and she said the person's name. "This guy calls me every year," Bruce said. A syrup trader from Quebec. Because he was long, Bruce wasn't interested. "I get calls about Quebec syrup every week," he told the caller. "I've turned away a lot of Quebec syrup."

At the counter I chatted with Walt Lacey, a retired airline pilot who was buying a few metal buckets. Walt had a small sugarbush and sugarhouse on land his grandfather had farmed, near the city of Keene. Walt hung about 200 buckets on his trees and made about fifty gallons of maple syrup per year. He liked doing it the old-fashioned way. "I can't see putting in tubing," he said.

Another call came for Bruce, someone from Connecticut. "So you've been boiling, huh?" he said. Sugarmakers in Connecticut had been boiling since mid-January. I heard that some were having a very good year.

Bruce left to help a customer but told me the tapping crew was working in Ken's Lot, so I went out to see if I could find them there. By late morning the temperature was already into the forties. As I walked up the hill I turned to look at the view into Vermont. The trails on the ski slope at Stratton Mountain had snow on them, but it was man-made snow. Nevertheless, the view was inspiring. People in New Hampshire paid a surcharge on their taxes for views like these—a view tax it was called. A tax upon the eyes, and the spirit. Bruce's view tax must have been a pretty sum.

Ken's Lot is the sugarbush closest to the buildings and the lot named after Bruce's father, Ken Bascom, who ran this farm from the 1950s until he retired.

Ken's Lot ran along the eastern slope of Mount Kingsbury and curved around the northern part of the mountain. To get to the edge of it I walked up the hill and by what they called the "New Building," the warehouse with a giant refrigerated basement that Bruce erected in 2010. I came upon a stand of sixty-year-old maples, tall trees with straight trunks, well spaced apart, each with its own piece of ground and sky above. Tubing lines ran to all the maple trees, which gave the woods an industrial pallor, but they were still beautiful. Walking in these woods always brought me the feeling of peace, and another feeling I can't quite identify but associate with the idea of dignity.

I hadn't walked far when I heard the sound of the work, the tap of a hammer on a spout. I stopped and listened and heard the drill, and looked through the trees and saw one of the workers, one of the tapping crew. I headed that way and saw Gwen Hinman.

Gwen is a sheepshearer who takes time off each year when her work is slow to tap trees at Bascom's. When the sugar season gets underway she checks tubing lines for leaks. Over the last two years I saw Gwen work not only at tapping trees but also in some difficult situations after storms. After a snowstorm with winds, when trees and branches fell upon the tubing, I found her wading through deep snow to repair and refasten broken lines. After a heavy ice storm that caused worse damage and resulted in a week of repair work I followed Gwen as she raced through the woods checking tubing for leaks, and for spouts pulled out of the trees. She worked in a rainstorm that day and had to empty her boots and wring out her socks every once in a while. The first time I saw Gwen in the woods I walked right up to her out of the surprise of seeing a woman there, and I must have startled her. I asked her how long she had been doing this, and she first said, "I don't know." Then, after a moment, "about ten years."

A year ago, in this same lot when it was very cold, I watched Gwen tap trees while standing on two feet of frozen snow. Now there were only traces of snow on the ground. There had been two storms this season, a Nor'easter at the end of October that brought three feet of snow and another brief storm in mid-January. But in this section exposed to the now had all melted. Gwen was walking on leaf on this warming day.

"I see you again," I said. I told her she didn't have to stop working on my account, that I didn't want to prevent her from putting in her thousand taps, the number each member of the crew aimed for each day.

"That's okay," she answered. "I did twelve hundred a couple of days ago. I can miss a few."

She went to another maple tree and drilled a hole. She used a portable hand drill. The drill bits were just over a quarter inch in diameter, and a thin stream of shavings dropped to the ground. She set the drill into her tool belt, pulled out a hammer, pulled a spout from a belly pack, and set it into the hole. She gave it three taps. A woman named Deb Rhoades, who had been tapping for forty years, told me that three taps was just right and four was too many, though she could tell by the sound if the spout was driven correctly. The sound of the spout going in had a flutelike quality, and when a tapping crew worked in close proximity, the woods had a rhythm and ring. One time I had seen a distressed woodpecker come flying across a ravine to see what was going on, perching and watching for a while before flying away, cawing out its disapproval.

After she set the spout Gwen pulled from a fitting a looped eighteen-inch length of tubing, called a dropline, and attached it to the spout. Immediately sap flowed out of the maple and into the tube.

"It's really running," I said.

"Yes, it is," Gwen answered. "And the vacuum pumps haven't even been turned on. There are three thousand gallons in the tank at the sugarhouse now."

She stood casually with the drill in her hand, bit pointing upward, and said she had been working for four days. She was alone here, and three other tappers were on the northern side of Ken's Lot. She said, "It's good ground for tapping, especially compared to last year." The snow had been deep and frozen then. "They put me on level ground the first few days so I could get my legs in shape. I'm in better shape this year anyway because I've been playing hockey and shearing a lot of sheep."

Gwen was tall and slender, with greenish eyes and a splash of freckles on her cheeks. She wore black snow pants and a light jacket, a wool hat, and work boots. She was light on her feet and moved easily and quickly through the woods. Her father, a well-known shearer in New Hampshire and Vermont, had taught her the trade of shearing sheep. He was a schoolteacher; Gwen had attended a private preparatory school and then the University of New Hampshire, but she left after a year to shear sheep, going to New Zealand. When Gwen's father died in 2010 she had inherited his flock of more than a hundred animals. It was a good inheritance, a legacy, but an expensive one at first; during the winter of 2011 Gwen spent $500 a month feeding his flock. She couldn't let any of them go at first. She also inherited his work—"I'm saying yes to everything," she said then.

She liked the outdoors, obviously. For the last five years Gwen had been living in a tent on her mother's property, close enough to find refuge in her mother's house now and then. She was planning to build a house on her own land, and had put together a small sawmill to make the lumber, but the project was delayed with new fortunes. "A lot has been going on," she said when I asked about the house.

I followed her from tree to tree as she drilled holes and drove spouts, and in all of them the sap leapt into the tubing lines. The trees were "shocked," to use one of the scientific terms, by the sunlight and the current of warm air passing through New England. There was a formula to describe this principle, developed by a maple researcher at the University of Vermont, a poetic line that went, "The extent of the shock is equivalent to the rate of the flow." I assumed that meant that the thermodynamic energy of the sun resulted in an equivalent amount of sap flowing in and from the tree. Or, more simply, it seemed that sunlight and sap were intimately related in this realm of life.

Gwen worked her way down the slope at Ken's Lot until she reached a section another worker had already tapped. She then moved northward, over to another section of trees. There was more shade in these woods and more snow. We walked along a road once used for gathering, back when they used horses at Bascom's. We climbed over a sizeable stonewall that followed the uneven and steep slope, a wall almost completely intact after two centuries, from the days when they raised sheep in these hills during the first economic boom in New England and a time when this land was almost completely cleared of trees.

On the north side in the shaded woods we were soon walking entirely on snow that had been in place since October after the big storm. Gwen found a block of tubing and followed the lines. She drilled a hole and set a spout, but this time the sap didn't run out of the tree. The same was true for the next spout, and then another.

"These trees are frozen," she said. From the perspective of a maple syrup producer in New Hampshire on February first, that was probably a good thing.

2

THE PUBLIC STILL THINKS
WE'RE DOING IT IN
THE MYTHIC WAY

I HAD TALKED TO Bruce Bascom for the first time after learning about an insect found in Worcester, Massachusetts, an invasive species called the Asian longhorned beetle (ALB). The ALB had moved from packing crates into trees in the city. It would attack any leafy tree but had a preference for maples, and I had heard that it loved sugar maples. There was a quarantine, and 20,000 trees were destroyed. The alarm was obvious—what would happen if the ALB got into the northern maple regions? How would the maple syrup industry be affected? Or the fall foliage?

We had moved to New Hampshire so my wife could begin a new career as a teacher, and her third-grade class visited a maple sugarhouse every spring. The trips were part of the social studies curriculum, part of an effort to learn about local economic culture. The sugarhouse they visited was on a dairy farm, so they had the opportunity to learn about that too. The kids gathered at picnic tables in the sugarhouse and sampled the new syrup, poured over ice cream. It was a special time of the year for them as well as for the community. My wife and I began to visit other sugarhouses on weekends, and this became a spring ritual for us.

The maple sugaring season, or rather, the sap flow, also meant the end of winter. Anyone who has lived in northern New England knows that the winters are long and sometimes harsh. My wife noticed that red-winged blackbirds arrived on our hill between March 6 and March 9 every year, calling out their *koo-ree* even when there was ice on the pond. At about the same time the sap buckets went up on the trees. Another thing I noticed along the roads was that the sunlight coming through the tubing lines would glisten through the sap inside. This became the earliest sign of spring, this indication that liquid was moving underground and through the trees.

Fortunately the ALB can fly only short distances and so migrates slowly. The quarantine seems to have prevented its movement outside of the zone around Worcester. Not that there isn't concern. When I went to Bascom's for the first time and met Bruce, we talked about the ALB, and Bruce pointed out some identification cards there for the taking. But he talked about much more and at length, and he showed such a passion for the history, lore, and culture of making maple syrup that I wanted to keep listening.

Bruce gave me his short talk on the history of the maple syrup industry in the United States. It peaked around the time of the Civil War, when maple syrup was associated with the abolitionist movement. "No sugar made by slaves," went the slogan. Sugarmakers actually made sugar then, dry or partially wet. For most families in those regions maple sugar was the primary sweetener. After the war, when the tariff on white sugar was reduced, dry maple sugar could no longer compete broadly in the marketplace. Still, at the time of the US centennial in 1876 there were 154 "sugar places" in the town of Acworth, which produced 214,000 pounds of dry maple sugar. In the early 1900s Bruce's grandfather and his brother held "buy days," when they collected dry maple sugar from other farmers and carried it by horse and wagon to the train station on the other side of the Connecticut River in Bellows Falls, Vermont. Gradually the industry went into decline as the prices fell. Some farmers liquidated their sugar orchards, selling their trees to mills that specialized in rock maple wood. A hurricane in 1938 destroyed many remaining maple groves. By the 1960s, when Bruce was a teenager, the industry had fallen to ten percent of what it had been a century before. But in the 1960s plastic tubing began to be used in maple orchards. Some sugarmakers would never use it, would never suck sap out of their trees, but plastic tubing saved the industry, Bruce said, and made possible a new level of pure maple syrup production.

When we talked that first time, standing in the store, Bruce said something he would repeat: "There is more to the maple industry than people realize." I wondered whether he was talking to me because of some deep feelings for the industry—it was easy to see he had them. The month was February 2010, and they had just started tapping trees. On the spur of the moment I asked if I could watch. Bruce said, "Show up and see what happens."

A FEW MONTHS LATER Bruce was inducted into the Maple
Hall of Fame—yes, there is such a thing—at the American
Maple Museum, in Croghan, New York. The ceremony is
held each year in May after the season is over and when the
equipment has been put away, and it was held during a pag-
eant for the Maple Queen of New York—yes, there is such a
young woman—who goes to agricultural fairs around the
state. Bruce's sales manager, Arnold Coombs, introduced him
to the audience. Arnold told of how, when Bruce was in college, his mother pleaded with him not to come back to the
farm and to get a job at a corporation instead. Arnold said,
"If only she could see you now." He said that in his reading
about successful people, they all shared the characteristic of
intense curiosity, and Bruce had that. Arnold said that when
he was in the business of trading syrup on the bulk market,
he and Bruce met every year to work out terms and signed
their contract on a napkin. Arnold talked about the equipment store, said it was the "Walmart of maple equipment
stores," and this brought a few laughs.

I kept returning to Bascom's, following the crew as they
tapped, watching them clean up after storms and as they
checked tubing during the sugar season. I was happy to tag
along—it provided me with a reason to get out into the
woods. I followed the 2010 season, which started off strong
during late February but then suddenly turned warm. I
talked often with Bruce and occasionally went places with
him, mostly to the area of northern Vermont that has the
richest maple culture in the United States.

I soon realized that the equipment store at Bascom's
served the function of a normal sugarhouse, in that people
came and socialized. I saw that Saturdays, when Bruce

worked in the store, was the best time to talk and to meet other sugarmakers.

Customers with large sugarbushes would come to buy barrels or tanks, fittings for tubing or pumps, spouts or containers, or any of the many other esoteric items. Bruce would sometimes greet them jocularly by way of introducing them to me. One Saturday he called out, "Here's someone with a big sugarbush!" That was Dan Crocker of Sidelands Sugarbush in Westminster, Vermont. Crocker was well known for his expertise and his manic energy and for his evaporation system that ran on reclaimed vegetable oil and smelled like a hamburger joint. "My trees are really good," Crocker said. And they were, as I later saw when I went to his well-groomed orchard with Bruce. "Everything goes straight into my sugarhouse. I don't have to do any gathering. My woods are clean." Crocker had 25,000 taps. He and Bruce talked about "syrup fever," an affliction that caused people to invest large sums in their operations. It was a deadly disease, they said. You needed to have a good job in order to support it.

"Hey, you should meet this guy!" Bruce said on another day. "His parents have a trailer they take to the fairs where they make maple cotton candy!" Then a shy, bearded sugarmaker told me with pride that his father and mother had started the business by erecting a sugarhouse on a trailer, from which they sold maple products—syrup, maple candy, ice cream, and that special fair food, cotton candy.

Late one morning on another Saturday a man arrived from New Jersey, driving a Toyota Prius, happy with his gas mileage and cranked up from his five-hour drive. He lived in the central part of the state near Princeton, he said, and had planted his maple trees in rows like an apple orchard.

"They'll be ready to tap in forty years," Bruce said. "You'll be dead by then." He told him the trees should be sixty feet apart and the rows should be staggered. The man hadn't done that, but he was going to feed and irrigate the trees and expected they would yield before forty years. He had bought some "super-sweet" clones from a company in New York, trees that promised to produce sap with a sugar content of up to eight percent. He sugared with 120 taps and made about thirty gallons of syrup. "My season starts in January and I'm done by March," he said. His thirty gallons weren't enough to supply his farm store so he drove to Bascom's to buy a set of five five-gallon containers at a price of $990. Out of this man's earshot Bruce said, "He'll hardly make a profit, driving all the way up here." But the man thought he would—"I sell it for seven dollars a half-pint, twenty-eight dollars a quart. That's a hundred and twenty-eight dollars a gallon." He stood to triple his money, far more than enough to pay for his gas. Off he went, enthusiastic maple farmer, back in New Jersey by late afternoon.

A couple came in from Farmington, Maine, after a four-hour drive, to buy an evaporating pan. They had made some syrup on their kitchen stove the year before. Now they were going to increase to fifty taps, string some tubing, and boil nights after work using their new three-foot-by-four-foot pan. Bruce talked them through the whole process, showing them what tubing to buy and what fittings to use and explaining drop lines and how they work. He showed them how to use a hydrometer to measure sugar content. He estimated their production possibilities—fifty taps at one quart of syrup per tap could amount to twelve and a half gallons. "That's more than we can use," the man said. Bruce followed with a story—he knew a couple who made syrup for their family, but after the kids grew up they had too much on their hands. "So they sold it to me," Bruce said. He spent an hour with them— if this was the Walmart of maple equipment stores, then this couple was getting the attention of Mr. Walton himself. Bruce even carried the evaporating pan to their car.

Another time I met Bruce as he was coming out of the store with a scrap of paper in his hand. He was on the way to the warehouse to find a sap intake valve for a customer in Pennsylvania. That customer was an Amishman, Bruce said, not able to have a telephone, so he had gone to his neighbor's to call him. As we walked to the warehouse he told me tubing sales were brisk. "Half the tubing sales are made in February. People in this business forget there are twelve months in the year and that you can plan ahead. The average person who comes into this store . . . actually they are not the average kind of person. They tend to be self-employed. Someone who has four thousand taps and wants to have a small business. Someone who wants a little pain in his life."

At the doorway Bruce came upon a man who may have been in that category. He had some coils of tubing in the back of his car. He was young, blond, goateed. "Do you work here?" he asked Bruce. "Yes, I work here. They even give me a hat for this." The young man said he paid for 500 feet of tubing but only received 400. Bruce leaned into the car, read the labels, and saw that one roll had 300 feet, another 200. "My bad," the customer said. Bruce went into the warehouse with his paper, but I stayed and talked for a few minutes. He was from Randolph, Vermont. He and his father owned a sugarbush with a few hundred taps. They were using buckets but would now switch to tubing. They had been making a few gallons a year but were hoping for much more.

On another Saturday I heard Bruce say to an older retired man in the doorway, "Do you want me to look at your rig?" They went to the warehouse, the part where used equipment was stored, most of it taken in on trade. Some of the evaporators were relics, such as the old gargantuan King Company model, with dollar signs on the firebox doors—the idea was that when the fire got hot enough the dollar signs glowed, which meant you were making money. This customer, from Westmoreland, a town a few miles south on the Connecticut River, had brought in a worn-out evaporator with a firebox made of a steel barrel. He had been using it for forty years. An evaporator pan fit on top of the barrel, and on the pan was a metal box with a spout for preheating sap. The barrel was rusted through. Bruce helped lift the evaporator from the man's truck, and they wheeled it into the warehouse on a dolly. A process of bargaining began. The old unit would leak, Bruce said. To me he remarked, "I told him I'd give him fifty bucks for the pan but more if he brought the whole unit in."

The old man said, "Saves me from having to take it to the dump."

I said to him, "That's not a good bargaining position."

Bruce looked it over, thought about it some more, and said, "A hundred and twenty bucks. If I can get a hundred and thirty for it I'll break even." The man looked surprised and said, "Okay."

In the store the old man told me he sugared to make about fifteen gallons of syrup and gave it away. His wife told him he was working for nothing, but he figured that the gifts were a form of money. Now he put his $120 toward a brand-new evaporator, a "Half-Pint," made by Leader Evaporator. Their beginning model, it would handle fifty taps and boil four gallons of sap per hour. Because it retailed for about $1000 and Bruce was a major shareholder in Leader, with a premium discount, both sides were pleased with this deal.

Finally, one Saturday near the end of 2010 I was in the store and looking at a large painting, something Bruce picked up at an auction. It was a scene of sugaring from a century or maybe a half-century ago: a grove of mature maples, a mountain in the background, wooden buckets on the tree, a team of oxen pulling a sled, someone pouring sap into a gathering tank, someone else carrying buckets with a shoulder yoke.

"The public out there still thinks we're doing it in the mythic way with oxen and buckets," Bruce said. "We can't put a picture of tubing and vacuum on that jug of syrup." It was true. Not many people knew about tubing and vacuum, reverse-osmosis machines, or steam-powered evaporators of the kind Bascom's used. Or about the scale on which Bruce was operating.

Bruce mentioned a company that I will call Gold Coast, a hip grocery chain that makes a practice of not revealing the source of their supply, all of which has the Gold Coast label.

"The order came through," he said.

I knew that the Gold Coast order was a big deal for Bascom's. Bruce said the bottling crew was working on this Saturday, filling the initial order in preparation for shipment. He asked if I wanted to see the work.

We went to the bottom floor near the evaporator, where five men wearing hairnets and white coats were at their stations. Plastic jugs wobbled along conveyors and were filled with hot and filtered syrup. Further down the line a machine spun plastic caps on the jugs. The jugs spun through a machine that attached labels, then the final march to cardboard boxes. One worker placed the jugs on the line, others monitored the filling and labeling, and another placed the jugs in boxes. We watched this hum that smelled of syrup and money. Bruce smiled and said, "They want to work today because they're being paid overtime." David Bascom, Bruce's cousin and the operations manager, joined us. David was pleased with the progress of the work. This initial order was for six trailer truckloads of syrup, and it looked like they would have them on the road ahead of schedule.

The order was actually for a single quart of syrup that would sit among other quarts of maple syrup, all with Gold Coast labels, in stores nationwide. In order to completely stock that shelf in all the Gold Coast stores and to have enough replacement stock to last a couple of weeks, Bascom's had to ship almost 70,000 quarts.

Bruce explained the numbers:

11,520 quarts per trailer load
69,520 quarts for the initial order of six trailer loads
5,760 quarts per week to resupply

Because of the other competition for attention on that rack of maple syrup in the Gold Coast stores, the label on the jug had to be appealing. This label was just that—gentle waves of color, browns and reds, a motif suggesting the forest but with an artful design, like something from the scissors of Matisse, sure to appeal to the hip Gold Coast shopper.

There was one very important word on that label that meant some heavy lifting for Bruce. One line of the label read "Vermont Maple Syrup," the state synonymous with maple syrup in the minds of many. Vermont produced forty percent of the maple syrup crop in the United States. Bruce needed to find enough Vermont maple syrup to fill those tens of thousands of jugs. He had some on hand already, but he was working the phone lines to find more.

The Gold Coast order was the achievement of Arnold Coombs, Bruce's sales manager, and it came through at just the right time. The order would help pay for the new building, and the new building was all about orders like the one from Gold Coast.

3

EARLIEST BOIL EVER

THE AMOUNT OF MAPLE SYRUP produced at Bascom's is less than three percent of what they sell, but it is still a substantial amount. They made 23,900 gallons in 2010, more than a fourth of the maple syrup crop for the state of New Hampshire.

Bruce's cousin Kevin Bascom "ran the woods" and did all the boiling. Kevin hadn't grown up at the farm in Acworth as Bruce had. Instead, he grew up in Nottingham, near the University of New Hampshire (UNH), where his father, Rodney Bascom, taught forestry and mechanics at the farm school. His family spent a few weeks every summer in Acworth, camping out near the farm that Rodney owned and where they cut about forty cords of firewood for the tenants there. Kevin came from a large family. His father and mother, Frances, bore nine children of their own and adopted a girl. In addition they took in forty-five foster children, mostly on a long-term basis. Their house was affectionately referred to as "the place of constantly slamming screen doors." When Rodney died in 2010 more than 200 people attended his funeral, where his brother Reverend Eric Bascom spoke, and

Kevin's son met children of Rodney and Frances that he didn't even know existed.

After attending the farm school at UNH, Kevin moved to Acworth in 1979 and began working for Bruce's father, Ken Bascom. David Bascom, Kevin's older brother, moved there a few years later after running a logging business. For a time Kevin, David, and Bruce were the primary workforce on the farm. They worked in the fields and cut wood. Kevin helped Ken improve the evaporation system and integrate reverse-osmosis machines. As the business grew, David moved indoors to manage operations, but Kevin continued to work in the farming operation and run the woods.

Over the years Kevin and, lately, his son Greg had been expanding and improving the tubing systems as well as the vacuum technology that went along with them. Periodically they replaced old tubing with new and rearranged the configurations for a better flow. Kevin set up the tubing systems according to the feel of the land, following the sags to take advantage of gravity.

Now in 2012 Bascom's managed sixteen sugaring lots. Bascom's owned the majority, and some were leased. Bruce paid 75 cents a tap for the leased lots, and for a landowner, over the course of, say, 4000 taps, this could add up enough to accept the sight of tubing lines in the woods. Bascom's also bought sap from some producers; Bruce's friends Peter and Deb Rhoades were one of that group. The lots covered about 800 acres and comprised a vast patchwork spreading out from Mount Kingsbury, with a few satellite lots. In all, factoring in those who sold sap to Bascom's, there were 68,573 taps feeding into the sugarhouse in 2012.

As for the total length of tubing on those 800 acres, Kevin calculated by multiplying the average length of tubing per tap, 30 feet including the mainlines, by the total tap count. This put the total tubing length at 1,755,450 feet. That amounted to 332 miles, equivalent to the distance from Acworth to Philadelphia.

When I mentioned that figure to Gwen Hinman she said, "And we have to walk that three or four times a year." It was all the more mind-boggling and weirdly impressive when you considered that all of that tubing, those 1.75 million feet, were designed to be airtight and under a vacuum pressure far lower than that of the air outside.

Regarding the strength of the vacuum pressure, Kevin told me about steel tanks that had been left empty for too long and collapsed like beer cans. Timothy Prescott, director of the Proctor Maple Research Center at the University of Vermont and an expert on vacuum, told me that contemporary vacuum systems could pull water out of the ground through the trees' roots, like a sucking straw. He also qualified that statement by adding that vacuum pressure did not harm the tree. Another scientist and former director of the Proctor Center, Mel Tyree, a specialist in sap hydraulics, agreed. He told me that a tree generates negative pressures of its own far greater than those that vacuum pumps apply. He told me that the tree's ability to transport liquids under negative pressures is a wonder of nature.

ON JANUARY 26, when the temperature ranged from 25° in the morning and got up to 45° in the afternoon, Kevin noted on his production chart that the sap "ran a little." For Kevin, "ran a little" was a relative term. In 2010 they dumped 500 gallons on the ground after a little run in February. Kevin liked to have at least 17,000 gallons on hand before he fired up his evaporator. That would yield about 300 to 400 gallons of syrup, depending on the sugar content of the sap.

Kevin didn't want the tapping crew to begin too soon because he didn't want the tap holes to dry out, for the wood to seal in the drilled holes. But his son Greg, who left a construction job each sugar season to come to work at Bascom's for his father, said they needed to begin because they had a short crew and would never finish otherwise. They started on January 23 and three days later finished the Pond Lot, putting in 6,022 taps. On January 30 they finished Hall's Lot, raising the count to 11,425.

The trees didn't freeze on the night of February 1, after the temperature got up to 48° in the afternoon. When Kevin checked the temperature early the next morning it was at 33°. The crew finished tapping Ken's Lot that day, putting the count at 13,907. They moved to Glenn's Lot, a section on the south side of Mount Kingsbury, and finished tapping there by February 3, bringing the total tap count to 17,105. They were one-fourth done.

Kevin didn't think there was a need to hurry because he was more than two weeks ahead of the earliest date he had ever boiled. But during those two days, on February 1 and 2, when warm air flowed up from the south, the trees awakened, and there was a major sap flow from Connecticut well into Quebec. At Bascom's they gathered 10,000 gallons of sap.

And so Kevin made his first boil of 2012 on February 3. From those 10,000 gallons, which had an average sugar

content of 1.7 percent, he made 166 gallons of syrup. Many
other sugarmakers over the region also boiled on February 3.

For many sugarmakers, using a wood-fired evaporator
and not in possession of reverse-osmosis machines that
concentrated sap, 166 gallons would have been a good year.
They would have boiled those 10,000 gallons over many
winter days and nights. But 166 gallons at Bascom's was, to
use a familiar term, a drop in the bucket.

I could hear Bruce's words, saying that 166 gallons, at a
wholesale price of $35 a gallon, were worth a total of $5,810,
which was not so bad for a day's effort at the evaporator.
Though, actually, the production on February 3 was not a full
day's effort. Kevin would have produced those 166 gallons in
less than one hour.

4

STRAIGHT AT IT

AND ALL OUT

PETER RHOADES, a forester and Bruce's closest friend, who had gathered sap with him as a boy, been his college roommate, and put together timber plans for him over the years, said that Bruce built the new building "so he could compete." Peter knew about all the past constructions and additions at Bascom's, how Bruce had added on to the sugarhouse six or seven times and then had torn everything down and started over. Peter said, "It hasn't worked out well for Bruce to go slowly and wait. It's been best for him to go straight at it and all out."

Of course Bruce had already been competing. Bruce operated in what was deemed the "second tier" of maple companies, composed primarily of single-owner proprietor businesses. Bruce's primary competitor in the second tier was David Marvin of Butternut Mountain Farms in Morrisville, Vermont. They ran neck and neck, or hand in hand, depending on the situation. Others in the second tier were McClure's Maple (which was bought by Dutch Gold when David McClure retired), Anderson's in Cumberland, Wisconsin, and

Highland Sugarworks in Barre, Vermont. There were also a few Canadian companies in the second tier, such as Bolduc's Maple, Bernard & Sons, and others in the maple-rich region of Beauce County, Quebec.

Arnold Coombs had a description for the type of individual who owned these companies and played in the field of the second tier. He was a person who could manage risk, and also someone who could manage a large number of relationships. In Arnold's words, "He's the type of person who can borrow ten million dollars and put his house on the line." Arnold said that person also needed a wife who could stomach those risks.

But Bruce did not put up the new building to compete in the second tier. He was aiming for the first tier. For him that meant Maple Grove, the largest maple syrup distributor in the United States. Maple Grove is based in St. Johnsbury, Vermont, and has a long history of owners. Maple Grove is now owned by B&G Foods, the food products corporation that owns Ortega, Polaner, and Vermont Maid, an artificial pancake syrup. Maple Grove has sales of $80 million per year, and people on Wall Street read B&G Foods' financial reports to see how the maple syrup industry is doing. Maple Grove supplies Walmart. They sell 40 million of those 1.5-ounce bottles of syrup each year, primarily to the Cracker Barrel Restaurants. Those nips contained pure maple syrup until the shortage of 2008, when, out of necessity, Maple Grove blended with other sugars. After the shortage passed, Maple Grove continued to blend because it would have cost several million dollars to return to pure maple syrup. For Bruce, Maple Grove had long been a model. He used to go on tours of Maple Grove, look at the machinery, memorize the names and numbers, and then slip out to his car to write down the information.

He didn't ever directly say that he wanted to overtake Maple Grove; in fact, he said it would never happen in his lifetime, though he didn't actually mean it. He would say that someone else was going to: "I predict that David Marvin will overtake Maple Grove one day," he told me more than once. It took a while for me to understand that, by that statement, Bruce also meant himself. Once, when he gave me a tour of the new building when the foundation was being poured, we were looking down at the deep hole in the ground, at what would be a storage area for syrup, and I asked, "So will this put you in the first tier?"

"Oh yeah," he said.

They started clearing the site for the new building the week before Bruce was inducted into the Hall of Fame. The trees were in Ken's Lot, and because Bruce often talked about the difficult relationship he had with his dad, who was a tyrant to work for, there was a shade of symbolism hanging in the air that week. Once, when Bruce saw me coming from Ken's Lot, he leveled a look at me and said, "You've probably been over there watching them cut those trees." They were trees that Bruce knew very well, having grown up in the house that stood next to them. When Bruce returned from college he and Peter Rhoades inspected those trees and tested the sugar content of their sap, writing the percentages on the trunks and thinning the orchard to leave the sweetest trees.

"Did it work?" I asked.

"We'll never know," he answered. They conducted that experiment before reverse-osmosis machines came along and made high-sugar content redundant.

Some of the trees would be cut for firewood. Others would be shipped to a mill in Brattleboro, to be marketed as "taphole maple." Taphole maple could be an appealing wood, with its holes suggesting another time and the work of the sugarmaker. The equipment store was paneled with taphole maple.

George Hodskins cut the trees in Ken's Lot. George had been working at Bascom's from the time he was nineteen, more than twenty years ago. His primary function was as a logger, and he owned a log skidder, a tractor designed to work in the woods, that he leased to Bruce. As the maples on the flatter part of the ground were removed, the others on the steep bank stood out in relief. They looked beautiful to me, perched alone on the hillside, and I pointed them out to George. He thought they didn't look so great. Their crowns were too thin, he said. From a producer's standpoint, the crowns of trees produce leaves and the leaves make carbo-hydrates, which are then converted into sugar once the thaw begins. Good maples need golden crowns.

George started working after Ken Bascom transferred the business to Bruce and went into semiretirement. Ken wanted to fire George, but Bruce wouldn't do it. Ken Bascom was quick to fire people, I had been told. He couldn't manage help, as Bruce had told me many times. George placed Ken Bascom in that generation of farmers who had a lot to teach but who yelled a lot. "He shouted like all these farmers around here. You could learn from them, but you learned at high volume."

Ken was a hard guy to figure out. "A very nice guy, very charming, put on sugar parties for the kids, have lots of people up to the sugarhouse, but to work for him, he was a driver.

He would yell about the oddest things," George said. "You could let a truck roll across the parking lot and he wouldn't say anything. But if you did something like leave a door open, he'd yell at you. He said to me once, 'If I was running things around here I'd fire you.' Eventually I just ignored him and did my own thing. He complained about that too."

The excavating crew came in, dug a deep hole, removed the sand, and crushed the big rocks. The concrete workers followed and built walls fourteen feet high, with a basement floor canted toward the middle, with drains in the event of a syrup spill. They installed girders and laid concrete planks to build the upper floor, then poured concrete over the planks and buffed the floor to a glassy smoothness. The construction workers assembled supports for the walls and arches for the roof, and as winter approached they covered the sides with steel panels painted the red color of the barns in New England. Bruce was pleased with that color. They built four loading docks for semis, three opening into the second floor warehouse and the fourth into the basement. Plumbers hooked up a sophisticated network of piping, leading from the silos to the new bottling room. Bottling machines arrived that were much like the machines at Maple Grove. Running at top capacity they would be able to fill eighty quarts per minute. In the basement a plumber and maple syrup producer named Jack Fuller installed an air-conditioning system that would lower the temperature to 40°.

One Saturday morning when the building was near completion Bruce gave me a tour of this basement. As we approached, he clapped his hands to show how the motion-sensitive and energy-efficient LED lighting system performed. We walked down a ramp into the cooler, the "New

Cooler," as this would be called. (There was also an "Old Cooler" and a "Middle Cooler.") The New Cooler was 100 feet wide and 210 feet long; if you took into account the 14-foot ceilings, the New Cooler was a 294,000-cubic-foot refrigerator. You could have played a hockey game in that basement and had room for bleachers.

"We will be able to store eight million pounds of syrup here," Bruce said. "About sixteen thousand drums."

Eight million pounds of syrup. The US crop in 2010 was 20 million pounds. Therefore, in this basement Bruce would be able to store more than a third of the syrup made in the United States in 2010. He could have stored one-fourth of the greater 2011 crop. But Bruce would not be storing just US syrup in the New Cooler; about half would come from Canada. The retail value of 8 million pounds of syrup at $55 per gallon would be $80 million.

At this point Bruce couldn't afford to buy 8 million pounds of syrup, but he intended to grow into his new basement. "I will be able to fill this cooler in about five years," he said. "That is, if the bank will give me more gas." That was how he saw himself, as an engine running on the gasoline of money.

Arnold Coombs was also driving the construction of the new building. Arnold wanted to increase sales by twenty-five percent a year, from his $40 million in sales in 2010. Bruce's job was to provide the syrup, in ever-increasing quantities.

BRUCE TOOK OUT a short-term loan, seven years in duration, because he wanted to pay the building off as soon as possible. He had turned sixty in 2010. "My retirement will be spent paying for this new building," he said, though actually the loan would be paid by the time he was sixty-seven. Time was a factor, though. "The future is my biggest problem," he said. What he meant was that he didn't have offspring coming into the business, neither of his two kids was interested, and he had no hard plan for what would happen to the company should something happen to him. "Fifty people would be looking for something to do," he said. Not that he hadn't been thinking about the succession problem; in 2010 he had hired a consultant from the business school at the University of Vermont to come in and examine the company regarding the matter of succession. She determined that Bruce, as the buyer of syrup in the field, was the one irreplaceable part.

He put up this new building during a recession. Bruce thought it was an advantageous time to build because construction companies would make low bids to get the work. There were those who disagreed with his decision. For his family members who lived nearby, the new building meant an ultimate departure from the kind of family farm Bascom's had once been. They also wondered what would happen should Bruce depart. He got several requests from relatives for options on land, should he pass away. Bruce ignored them. His accountant said he should not take a risk on a building project at this time, but Bruce dismissed that advice on the belief that accountants were, by nature, overly cautious.

For a while it looked like the accountant was right. Bascom's struggled during the summer of 2010 and in July, for the first time in many years, lost money. Bruce had developed a large enterprise with equally large expenses. "I have to sell a million dollars worth every month just to keep things running," he said one afternoon. During that summer he put some of the employees on partial furlough, four-day weeks.

I then asked if he regretted taking on the new project.

"Absolutely not."

When Arnold secured the Gold Coast order the whole outlook changed. Going into the fall Bruce scoured about looking for Vermont syrup and put a statement in his catalogue that he was "looking for Vermont." He made calls from the office and took drives up north. But the need was too great to fill by calling individual sugarhouses. Ultimately he called on his counterpart, David Marvin of Butternut Mountain Farms, who controlled the supply in northern Vermont—had it locked up, Bruce liked to say. Actually, Marvin controlled fifty percent of the syrup in Vermont. He came to Bruce's aid, selling him eighteen trailer loads, a couple of million dollars worth—65,000 gallons. He was happy to move out inventory to make room for the next year's crop.

By the summer of 2011, a year after beginning construction on the new building, Bruce had 5.5 million pounds of syrup in storage—not enough to fill the basement but enough, he figured, to carry him to the end of the year.

WORD TRAVELS FAST in the maple syrup industry, and as the 2012 season approached, Bruce received inquiries about his company. He got an offer from the head of a venture capital firm that entered into the maple business by purchasing a Canadian maple company named L.B. Maple Treats. Now that the financial situation had changed between Canada and the United States due to the monetary exchange rate, L.B. Treats was looking for a footprint in the United States and wanted to buy American syrup. "It would have made me a very rich man," Bruce said of the offer, "but I would never sell." He also received a proposal to manage the company from a Canadian named Tom Zaffis, the previous manager of L.B. Treats who was now managing the equipment division of LaPierre Company in Quebec. Zaffis believed Bascom's would keep him interested for a long time, and his proposal to become second-in-command had left Bruce feeling very excited. He had received a similar offer from a manager in Ontario who heard of the new developments.

During that time, late in 2011, one of the companies in the second tier, Highland Sugarworks, underwent a traumatic change when its owner, Jim MacIsaac, died in the woods. MacIsaac was the newest presence in the second tier and coming on fast after starting his company twenty-five years ago, after attending the University of Vermont. MacIsaac had taken on a lot of producers and was competing with Bruce for supply in the St. Aurelie region of Maine and in Vermont. MacIsaac enjoyed working in the woods, and one afternoon in November he went out on a four-wheeler with a chainsaw to cut a tree. As it fell, the trunk bounced back into his chest. Though he tried, he didn't make it out of the woods. "They lost their fearless leader," Bruce said, and though the employees promised to continue as before, the future of Highland was in question.

A few days after the funeral Bruce was in the store when a young man, about twenty years old, came in with his parents. He had started sugaring the year before, putting in 175 taps. Now he was thinking about getting involved in a more serious way. They asked a lot of questions.

"How many gallons of syrup can you make with a cord of firewood?" the young man's father asked. A cord of firewood is a stack of wood eight feet long, four feet high, and four feet wide.

"About thirteen to twenty-five gallons, depending on the kind of wood you use," Bruce said. "There can be a lot of variation, depending on whether you use dry hardwood or softwood like pine, or mixed wood, or the trashwood you cut when pruning an orchard. There was a sugarhouse in Vermont that used dry hardwood that was two years old. It takes two years to really dry hardwood. They had two woodsheds, each with a hundred or so cords, and they filled one each year." Bruce could have been describing the farm he grew up on.

They looked at tubing and fittings, and they talked about evaporators. They wanted to know about boiling times. "Most people can boil six hours," Bruce said. "They don't want to boil for twelve."

He told the family that Bascom's was hosting a boiling seminar the next week and invited them. While they were looking at the evaporators Bruce came to me and mentioned the Tom Zaffis proposal, saying, "There's been a new development. It will result in a major change in the industry."

The winter of 2012 was looking promising after three feet of snow fell in late October. On the day of the boiling seminar the trucks and cars were streaming up the hill early in the morning. A worker was moved from the warehouse to direct the cars into the cornfield. Women from the office and the sugar-making section were moved to the new building to serve lunch. The guys in the Cooler were ready to take in the syrup that some of the attendees were bringing in to sell. Bruce and David Bascom had estimated that about 250 people would attend, but they rented 400 chairs to be on the safe side. As the talk began, Bruce noticed there were no empty chairs.

The seminar was held in the new building, and crates and pallets were moved to make room for the chairs and the speaker. Brad Gillian was a young sales representative at Leader Evaporator and a talented speaker and storyteller. He began by talking about his grandfather, who, he said, was an old-time Vermont sugarmaker. "He made better syrup than you could today, on a flat pan over an open fire on a brick arch." Gillian said he had been the taste-tester in the sugarhouse, a job that often fell to children. His grandfather had no electricity in that sugarhouse and boiled by the light of a wood fire. Doing that caused you to listen to the boil, Gillian said. "My grandfather said the evaporator will talk to you. You just have to listen."

He asked for a show of hands. "How many of you are burning wood?" About half the people raised their hands. They were an old-fashioned woodsy crowd, but there were many among them who wanted to expand.

I had been up late the night before, and went to get some coffee at the stand set up in the new bottling room. What a room it was—open and spacious with plenty of light and a view of the distant mountains. The conveyors, the fillers, the packing tables—all were fresh and new and promising.

I walked out, sipped the coffee, and looked at the crowd. It seemed to me that these seminars and also the open house Bascom's held in the spring were an outgrowth of the sugar parties I had heard about, the parties Ken and Ruth Bascom had hosted during the sugar season each year. During those times cars were lined up all along the road. The visitors drank coffee and ate pastries, sampled the new syrup, and talked to Ken Bascom at the evaporator. There was no evaporator on this day, but the event brought people together, and Bruce was roaming about, talking to this one and that.

I saw Bruce walking my way. I didn't know whether he wanted to talk to me, and it seemed he didn't because he walked past me, but then he turned and said something. Tom Zaffis was "sixty-forty," he said. Maybe he would come, maybe not. In time, for personal reasons, the Zaffis proposal would fade away. But Bruce's excitement was still fresh on this day, and the success of the boiling seminar had intensified his feelings.

He said, while looking at the crowd, "This is why he wants to come here! This is the value of the name!"

5

THE FIRST FULL-TIME

SUGARMAKER

To BRUCE'S RECOLLECTION Ken Bascom never said one way or the other whether he wanted Bruce to return to the farm. One day I asked Bruce, "If your father was silent about your return and your mother begged you not to do it, why did you come back?" For a moment Bruce's face reddened and his eyes went wide, like I was a teacher calling on him in English class. But then the look turned to amusement, which I thought was the difference between then and now.

"I wanted to prove I could do it better than him," he said.

In 1965, a few months after Ken Bascom became a full-time sugarmaker, an article about him and his family appeared in a magazine called *Food Marketing in New England,* published by the First National Food Stores. The story took the form of a defense, and celebrated the farmer and his wife who were making a go of maple syrup production against the claims of a city dweller who stated that it was a thing of the past, strictly for fuddy-duddies, that young people didn't care about it anymore. "'Well,' we said, 'it *is* old, as years go, one of the few arts taught the white man by his

Indian predecessors on this Continent. But we can't disagree with you too violently on the matter of giving it attention. It's ... Spring around the corner ... it's new life rising ... and it's a field of human endeavor about which there still is much deep and moving mystery.'"

The editors intended to send the Bascom piece to their cynical friend, with a circle in red pencil around the words, "young people don't, etc."

For Kenneth Bascom is a young man and his wife Ruth is a young woman, and if it doesn't embarrass them too much to say it (they're real New Hampshire people, who are not the expostulating kind)—we rate them as being as high a type of young people as the U.S. produces on any level you care to name. Ken Bascom isn't shuffling his feet in this maple business. He's enthusiastic. So is Ruth. And they work their heads off at it, and succeed at it, and plan to double it. Ken sold his herd of cows last October. They were doing well too, eighty Holsteins, forty-five milking, and at the time they were sold, Ken was making a ton of milk a day and the herd production was 520 pounds butter fat, 13,000 milk. But maple trees interested him most, and the opportunity ahead, he feels, is great and the whole sugaring enterprise stimulating. This is thinking against a trend, an individualistic thinking, planning and operating which make our country what it is—the sort of thing that showed to the Russians who read the magazine article above that what makes America tick is people free to go against, as well as with, the tide.

Ken was hanging 6500 buckets, so many, the article stated, that stacked end to end they would stretch more than a mile.

He also had 500 taps on tubing as an experiment. Ken bought sap from other sugarmakers who delivered it to his sugarhouse, and he also bought syrup. He bought it in thirty-gallon drums and paid for it by the pound. The article stated that Ken hoped someday not to have to buy syrup, once he further expanded the operation. Ken would continue to farm. He had about 600 acres under production, 150 on which he would raise hay and clover. He would also cut 200 cords of wood a year—100 cords for sale and another 100 to be used to boil sap. Two hundred cords of wood at four feet wide and four feet high would stretch 1600 feet, about three-tenths of a mile.

The article focused on the maple sugar parties that the Bascoms held at their sugarhouse each year. The parties were very successful—in 1964 there were 500 visitors. On those weekends the Chevys, Pontiacs, Buicks, and Fords were lined up along Sugar House Road, and tour buses came from Boston. To advertise the parties, Ken and Ruth had produced an informational brochure that they mailed to prospective visitors. It read,

> During the season (approximately March 13–April 18) we will be serving sugar on snow, hot fried doughboys and syrup, pickles and coffee at our sugarhouse. Not every day but on the days and nights the evaporators are working. The charge is $1.00. We must have a reservation for large groups. A few days notice is sufficient. (Tel. 835-2230)
>
> WHAT YOU WILL SEE IF YOU VISIT US:
>
> - 50 mile view of fields, valleys and mountains. evaporators.
> - Gathering and/or boiling of sap.

- Filtering of maple syrup.
- Wooden, metal, plastic buckets, new plastic tubing systems.
- Complete line of delicious maple products.

WHAT YOU WILL HEAR:

- The putt-putt of tractors.
- The drip-drip of sap in metal buckets.
- The rush of sap on its way to the evaporator.
- The roar of the fires.
- Explanation of the sugaring process.
- The toot of the steam whistle announcing that syrup is being drawn off.

We do not have Florida's climate, but we do have clean, fresh air aplenty atop our 1,500 foot Mt. Kingsbury. For this reason we suggest an extra sweater. Be sure to bring boots. We still have snow in the Spring! And don't forget your camera!

This was a family affair, the article said. There was a portrait photograph of the three kids, of Bruce, fourteen, a high school freshman, and Judy, twelve, a seventh grader, and Nancy, ten, a fifth grader, sitting around a table having a private sugar party. A pile of doughboys—doughnuts without holes—in a bowl. A bowl of pickles nearby. Judy looks into a tea cup while Nancy samples a doughboy, and Bruce seems to be lifting a piece of maple taffy from a pan of snow—sugar on snow.

Ruth Bascom was a town girl from Milford, Massachusetts, who had been a secretary before she met Ken. The article stated, "On the maple side, all the family pitch in. With

Mother Ruth as the head chef, the maple products are turned out in the family kitchen. Ruth brings her business training to play on the books of the maple business. She receives no pay. Ken says he figures she deserves the latest in kitchen and household appliances. One year she went without however—'I was broke. I had bought a bulldozer,' he says, grinning."

The Bascoms were active in their church and in community organizations. The Acworth 4-H club met in their living room, but it had grown so large that Ken built a garage with a room above where the club could meet. Ken held offices in the Grange, served as an Acworth selectman, as the director of the Farm Bureau, and was a member of the advisory board for the State Department of Agriculture. He was president of the New Hampshire Maple Syrup Producers Association and active in the North American Maple Syrup Council.

The article closed with a note about the extent of the work on a maple farm. It took two days for the three- to five-man sugaring crew to get to all the 7000 buckets. In a normal season of six weeks, buckets were emptied from six to as many as twelve times—42,000 to 84,000 times in all.

KEN BASCOM'S FATHER, Eric Bascom, was born on a farm about a mile away from the maple farm, on the other side of Langdon Woods. His father, James Bascom, was a farmer noted for his cleverness—he made a windmill from a wagon wheel—and for his ability to produce light-colored maple syrup. Eric Bascom attended a theological school in Maine, where he met his wife, Elida Frost. Ken Bascom was born there, in 1925. Eric and Elida became ordained ministers; Elida was the first female ordained minister in New Hampshire. They had four more children. Eric Jr. became an ordained minister in Springfield, Massachusetts. Rodney became a farmer and logger and taught at the University of New Hampshire. Paul became an agricultural statistician with the US Department of Agriculture. A sister, Shirley, raised a family in Tilton, New Hampshire.

In the late 1920s Eric Bascom bought the farm on Mount Kingsbury for $2500, paying $30 down and $30 a month to the widow who owned it. The place was called the Stone House Farm because of the smart-looking stone house built in 1837 by Zenas Slader, who cut slabs from a seam on top of the mountain and moved them to the site with a team of oxen. Eric's brother Glenn owned the farm further down the hill. At the time of his purchase Eric was a minister in Canterbury, New Hampshire. He arranged for a tenant to manage the farm but returned in the spring to make maple syrup and grow a crop of potatoes with his brother Glenn. Eric sold his maple syrup to parishioners and, in the 1930s, during the Great Depression, peddled it house to house.

The Depression made life difficult for most everyone but none more so than ministers of churches that depended on weekly donations. In 1938 Eric Bascom's yearly salary was reduced from $1200 to $750. In the fall one of the worst hurricanes in history hit the Northeast, with winds of 160 miles per hour cutting a swath 400 miles wide, leaving 500 people dead. The hurricane blew away barns and livestock and leveled millions of trees, destroying many sugar orchards. Hummocks, the mounds and hollows from tree trunks and roots, can still be seen in the woods of New Hampshire today.

Eric and Elida decided to move their family to the farm in Acworth, arriving early enough to plant crops in the spring. Ken stayed in Canterbury to finish eighth grade but worked in the fields that summer. When it came time to gather hay, Ken received a quick driving lesson and, at age thirteen, drove a Chevy truck while his father arranged the loads of hay. Eric continued to grow potatoes with his brother Glenn, started raising chickens, and began building a dairy herd.

Maple syrup was a crucial part of the farm. Later in his life Ken Bascom wrote about this in an article for a farming publication: "I was thirteen upon moving to the farm and descended from several generations of sugarmakers. We had 600 old metal buckets, a team of horses, a sled with a five-barrel tank, and a rough-boarded sap house. There was a 20-barrel storage tank and a 2½ by 8-foot evaporator. Being the oldest of five children, it became the lot of 'Yours Truly' to drill the holes and to tap in the metal spouts."

Ken's brother, Eric Bascom Jr., also wrote about this work in an article in the *Keene Sentinel*, looking back at the year of 1942 during the Second World War: "The sap spouts are those tubular tin pegs and tap into holes in the trees. Usually Kenneth drills the holes. Rodney sets and spouts and I, the beast of burden, follow with a stack of metal buckets, at least one for every tree. Last year when we tapped, the snow was up to our hips. This year it's only up to our knees."

Price controls were in place during the war, and maple syrup was set at a price of $3.30 a gallon. "Even so, Dad's expanding," Eric wrote. "If the war ever ends, the price will go up. Last year we tapped maybe 1,200 trees. This year he plans to tap 2,000."

To Eric, their sugarhouse seemed like a "clipper ship with crowded sails plowing." There were other vessels on those seas, and he could see steam rising, "from my uncle's shack, and Roy Clark's. We have plumes from Gerard and Chester Mason's in the hollow, and in the southwest, Uncle Cal's and old Fred Green's. There are literally hundreds of small producers around us who love the tradition and supply their own kitchens and a few village stores."

He described the long days gathering sap:

Each of us has a pair of 16-quart gathering pails. The sides taper in at the top, with a flared rim that allows emptying a 12-quart bucket with minimum spillage. We stumble up and down banks and trek from tree to tree to sled. The steel gathering tank holds three hundred gallons, but the tank is full before we're halfway through the section. We'll have to return to get the rest and that's too bad because, as we head for home, the horses think they're done for the day. They're pulling 2,400 pounds of sap, all uphill, yet we're at the sugarhouse in short order. This load and the rest will keep dad boiling half the night. It is a night and day operation that blots out everything else. When we get back to the barn we'll have nothing to do except rub down the horses, milk the cows, clean the stables and feed the stock.

In 1942 the Bascoms made 600 gallons of syrup, doubling the previous year's crop. That meant a return of about $2000, which seemed like a very large sum to the twelve-year-old boy, as he told his father.

"About half of which is due to the bank," his father had answered.

AFTER HIGH SCHOOL Ken Bascom served in the Army, stationed in Italy for eighteen months, until the war ended. He then attended the agricultural college at the University of New Hampshire, completing the two-year program. Ken considered staying to complete the four-year program but thought the final two years would be more theoretical than practical. He wanted to begin working on the farm, and by then he was married.

Ken met Ruth Baker during the summer of 1947 at a square dance in Acworth. She had come from Massachusetts to visit some relatives. At the dance the Bascom brothers announced their presence by stomping their feet all at once, something they may have learned when they lived in Canterbury near the Shaker colony. Ruth was impressed, and also impressed with the ambition of the young farmer. They were in many ways a compatible couple. She had attended Houghton College and studied business and also studied religion at the Providence Bible Institute. The wedding was held in Massachusetts, with all of Ken's siblings taking part and with Eric officiating.

In 1950 Ken bought the farm from his father for $25,000. As planned, with their children full grown, Eric and Elida returned to the ministry. That same year Ken and Ruth built a new house, 800 feet away from the stone house and on the opposite side of the sugarhouse. Glenn Bascom sawed out the lumber at his mill. Friends and family helped raise the building. Ken named the place "Happiness Lodge." In November Bruce was born.

A photograph from 1956 speaks to the name Ken Bascom gave to his home and to his maple syrup business and sugarhouse—a Sunday morning breakfast scene, with Ruth wearing a red dress, ladling syrup over a pan of baked French toast. Ken, wearing a white shirt and dress pants with his hair combed back, leans over the table to cut portions for the kids. Bruce, almost six years old, is sitting on the chair with his legs drawn under him, anticipation on his face. Judy, age four, waits politely. Nancy, a toddler, pulls at the tablecloth and tries to climb up on the table. This too seems to be among the best America has to offer—their own maple syrup, their eggs, their milk, their Sunday—and Ruth, in her amusement, seems to know completely.

By then the Bascoms had hosted the sugar parties for more than half a decade, and they kept improving upon them. They were building a mailing list that would reach a thousand names for the parties and for mail-order business. Their brochure for 1957 listed syrup at $5.75 per gallon and $1.75 per quart. As the kids grew older, they began to help at the parties. They could gather snow in baking pans for sugar on snow. They could help make maple candy and maple cream. They could wipe the syrup off the tablecloths. They could gather sap.

Ken had a serious accident in 1958 while working in the woods, when he cut down a tree and a heavy limb hit him on the forehead. His brother Rodney found him lying unconscious, his face blackened. At the hospital his pain was so intense that Ken asked someone to bring him a gun, half-joking—they realized that if he could joke about, it he would probably be okay. Eric Sr. and Uncle Glenn boiled that year, while brother Rodney managed the farm. Ken and Rodney were working in partnership, managing two farms, but they weren't making much of a profit. Then, in one of those moments that changes everything, Ken neglected to thank Rodney for doing all of the work while he healed, and Rodney took offense. It didn't help that the year before when they were gathering sap Ken forgot to tell Rodney that his wife was in labor, with Kevin. Rodney moved his family to Concord and worked on a dairy farm, then at the farm at the University of New Hampshire. He created a sugarbush in the town of Nottingham.

Ken was back in full force the next year in 1959. He tore down the sugarhouse his father built and constructed a new one on the same site, with a concrete floor. The building looked like a barn, or even a house, but with doors in the roof that opened to vent out maple steam. He painted the building brown with yellow trim and red doors. At one end of the building Ken erected a sizeable smoke stack, thirty feet tall and thirty inches in diameter. He bought a used steam boiler from a laundry near Lake Winnipesaukee and converted it to be heated by wood. Steam at 325° could bring sap to a boil almost instantly. Ken engineered the plumbing of the steam system himself. The steam pipes sat within an evaporating pan four feet wide and ten feet long. He built the sugarhouse large enough to hold fifty visitors and made ten picnic tables to seat them. For the parties they covered the tables with red-checkered tablecloths, according to tradition.

Ken was constantly thinking about ways to improve the systems and increase the capacity of the sugarhouse to accommodate more taps. By 1965 he had added a second evaporator, this one oil-fired with a five-foot by ten-foot pan. It was highly state of the art for its time, this pair of evaporators working in sequence, with the oil-fired unit doing the first part of the boil and the wood-fired steam evaporator finishing off the syrup. The system doubled his production per hour. For a touch of fun, Ken rigged up a steam whistle that he blew when the syrup was ready to be poured, and that could be heard miles away. The guests, wandering around looking at the buckets, taking in the view, knew when to come to sample the new syrup.

The decision Ken made to leave dairy farming and go into maple production did not come easily. Where Ken lived, no one had done it before even though the region around Acworth was the most productive in New Hampshire. But Ken knew someone who succeeded full time in the maple business, Bob Coombs, in Jamaica, Vermont. Not only was Coombs running a large syrup production operation with more than 20,000 buckets, he was selling equipment as well. Coombs also bought syrup from other producers, with many loyal suppliers who would sell only to him spread out through New England and upstate New York. He packed syrup for stores and sold it wholesale on the bulk market. Coombs had two trucks running routes throughout New England. His son Arnold began making deliveries as a teenager, driving to pick up barrels of bulk syrup in New York when he was only sixteen.

Ken had seen that the future in dairying had limitations. He had also come to a point where he didn't want to work with animals anymore. He wanted to work with trees. Ken sold his horses first of all, the workhorses that pulled a wagon with a sap tank. He butchered his chickens and hung them from the clotheslines to drain. That was part of life on the farm. When Ken butchered a cow occasionally, he did the killing in the barn but cut the meat on the kitchen table. The work left saw marks on the table, but later they bought a new one. In Ken's mind his dairy cows were his meal ticket, and he had developed the herd his father started those years ago to a prime condition. He sold them in October 1964. A month later, as though to mark the new era, Ruth gave birth to their fourth child, Bradford.

There was another reason for the change. Ken Bascom was an athlete when it came to the work of farming. He would have made the national team if there were one. Ken worked seventy to eighty hours a week, six days a week, with a half-day off on Sunday for church except during sap season, and there were few who could keep up with him. But Ken expected others to keep up, including the tenant farmers who lived in the stone house. Ken fired anyone who didn't measure up. He fired workers who smoked because he didn't want to pay for cigarette breaks. He was in that generation of farmers who yelled a lot. In that year before he sold his cows, five tenant families moved on and off the farm.

"Because he expected them to work eighty hours a week just like he did," Bruce said. "My father's main problem was that he couldn't manage help. He was a tyrant to work for."

Of course, no one worked more for him than Bruce did.

6

A GALLON EVERY

22 SECONDS

KEVIN MADE HIS SECOND BOIL of 2012 on February 10. It would have been his earliest boil ever, except for the one the week before on February 3. On February 10 Kevin made 451 gallons of syrup, bringing the total for 2012 to 617 gallons. On February 10 the temperatures at Bascom's went from 25° in the morning to 41° in the afternoon. The tapping crew of four people worked all that day, finishing Putnam's Lot, raising their total tap count to 33,700.

Two days later, on February 12, the temperature was 6° in the morning, getting up to only 12° in the afternoon, and the sap run halted for four days.

Nevertheless some meteorologists were describing this as "the non-winter of 2012." Partly this was because of a lack of snow—there was a snow drought. Going into the last winter Kevin plowed the parking lot and Sugar House Road sixteen times by January 1. But this year he had plowed only four times going into February, and that included when he plowed after the big snowstorm in October. Meteorologists claimed that the cause of the drought and the warm weather was due to an unusual positioning of the jet stream, which had looped far to the north in North America and, conversely, far to the south in Europe. Because the jet stream acts as a boundary for weather fronts, warm air spread northward in the United States and Canada while polar air moved southward through Europe. During those two days when a heat wave passed through New England on February 1 and 2, bringing temperatures in the 40s and 50s, temperatures in the Ukraine dropped to −28° Fahrenheit.

On Thursday, February 16, the temperatures ranged from 29° to 42°, starting a new sap run. Kevin Bascom boiled for the third time the next day on February 17, his third Friday in a row, and made 621 gallons. He boiled again on Saturday, Sunday, and Monday, bringing the total production for 2012 to 2362 gallons. On Monday it turned cold again and the trees shut down for two days.

On Wednesday morning there was a half-inch of snow, followed by a warm afternoon in the midforties, and that triggered a sizeable run. Kevin boiled for seven hours the next day, making a whopping 1373 gallons, which only a few years ago would have been a record day. It only got up to 38° that day, which put a brake on the sap run. Kevin's boil the next day, on Friday, February 24, produced a modest 283 gallons of syrup. His total production then stood at 4018 gallons.

Some sugarmakers called this period from February 16 to February 24 "the big run." Some said they had missed it. But another much bigger run was about to come.

Because of the early start of the season, the tapping crew completed their work near the end of the big run. As of February 23 there were 63,865 taps feeding into the Bascom sugarhouse.

You COULD TELL that Kevin was boiling when you arrived at the parking lot and saw the broad column of steam shooting through the sugarhouse roof. That steam was scented with maple, and as soon as I got out of the car and stood in the open air I encountered the sweet smell. I liked this idea of standing in a maple-scented mist at the top of a mountain.

Inside the sugarhouse Kevin was at the evaporator. Kevin is slight of build, quiet of voice, but he was running a high-powered, finely tuned machine, with its rows of steam pipes, pulsing hoses, fervid boiling and the fans throwing off sap steam, the water condensing and dripping, the syrup flowing out, and the reverse-osmosis machines in an adjacent room whirring at a high-tech pitch. I tried talking to Kevin at the evaporator, but there always was too much noise, and his voice was too soft to follow over the kaleidoscopic sound. But at intervals, twenty-five feet away in another room by the filter presses as he poured syrup from a hose into a fifty-five-gallon drum, you could hear Kevin talk. He was experiencing the pleasure of the harvest there.

I said to him once, "Some people work all year to get two hundred gallons. It's like you're flying the Concorde and they are in little Cessnas."

"It's like flying the Concorde with one person," he said with a burry laugh.

BOILING HAD COME a long way over the last 400 years. Native Americans boiled sap in hollowed-out logs, into which they placed hot rocks—they made great quantities of sugar this way. European settlers used iron kettles, a single kettle to which they added fresh sap to the thickening, blackening syrup. Sometimes they used two or three kettles heated over an open fire, with sugar solutions of different stages in each kettle. In the mid-1800s sugarmakers began to use flat pans, rectangular and as much as six feet long, boiling the sap over a stone or brick fireplace—an arch, this fireplace was called. Remnants of those stone or brick arches can be found in the woods today, sometimes even in places where maples no longer stand.

In the latter part of the nineteenth century modern evaporators were developed, with metal fireboxes, also called arches, with two pans on top. One pan was for rapid boiling, the other for finishing syrup. Eventually the boiling pan developed so as to be fluted with deep troughs so as to have more surface area to transmit heat. As the sap boiled and thickened, it was transferred from the flue pan to the syrup pan.

In the syrup pan the thickening syrup moved along by means of a density gradient, the peculiar principle in which thinner syrup pushed thicker syrup ahead. At the final stage, when the syrup was at a density of two-thirds sugar, it was then "taken off," strained, and filtered.

The fuel for the fire was wood. Generally a sugarmaker could produce a few gallons of syrup per hour, depending on the size of the evaporator, the sugar content of the sap, the properties of the wood, and the skill and effort of the person feeding the fire.

A researcher at the University of Vermont devised a formula known as the "Rule of 86" to determine how many gallons of sap needed to be boiled to make a gallon of maple syrup. The principle was mysterious and simple: if the sap was at one percent sugar content, it took 86 gallons to make a gallon of syrup. But by doubling the sugar content to two percent, the work on the other end was essentially halved, now taking 43 gallons of sap at two percent sugar content to make a gallon of syrup. I found it interesting to multiply the work out—a crop of 1000 gallons of syrup made from two percent sap (often the normal content) would require the boiling of 43,000 gallons of sap. The Bascom crop of about 24,000 gallons would necessitate the boiling of 1,032,000 gallons of sap. Though what they do is actually processing.

When Kevin Bascom came to work on the farm in 1979 Bascom's had about 30,000 taps on tubing. Bruce had been developing the system for six years. Ken Bascom was well ahead of most sugarmakers because he was boiling by using steam in pipes under high pressure. By 1979 Ken had added to his sugarhouse two oil-fired evaporators that did the bulk of the boiling, feeding reduced sap to the steam-powered evaporator that then finished syrup quickly.

The cost of making syrup increased suddenly during the fuel crisis of 1973 and 1974, when the price of oil quadrupled. Ken had used oil because it was relatively inexpensive and reduced the labor of cutting wood. At that time Ken was burning about four gallons of oil to make a gallon of syrup. That cost was feasible when oil was 25 to 40 cents a gallon, but not at $1.60.

The fuel crisis intensified efforts to make the evaporation process more efficient. As it happened, around 1974 the first reverse-osmosis machines became available for maple syrup production. Reverse-osmosis machines are essentially desalinization machines working, as their name implies, in a reverse way. Rather than save the fresh water and discard the salty brine as they do at sea, maple syrup producers discard the pure water—or permeate, as they call it—and use the sugar solution, the concentrate, for syrup.

The possibilities of reverse osmosis were irresistible to sugarmakers who were making a business of producing maple syrup. When a producer could concentrate maple sap at two percent sugar to eight percent by running it through an R.O., as they call them, he would have to boil only about ten gallons of water rather than forty-three. The syrup that cost the equivalent of four gallons of oil to produce would now only require one gallon of oil, with sap at eight percent sugar. The Bascoms added their first R.O. machine in 1977.

Ken Bascom boiled for more than forty years, and when he retired Kevin took over. Ken might boil on the weekends when visitors came by, but Kevin put in the long hours. "I used to boil sixteen hours a day," he said. "I used to be here at nine o'clock every night. Eventually we had two shifts. I would boil in the morning and through the day and someone would replace me at night." During the night shift Kevin was usually at the R.O., concentrating sap for the next day's boil.

Some sugarmakers run sap through an R.O. and concentrate it to eight percent and take it no further, content to boil off ten gallons of water to make their syrup. Other sugarmakers, those like Kevin, take the sap to higher concentrations. They run the sap through the R.O. a second time and possibly bring it to twelve percent. Or, if they have reverse-osmosis machines with a higher number of membranes like Kevin has, they bring the concentrate up to eighteen or twenty percent on that second pass. At a concentration of twenty percent, the sugarmaker only has to boil off three and a third gallons of water.

Using an evaporator with high-pressure steam like the one at Bascom's, where the temperature in the steam pipes reaches 350°, and with highly concentrated sap, it takes only a pint of oil to make a gallon of syrup. The four gallons of oil that produced one gallon of syrup during Ken Bascom's time can produce thirty-two gallons of syrup in the system Kevin runs.

Because of the power of high-pressure steam, Bascom's is able to use an evaporator half the size they would need otherwise. Their processing has followed a path of reduction in step with their improvements. With sap at twelve percent, Kevin can fill a 55-gallon drum every half hour. With sap at twenty percent, he fills a drum every twenty minutes. That is 55 gallons of syrup produced in only twenty minutes. That is 2.75 gallons per minute—a gallon about every twenty-two seconds.

The membranes in an R.O., membranes that are fine enough for water to pass through but not as easy for sugar molecules, require a lot of care and attention. Kevin cleans his at least once a day, using the permeate separated from the sap.

Before raw sap ever reaches the membranes, it is filtered several times. From the storage tanks behind the sugarhouse the raw sap first passes through a filter of diatomaceous earth (fossilized remains of diatoms, often used in swimming pool filters) that removes large particles. The sap passes through a bag filter, then through a prefilter attached to the R.O. Using a pair of reverse-osmosis units on the first pass, Kevin processes 8000 gallons per hour, bringing it to a concentration of eight percent.

He then routes the sap outdoors to a storage tank where it cools. Kevin usually makes the final concentrate at night. The sap is filtered again, passing through a bag filter and then a cartridge filter before passing it through the membranes on the R.O. Kevin slows down the flow rate, and the sap emerges at eighteen to twenty percent.

In the morning he starts up the evaporator again, charging it with steam from the boilers in the basement. He moves the concentrate through a preheating unit, a box above the evaporator that the escaping steam from below heats—a "steam-away" this is called. The sap then enters the evaporator near the boiling point. Less than a minute later it's maple syrup.

7

A SUGARHOUSE FULL

OF SOUND AND EVERYBODY

COMING AROUND

O N THE SOUTHERN WALL of his new sugarhouse Ken Bascom attached two wooden signs shaped like maple leafs. On one he wrote, "Happiness Lodge Maple Products," and on another that overlapped the first he wrote, "Ruth and Ken Bascom." In 1967 he put up four smaller leafs, one for each of his kids.

Ruth Bascom took a photo of her family in front of the signs that year. Ken stood in front of the Happiness Lodge sign, leaving space so his wife's name and his could be seen. Standing proudly, he is forty-two years old but seems like he could be much older. Bruce stands next to him, the same height, a hand raised to touch the leaf with his name—his is the largest leaf and the one that is the highest up. In jeans worn at the knee, a wool jacket, and a wool cap, Bruce stands straight and lean—he has the look of a farm boy who has done a lot of work, the kind of kid who drives a tractor at a young age. Nancy is beside him, in a crouch, below her leaf, the third one down. She is a tomboy and Bruce's shadow; she will spend the summer stacking hay bales with him even though she weighs only seventy pounds. Brad, at two years old, stands with his head below his leaf, the smallest and furthest down on the wall. At the end of the line, standing below her leaf, is Judy, nearly as tall as Bruce and not a tomboy; Judy likes working at the sugar parties, making the doughboys, collecting the snow, eating a leftover doughboy or piece of sugar-on-snow, and having a little fun with the other kids when the day in the sugarhouse is over. The parties give her a family feeling she enjoys.

The departure from dairy farming to full-time maple also meant a profound change for Bruce. Previously he had fed the cows, helped with the milking, taken care of the new calves, and worked in the fields. Bruce was driving a tractor from the time he could reach the pedals, from about the age of twelve. The daily chores of the farm were also Bruce's daily chores. When his father went into the maple business full time Bruce thought that he too might make a living from maple someday, though he didn't say much about it.

Bruce had difficulty saying much at all, in that he had a severe stutter. Bruce said that his stutter defined the early part of his life, that he confronted it every day and in every interaction. For someone with relentless verbal energy, a stutter like his was the worst of impediments. His classes at school, especially his English classes, were an exercise in torture. He was permitted to drop the mandatory French class. One classmate remembers Bruce as the red-faced kid with a stutter who gained a whole lot of confidence in college, though Bruce said the stutter wasn't about confidence at all. The strain was hard on the father-and-son relationship—

Ken would stand in front of Bruce waiting for him to get the words out and sometimes walk away before he did. This was, of course, hard for his mother to see. Ruth took him to the medical center associated with Dartmouth College for therapy, and Bruce was given exercises to help him to speak. One was simply to relax and breathe. Bruce's sisters knew not to bother him when he was doing his exercises in his room. He memorized limericks and made some up: "There once was a man from Seattle, who had a beard that would rattle. He eventually found, when the time came around, with his beard he could call in the cattle." He could still recite them.

Bruce had a precocious talent for business and for driving. His sisters remember him driving at ten, but Bruce thinks it was closer to twelve. He was twelve when he started an apple cider business after he saw an ad for a cider press. Ken lent him the $25 to buy it, taking cider in payment. He gave Bruce a motor to run the press and took cider payment for that as well. In the fall, when the apples ripened, Bruce and the girls would get into the family car—he was twelve, Judy ten, and Nancy eight—to drive to abandoned orchards and find rogue trees to gather apples. They pressed, filtered, and bottled the cider in the dairy barn. They found customers by phone calls and by knocking on doors, though Bruce's sisters did that work because Bruce couldn't talk on the phone or knock on anyone's door. He sold the cider for 75 cents a gallon, sometimes carrying it to school on the bus to pass to his customers' children. He was clever enough to offer Judy and Nancy a 10-cent commission on the empty jugs, which ensured a steady supply. Bruce kept up the cider business into high school, accumulating a $600 savings account.

Driving a car at ten, a tractor at twelve, and running the evaporator at about the age of ten could be hazardous. Bruce's way of saying this was, "I wasn't an inexpensive kid." He destroyed a couple of trucks, and he tipped over the tractor, almost severely injuring his leg. Ken built a stand for Bruce so that he could see into the evaporating pan. A couple of times he let the sap get too low in the pan, which scorched and opened up leaks. Ken lectured him at high volume, repaired the pan with hacksaw blades and epoxy, and, after the season, bought a new one. When it came time for Bruce to take the test for his driver's license, Ken sent him to Keene alone in the farm pickup, saying there was no point in wasting an afternoon. When the registry officer asked Bruce what he would do if he failed the test, Bruce answered that he would probably just drive home.

Bascom family vacations were usually spent at maple meetings. If the meeting was in, say, central New York, Ken got everyone up at 3:00 in the morning, loaded up the car, and drove until they reached Binghamton or Syracuse or Croghan, talking maple all the way. Bruce remembered loving it. At the meeting Bruce would absorb as much as he could, but in his memory he was the boy standing in the shadows, unable to get out a complete sentence.

Ken set the schedules for his kids. They worked on the farm after school and on weekends. None could play sports because they were a waste of time. Each child played in the school band because Ken believed that art had value in a child's development. Once they started they weren't allowed to quit. Bruce played drums.

When the time came to tap the trees the family worked in the woods, except for Ruth. They started at 7:30 in the

morning and worked until dark, with a tiered level of responsibility. Ken drilled the holes while another older
worker might set the spouts. Bruce hung the buckets, and
Judy and Nancy put on the lids. This meant slogging through
the snow all day. Back at home at night they stood by the
heating registers trying to warm their feet.

As Bruce grew older, Ken scheduled the tapping around
the school vacations in mid-February, even though that was
early to begin tapping trees. School kids were an important
part of Ken's labor force, as was true for many sugarmakers
with thousands of buckets. By normal standards, a producer
would employ one worker for every 500 buckets, which
meant Ken would have twelve to fourteen people working
for him, but it was more like two or three men and a group
of kids. When the flow began Bruce brought friends home
from school to earn a little money emptying buckets. The
memory of this time was one of Bruce's favorites—the
skilled old men Ken hired to tap and drive spouts, the sight
of the tractors pointed toward the woods, he and his friends
arriving after school. The boys running to empty the buckets,
trying to impress the older men, wearing themselves out after three hours.

I think it is difficult to comprehend the frenetic anxiety of
someone who made most of his year's wages in those six
weeks of the sap run and who had to get the supply to fill
his regular accounts. Sometimes, when help wasn't available
and the crew was undermanned, the work fell upon Bruce.
Ken had him up at 5:30 on some days and in the woods by
6:00, and kept Bruce out gathering until after dark, only to
have him up again at 5:30 the next morning. Slogging
through snow, carrying heavy buckets that sometimes

spilled on legs and into boots or doused the gloves on freezing March days. Such was the life of the son of the first full-time sugarmaker. But as Peter Rhoades, who was one of those boys, said when I asked if this was especially hard work, "We always worked hard, it was just a part of our lives."

When the season was over, Bruce cut wood, those 200 cords, alongside his father. Ken Bascom was producing about 20,000 bales of hay each summer, and later as many as 30,000 bales. They would load hay all day and into the night and then deliver it the next morning. Making hay, like making syrup, is a burst activity. On some days Ken delivered syrup packed in jugs to his customers at retail stores, gift shops, and farm stands in New Hampshire and Vermont. He made his deliveries in what they called "the boat," the poor man's pickup truck, a secondhand station wagon loaded to the limit of its suspension system. Ken and Ruth sold syrup from their house too.

In those years, when his maple crop wasn't enough to fill his accounts, Ken drove to Quebec and bought a few barrels of bulk syrup to make up the difference. Sometimes it was cheaper to buy Canadian than to produce it at home. Ken wasn't the only one doing this. Large distribution companies in the United States took advantage of the cheap supply of Canadian syrup, companies like Maple Grove, American Maple, and, eventually, Springtree in Brattleboro, Vermont, which supplied large grocery chains and helped develop national markets. Bruce rode with Ken on some of these trips to Canada.

Bruce attended the University of New Hampshire. His grades were poor at first, especially in freshman English, which was another exercise in torture. He took two forestry courses along with Peter Rhoades and thought about going into forestry, but he finally decided on the business school. Bruce got As in most of his business courses.

During the sugar season he went home on weekends. Ken was still using buckets, but Bruce was thinking a lot about tubing. Tubing was the way of the future. Operations with buckets depended on cheap labor, and he knew all about that. Bruce saw tubing as the economic replacement for the dependence upon cheap family labor. The quality of tubing had improved since Ken Bascom had tried it in the mid-1960s. As part of a research effort Bruce visited two maple farms in New Hampshire that had converted to tubing. During his spring vacation in his sophomore year Bruce traveled to Ontario and worked in a state-of-the-art tubing operation owned by the sugarmaker Dennis Nolet.

Bruce met his wife the same way his father met his, at a square dance at UNH. Her name was Liz Parker. She was a year ahead of him and studying history. Liz seemed everything that meant sophisticated to Bruce. Her family lived near Washington, DC, and her father was an educator with the US Agency for International Development. During her primary school years Liz lived in Vietnam and Thailand. Bruce was smitten and feeling like he could do just about anything.

Bruce brought Liz home to Acworth. Liz woke up early and went to the kitchen. Ken was there, waiting, she thought, and had all sorts of questions for her. Bruce worked in the fields that day, picking up rocks that had worked their way to the surface during the winter freeze. Picking rocks, with the bending and lifting, was the least desirable job on the farm. The wet rocks also tore up gloves and hands. But picking up rocks happened to be a time when Ken and Bruce talked to each other. On this day Bruce asked about some money he had lent to Ken, the $600 he saved from his cider business. Ken had been having financial difficulty. Later Bruce would see that his father was getting close to bankruptcy despite working eighty hours a week.

Ken asked what Bruce wanted it for, saying he didn't have that kind of money. "I want to buy an engagement ring," Bruce said.

Ruth was thrilled with the news. Two days later Ken gave Bruce a check for the full amount, plus interest compounded for the duration of the loan.

"Always with interest, that was his way."

During Bruce's senior year at UNH he took a course in entrepreneurial management, in which each student had to devise a business project. There were many interesting projects in the class, and each student made a presentation. Bruce had his usual difficulty making his, which was a design for a maple sugaring operation with 25,000 taps feeding into a central evaporation plant. There was a lot of interest among his classmates and some skepticism. They were New Hampshire kids, and they knew about maple. Some called it the "flubbing tubing project."

Ruth assumed that when Bruce went into the business school that he would eventually get a job with a corporation. Despite some evidence to the contrary, with Bruce's work in the sugarhouse and the trip to Ontario, she did not expect him to return to the farm and hoped he wouldn't. The economics of farming were too difficult, as was the relationship between father and son. When she realized during his senior year that he intended to work with Ken, she wrote a letter asking him to get a job with a corporation. When he didn't respond she drove to Durham, got a room, stayed for two days, and took Bruce out to dinner. At the restaurant she pleaded with him not to return to the farm. Get a job with IBM, she said.

For Ruth, farm life was a shock at times. Money was scarce. Ken was one not to spend on consumer goods or vacations, only on farm improvements. There was one car, but often it was being used to make deliveries, and so days passed without leaving the farm. Ruth could have put her education to use in the maple business and been a great asset, but Ken was too difficult to work for and she couldn't be part of the business. Eventually Ruth got a job off the farm, working for the 4-H organization and later for the school district.

Many farm wives had a list of things for their daughters to avoid or not learn how to do. Some would say, "Don't learn how to tap trees, because you'll end up out in the woods in the winter." Ruth's list for Judy and Nancy was

1. Don't learn how to drive a tractor.
2. Don't learn how to milk a cow.
3. Don't marry a farmer.

The wedding took place the weekend after Bruce's graduation from the University of New Hampshire. They scheduled it for that weekend because there were three other Bascom weddings that June. They held it at the church in Acworth, the one that sat high on a hill with a tall steeple. Eric Bascom Sr. officiated, just as he had for Ken and Ruth. A

Bascom uncle played the organ. Peter Rhoades was the best man. Peter's wife, Deb, was a maid of honor.

The new couple honeymooned in Bar Harbor, Maine. The weather brought clouds and rain, and after a few days Bruce thought it a good idea to cut the honeymoon short and return to the farm. Ruth was so annoyed that she wouldn't speak to him. Ken punished him by making him pick rocks the next day.

When Bruce and Liz moved into the stone house Ken set his salary at $75 a week. To be fair, he gave himself a salary of $75 too.

Bruce wanted to prove that he could do it better than his father, but he first had to prove he was capable. One thing he was now able to do was knock on doors. Bruce went to his neighbors and arranged to rent enough trees for 12,000 taps and paid rent of 10 cents per tap. He sold the sap to Ken, not thinking that he would overwhelm the evaporation system and keep Ken up all night boiling.

Bruce made an appointment at the farm credit bank to ask for a loan of $5000 to buy tubing and equipment. He took the project paper from his entrepreneurial course along, the one describing a 25,000-tap operation, the flubbing tubing project, and showed it to the bankers. They had heard about tubing but thought it would never be profitable.

The next day—there they were again, picking rocks—Ken asked Bruce how things went at the bank. After Bruce described the outcome Ken told him to send a thank-you note and ask for another appointment.

The next time the bankers showed a different regard. They asked how Bruce's grandfather was doing. They told him that the people who came back a second time were the ones they approved for loans. Though Bruce didn't figure out until later that his father made a call, he did sense the opportunity of the moment and doubled his request, asking for $10,000, and was approved.

Bruce then, with help from a cousin and Peter Rhoades, assembled a tubing system that was the largest in New Hampshire. For a while at Bascom's, buckets and tubing co-existed, but gradually the buckets diminished and would only be seen around the sugarhouse for the benefit of visitors. By 1975 Bruce increased the tap count to 23,000 and made nearly 7300 gallons of syrup. In 1978 they were at 30,000 taps and made 12,200 gallons. They were the largest producers not only in New Hampshire but perhaps in New England.

Still bent on proving himself and wanting to branch out, Bruce joined two other sugarmakers and bought an operation in Vermont called Saltash, and set up a sugarbush on a mountainside. He drove there regularly, along with his cousin Kevin, and they worked up the sugarbush and the tubing lines—they had large pipes running down the hill. Bruce would later call this "my first big mistake." The mountain had strange freezing patterns and stayed too cold. For two summers in a row caterpillars defoliated the trees.

With plastic tubing and reverse osmosis the industry had changed, but not a lot changed between father and son. They fought and fought some more, and they had shouting matches every morning before work. Outside, the workers would wait. They joked that the guy who won would come out and tell them what to do for the day. One said, "Why should we come in at seven-thirty when they always fight until eight? Why not just come in at eight?"

When Ken went into the maple business full time, he had Bob Coombs as a mentor, but Ken didn't model his own enterprise on that of Bob Coombs. He continued to be a farmer and focus on production of syrup and hay and firewood. He did, however, tell Bruce that he should model the business on the one Coombs developed, with all of its facets that included production, equipment, and bulk buying. Bruce termed this as "multiple complementary businesses going simultaneously," with all the pizzazz of a biz-school grad.

Ken raised Bruce's salary to $125 a week toward the end of the 1970s. In 1979 they drew up a formal partnership agreement by which Ken would sell the business to Bruce in 1989, under a financing arrangement with interest.

Until then Ken was in charge, but a kind of division of labor developed. Outside of the sugar season Ken ran the haying operation, making about 30,000 bales per year and selling the hay primarily to horse owners. Ken's focus was on production, but Bruce's was increasingly on profit. An older man who ran a maple company told Bruce he should get into the business of buying bulk syrup. Bruce followed his advice. He immediately liked the sport of it, of borrowing money and seeing how he could do trading syrup. They didn't yet have an office in the sugarhouse, so in the first years Bruce traded on the phone in his kitchen. He was still battling a stutter, and he made heavy use of that phone, walking and talking at the end of a cord. He walked and talked so much that he wore a semicircular path through the linoleum.

Behind the sugarhouse they erected a new structure, a building they called the Cooler. At the doorway was a ramp for unloading barrels. Inside was a platform scale. The concrete walls were insulated to keep the air-conditioned room cool and prevent syrup from fermenting. Kevin named this place "Bruce's Playroom." In the fields cutting and gathering hay, the joke among the workers was, "Bruce is on the phone."

Ken yelled at Bruce if he left lights on, but he liked hearing the war stories about buying and selling syrup. Ken was a risk taker himself—selling his cows had been a huge risk. Stories like the time when Bruce wrote a check for $700,000 to buy loads of syrup in Maine without the money in his account to cover it, and then having to hustle to the bank to convince them to honor the check until he made the deposit. Bruce made some good deals—sometimes he made more money in one day than he made in an entire year on the farm payroll. He turned his profits over to Ken, who used the money to make improvements. When, in the 1980s, the farm grossed a million dollars for the first time, Ken was shocked. It made him realize that the farm was going in a new direction.

The sugar parties flourished in the late 1960s and into the 1970s, as the kids passed through their teenage years and when their friends came to work in the sugarhouse. Ruth was responsible for arranging for tour buses to come to Bascom's and to the Clark sugarhouse next door. The buses came primarily from Hartford, Connecticut, filled with French-Canadian families displaced during the Depression and with fond memories of sugaring time in their homeland. Ken ran ads to attract them. The Bascom girls served sugar on snow, Ruth made maple candy and pecan pies, and sometimes Ken made butternut fudge from the butternut trees that grew there, from a recipe that was his alone. The steam whistle blew, and the guests tried the hot syrup and poured it on the doughboys. They watched the work and talked with Ken at the evaporator as he explained the process of making syrup, how the trees would run, just how much sap it took to make a gallon, how the syrup was graded according to color, and the other lore of syrup making.

When Bruce, Judy, and Nancy went to college they returned on weekends to help with the sugar parties, and Bruce was there on a daily basis after college. But as the industry began changing, and with Bruce in the forefront, putting up tubing and retiring buckets, so did the sugar parties change. Customers began asking why the buckets were no longer on the trees. And why all the tubing, which didn't look appealing at all. At the evaporator Ken heard them talking. They wanted pancakes. But the parties were a weekend operation. A pancake restaurant was not part of the plan.

The girls had always worked without pay as part of the family effort to run the farm. But as Judy Bascom said, "The women's movement had come along, and we were feeling that we needed to get paid. We didn't want to work for free anymore." Ruth knew the girls weren't going to stay on the farm. They took paying jobs and filled in at the parties when they could. For a few years Judy traveled by bus to get to the parties, and Bruce paid for her fare and her labor.

But another contrary development occurred. Though some visitors were disappointed to see plastic tubing, others came to learn about it. "Some customers came not to buy syrup," Judy remembered, "but to buy tubing and learn how to use it. A lot of little people wanted to get close to nature. Bruce said he would show them how. He wasn't going to tell them not to do it or that they couldn't make money at it. Years later some of them would have a big sugarbush."

That's how the equipment business started. Bruce sold tubing and even ran a tubing company for a while. He bought old evaporators and flat pans from sugarmakers and sold them at the farm. When he heard that Bob Coombs was selling his share of stock in the Leader Evaporator Company, Bruce lobbied hard to buy it. Leader had only a dozen shareholders. For Bruce the point of buying the shares was not so much to own the stock but to have access to information about the industry. The information was worth more than the stock, Bruce thought. Ken agreed, and Bruce became a part owner of the major evaporator company in the United States.

At the end of the 1980s Bruce went on a land-buying spree that had most everyone around him worried. The first piece he bought was the Cole's Lot, fifteen miles away but with a promising stand of maples. Part of the reason for buying land was to have collateral for loans—"You can buy a whole lot of syrup with a piece of land," he said. But the major reason was that large properties around the farm came up for sale, and at the same time. Bruce bought as many as he could. He bought the Westney property, a beautiful piece of land rising to a high hill with the best views in Acworth. To convince the bank of the property's worth he asked Peter Rhoades to draw up a timber assessment accounting for all the trees and their values, with a plan to harvest timber while the maple grew in for future syrup production. The bankers had planned to turn Bruce down, but Bruce drove with them to the top of the hill, and Peter spread out his color-coded assessment on the hood of the car while Bruce orated his plan with the long views behind him. He bought the Moody Lot that abutted Westney's and later purchased a block of three other farms that ran down the hill and abutted his Uncle Glenn's property. Glenn's dairy farm was then owned by his son Harvey, who had operated the farm for thirty-five years. When Harvey retired in 1990 Bruce bought the dairy farm too.

He alarmed his more pragmatic family members, and alarmed his bankers, especially when he borrowed money under his father's name because he knew the bank wouldn't lend him more money for land. They put Bruce into that special category of borrowers who received quarterly reviews. By way of retribution they gave him a short-term loan of seven years, expecting he wouldn't be able to pay it off, but Bruce paid the loan on time. In a relatively short period of time Bruce expanded the 280 acres his father owned to 2400 acres, an area, he said, "about a mile and a half wide and three miles long." He put most of the land under a conservation easement so that it would remain in agricultural use.

Ken had borrowed money and taken his own risks, but the way Bruce was leveraging himself unnerved him, and he decided to retire. Though Ken kept working. As Bruce said, "He retired to a forty-five-hour workweek." At times Ken worked with Liz in the mailroom, packaging up orders for syrup or equipment, though they rarely talked. According to Liz, she had only three conversations with Ken the entire time she knew him. At times Ken found the changes at the sugarhouse hard to accept, what with the movement to a corporate structure. At times he felt unwelcome there.

Another reason for Ken's departure was that in 1989 Ruth was diagnosed with cancer. She died in 1990. It was too soon, Bruce thought, and just as he was making the business successful.

In 1997 Ken Bascom was inducted into the Maple Hall of Fame in Croghan, New York. When Bruce was inducted in 2010 they formed one of three father-and-son pairs. When Bruce spoke at the induction he said he was happy to join his father. Privately Bruce said that his father was his major influence, that almost everything he did at the farm was in some way related to what he learned from Ken. They had fought, yes, every day, "But it was all forgotten the next day."

And of course Bruce had proved what he had set out to do.

Bruce's younger brother Brad felt somewhat similarly. Fourteen years younger than Bruce, Brad had a different kind of relationship with his father. Ken also set Brad's schedule and had him working seven days a week in the haying operation during high school and college. But Brad had fond memories of the time he spent with Ken, quiet times talking, and handing him wrenches while he worked on a machine or farm implement.

"I think of Bascom Maple Farms as something Ken Bascom built up," Brad said to me. "Eric had a one-room sugarhouse shack. My father was a farmer and an innovator. He engineered steam pipes, and he brought in the reverse-osmosis machines early on. He was a workaholic. Bruce was whispering in his ear, but Ken had control of the business in the 1970s. It was quite a scene then. You drove up the hill, and there was a hundred cords of wood. A wood-fired steam boiler, enormous with the sound of humming pipes, and the stack and the blower. A sugarhouse full of sound and everybody coming around. It was a romantic place to come to."

After Brad graduated from college he worked away from the farm for a few years. After Ken retired, Brad asked Bruce about the possibility of joining the farm as a partner. Bruce refused. He said he had just gotten out of a partnership with his father and didn't want to get into another one. Anyone who knew him could understand that but also wonder how things might have been, especially when Bruce began searching for the answer as to how the farm would run without him.

After Ruth died Ken turned to writing poetry. In a poem titled "The Old Timer," he wrote of her absence and the changes at the sugarhouse.

Of course she did not mean to go. God knows I wish it were
    not so!
But was naught that I could do and now I must go on.
It's memories and restlessness that get me up at four, I guess,
But nonetheless it lets me see the hopefulness of dawn. . .

. . . Somewhat sadly I recall the sturdy horses, tanks and pails.
Knee-deep in snow in early March we'd tap
and drive the horses out to open woodland trails
and back and forth would go the teams bringing in the sap.

I've done it all. The tapping, then collecting, aching legs,
all well recalled. Cutting, hauling, stacking wood,
the firing, boiling, the packing of the crop in bottle, jugs
    and kegs.
The "boys" now have it easier, the sweat removed, that is good.

Gradually I'd made the changes. Wood to oil, high pressured
    steam,
collecting tubes in networks many acres wide,
reverse osmosis bought to cope with our ever growing stream,
automatic filters and mechanized canners, all we took in stride.

The little one-room house my sugar-maker father made
was enlarged five different times and now unrecognized.
The sales room, the warehoused goods, now bring annual
  parade
of sugar-makers come to get their inventory of supplies.

My second cup of coffee down, I put boots on and out I go
to check on how it's going, what needs attention, if so, how.
The "boys" will have it all in hand I know,
for, as you see, I am the "Old Timer" now.

Ken married again. In 2005, when he took his wife to the
hospital, the doctor noticed that Ken was sweating profusely
and examined him. He was diagnosed with stomach cancer.
Near the end, in and out of consciousness, his brother Paul
asked Ken what it had been like to work with Bruce.

"Have you ever been on a runaway horse?"

"He meant it in a good way," Bruce said years later. He
liked the runaway horse comparison.

Bruce had never been able to speak in public, even up to
the time of Ken's death. But that changed, and a few years
later, in 2010, for the first time Bruce sat on a panel at
Leader Evaporator in Swanton, Vermont. The other panelist
was David Marvin, of Butternut Mountain Farms. The panel
was arranged by bankers from Yankee Farm Credit, who
wanted to know how to lend to sugarmakers. The industry
had changed, and bankers were now willing to lend to the
maple industry. Bruce joked about the day, saying, "I'm in the
big time now." And I think he meant it too.

8

SHORT, SWEET, AND

OF HIGH QUALITY

AFTER THE BIG RUN in February the temperatures dropped and the trees shut down for most of the next ten days. Kevin made only one boil during that time and only two boils until March 8, when another run began, what would be the most unusual run sugarmakers had ever seen.

When that first big run ended on February 24, when Kevin had produced 4018 gallons for the year, he was well ahead of his 2011 output for that same date. As of February 24, 2011, Kevin had produced only 648 gallons on a single boil. That didn't mean he was expressing a great deal of certainty about the 2012 season. When we stood in front of the production chart near the evaporator and looked at the season of 2012 so far, with the early boils, he just shook his head as though to say, "One never knows."

All sugarmakers kept some sort of records of their production, whether on scraps of paper or markings on the wall as I saw at one sugarhouse or the kind of complex and richly detailed narrative of the years as on the chart at Bascom's. Kevin kept the chart. Most prominent were two oversized daily calendars, one with the previous season and the other, ongoing, detailing the current season. Each day he recorded temperatures, notes about the weather, and the production of syrup in grade and pounds to the decimal point. Below those calendars were several years of daily records, reduced to single sheets of paper. Taking up half of this bulletin board was a set of bar graphs that recorded the history of production at Bascom's going back to 1954. In that year Ken Bascom hung 3900 buckets and made 825 gallons of syrup. He had a much better year a decade later in 1964 before making the leap as a full-time maple producer, with 6900 buckets and 2090 gallons.

In the year 2000, when I first learned that Bascom's was the largest producer in New Hampshire, they made 11,212 gallons on 35,000 taps. The next winter of 2001 was a very unusual one—eight feet of snow in February, and the workers had to go into the woods to dig snow from under the mainlines. They made only 4695 gallons that year. Toward the end of the decade came the boom years, after vamping up the R.O. system and switching to the use of new and clean spouts every year. In 2008, 22,500 gallons on 56,800 taps. In 2009, 23,916 gallons on 60,800 taps. In 2010, despite the warm winter, 22,540 gallons on 64,804 taps.

The 2011 season got a late start because of cold weather and an ice storm. In 2011 Kevin made his second boil of the season on March 6, a Sunday, but that night it began to rain heavily, and though the temperature stayed above freezing for most of the night, it plummeted toward morning and the rain began to freeze on the trees, coating the branches and everything else with ice—every blade of grass in the fields and every pine needle on the white pines. It was beautiful and calamitous. When the storm was over I walked through the woods and caught a strong scent of pine, then saw a small tree stripped of its needles, which were lying on the ground encased in ice like pendants. On that Monday morning and through the next day the trees around Bascom's were snapping with a sound like gunshot. On Monday morning I went over to have a look and had to drive under a massive white pine that fell on the road and stretched the power lines down with it.

Strangely enough the bottling crew made it into work that day at 6:00 to get an early start on a big order, just before the trees started falling. Few others made it in. George Hodskins had to cut his way to work, stopping with his chainsaw and removing fallen trees from the road. The tapping crew had finished the week before the storm and buttoned up the system, but with the fallen trees and the freezing rain, the mainlines came crashing down, pulling the tubing from the spouts, and other spouts simply popped out of the trunks. Additional workers went into the woods, breaking through the ice with hatchets and cutting the downed trees away before pulling up the mainlines. It was at the end of the week, on Friday, when I came upon Gwen in the woods during a rain, checking tubing and emptying the water from her boots every so often.

The electricity was out for two days, but the sap was running and they went to gather it. On that first day George went to Glenn's Lot to collect sap in a ten-wheel truck with a 3000-gallon plastic tank in the back, but he had to route around the dairy farm because of the trees straddled across Crane Brook Road. The hill going down to the tank is very steep, but George made it down without problems. Going back up the hill with a full tank was a different matter. George got partway up but began to slide backward on the ice, his truck turned into a 40,000-pound sled, with the 24,000-pound sap tank leading the way. One of his rear wheels hit a snow bank, which spun him around, facing forward and still going down until he hit a ditch. George walked down to Crane Brook Road, where he could get cell service, and called Kevin, who came with the tractor and pulled him out. George got into the bucket of the tractor with a chain saw, and they went along Crane Brook, cutting downed trees and opening the road.

By the end of that week the sap run let loose, and some monstrous days at the evaporator followed. On Saturday Kevin made 1200 gallons, on Sunday more than a thousand gallons. On Monday 720 gallons, on Tuesday 988 gallons, and on Wednesday, March 16, 1296 gallons. Kevin had his biggest day ever on March 17. He had produced concentrate the night before and drew from a tank of 10,000 gallons of sap at twenty percent sugar. He began boiling early in the morning, and when he used up the concentrate he continued with sap at eight percent. Kevin boiled until ten o'clock that night, until he had made 1736 gallons of syrup. His production for that week after the ice storm was also a record 7,642 gallons.

The 2011 season continued for another three and a half weeks, to a final boil on April 13.

BUSINESS AT THE STORE was brisk in 2012 during the last week of February, as people hurried to get fully tapped. I saw

Deb Rhoades at the store one afternoon. Deb ran a gardening business and Peter Rhoades was a forester, but they worked together during the sugar season, taking turns boiling at the old sugarhouse that Peter's grandparents owned. Deb and Peter also tapped their trees together, with Peter drilling the holes and Deb driving the spouts. They owned about 800 acres of woods that they managed not only for maple syrup but also for timber. They worked together at that too, with Peter cutting trees and Deb driving the log skidder. You wouldn't guess that Deb ran a log skidder; she was a bookish person with the look of a librarian, and she read two or three books a week. Deb and Peter had tapped trees for Bruce in the 1970s, with Deb the only woman on the crew. She remembered the long walks out of the woods at the end of the day as difficult—it wasn't easy keeping up with the long-legged men—but she tried to never let them know.

Deb told me that they were behind in their tapping work because of squirrel damage. "There's been an outbreak of squirrels this year," she said. "They've been biting through the lines." Animal damage was something every producer with tubing had to deal with. Squirrels, coyotes, bears, and porcupines were all known to gnaw into tubing for the taste of the sap or for entertainment. The holes caused leaks in the vacuum system and were not easy to find. Deb and Peter were repairing the holes from squirrel teeth with black electrician's tape. She told me that normally they bought a single roll of tape each season and didn't use it all, but this year they had gone through twelve rolls and bought twelve more.

Peter Rhoades and I had gotten to know each other over the past couple of years. When I had asked Bruce to put me in touch with someone who really knew the trees, he sent me to his old friend. I called Peter after I talked with Deb in the store.

"We haven't tried to catch any sap yet," Peter said. He hoped to have their system up and working in a few days. Which meant he would miss the early big sap run. "It's a nice year to be out in the woods, that's for sure," he said. "But I can't imagine we're going to have a good sugar season based on my experience. I've always found the best sugar seasons come after long, cold winters. I've never seen a winter like this one before. There's certainly the potential for the season to be short."

BRUCE WAS DEFINITELY showing an optimistic side when I saw him at the store on the last Saturday in February. He was wearing his boots, his wool jacket, his frayed khakis, and a playful smile. Throughout the morning he kept asking customers about their crops as soon as they passed through the doorway. "Fifteen percent of the crop in February," he kept saying that morning. Kevin had hit fifteen percent on Thursday, February 23, and the amount was written on a whiteboard near the cash register.

"Three thousand, seven hundred, and thirty-five gallons—fifteen percent of crop," Bruce said to another arrival. Though his announcement tended to bring silence because the Bascom figures were so out of whack with everyone else that it was impossible to make sense of them. It was like saying, "I jumped thirty-two feet high but can really jump ninety-six."

There was further reason for optimism, due to the inch of snow that had fallen the night before.

"A little bit of winter," Bruce said.

Aside from the weather, Bruce was puzzling over a possible syrup deal that morning. He said he was two months long, but because the season was beginning, he thought maybe he could afford to be one month long, and could therefore unload some of his supply. Bruce had been talking with Maple Grove about a deal for multiple truckloads. Maple Grove churned through huge amounts of syrup. Bruce didn't expect much of a profit, but that wasn't the point. He wanted a fresh credit line and a chance to acquire new producers. But the deal would be a gamble. If he sold his inventory and the 2012 season turned out to be a poor one, he might be in a bind.

"I have to decide," Bruce said.

"When?"

"When they call." He laughed.

Of course there would always be Canadian syrup to fall back on if the US crop was short. Bruce had many barrels from Quebec in his Cooler and thousands to come in the next months from his numerous suppliers there. One of the risks in that option was that Canadian syrup was tending to be more expensive, with the Federation price and the fluctuating exchange rate.

"Federation" referred to the Federation of Quebec Maple Syrup Producers, the agricultural union that controlled production and marketing of maple syrup in that province. The people of Quebec were passionate about the production of maple syrup, and the cultural tradition was as rich if not more so than that in the United States. The Federation had more than 7000 members in 2012. Quebec produced ninety percent of the Canadian crop and about eighty percent of the world crop—five times the production of the United States in 2010. In doing so, the Federation controlled the world market and also set the world price. It had stabilized an industry that often had wild swings in production and price due to the vagaries of winters. Bruce himself admitted that he and the industry had benefited from Federation policies, and he was deeply involved in that organization as a registered buyer in Quebec. But Bruce had also enjoyed speculating during the wild swings in price of past years, and he, like many others, was a critic of the Federation pricing structure, which, he claimed, was out of touch with the marketplace.

Bruce did what he often did when he started talking about the price differential and when I took on a confounded look: he grabbed a piece of paper and started scribbling. And as usual, when he finished, he crumpled it up and tossed it in the trash, as though it were secret information.

He wrote down the Federation price per pound, which would be $2.89 in 2012, per the Federation's recent announcement. Below that figure he wrote the cost for transportation and procurement, 12 cents a pound, which raised the total price to $3.01. At eleven pounds to the gallon, that meant a bulk price of $33.11 a gallon, which Bruce thought way too steep. To this figure Bruce factored in the exchange rate—at that moment the US dollar was worth 99 cents to the Canadian dollar. That brought the price to $3.05 per pound, Bruce said, which put the bulk price per gallon at $33.55, which was excessively high.

"The time to act is now," Bruce said. He tossed the paper and walked away to help a customer.

Because of the early sap runs, producers were arriving with barrels of syrup to sell to Bruce. This was encouraging even though it seemed far too early in the season. One producer drove from New York with a trailer loaded with barrels. He stopped in at the Cooler, got weighed and graded, then came to the store with a receipt that brought a $9000 check. Liz wrote it out while Bruce talked with the producer, who said, "I started tapping on January twenty-seven. I've never done that before."

Two other customers arrived, who had also driven from upstate New York. Bruce greeted one with, "How much have you made?"

"About five hundred gallons," he said. He was tall and bearded, wearing a hooded sweatshirt.

"That's about fifteen percent of crop, right?"

"Yeah," he answered. Bruce introduced us in his usual way. He told him, "You should talk to this guy," meaning me. "He's a writer, you might end up in a book."

He was from Glen Falls, New York, near the Vermont line, and he managed the sugaring operation for the other man he came with and who was now buying equipment. I asked what he thought of the weather as of late.

He told me he worked in construction and had been outdoors doing roofing. "It's the first winter ever I didn't have to wear long johns," he said. "We've been working in short sleeves."

I asked about his expectations of the season.

He smiled a little, and with an air of authority said, "It will be short, sweet, and of high quality."

Everyone seemed to be talking about the weather that morning. Bruce overheard me talking about it, and in a quieter moment made a comment.

"Maple producers are a bunch of worrywarts, you know that, right? This is the time of the year when they worry about the weather. They are like corn growers, saying that the crop is lost two or three times in a single year."

9

HERE FOR THE

HISTORY

THE FIRST TIME I saw Peter Rhoades at work in his sugarhouse was an afternoon in March, in the 2010 season, after we checked tubing. A bear had passed some time making holes in the lines at the uppermost reach of the system, and we found the leaks by listening for the hissing sounds. We came down through the woods, the yellow bright light on the branch tips, the sky a deep New Hampshire blue. We walked down through the field toward his grandfather's house, where his Aunt Margaret now lived, along the soft snow. Then we went to get his tractor, a 1947 Farmall, and we gathered sap, first from barrels and then from a steel tank, a milk tank. The tank was overflowing, due to a sudden run, so Peter called George at Bascom's to tell him he should make a pickup.

Peter's grandson, who was named after him and who they called Petey, went with us to gather sap and then back to the sugarhouse, staying there until he left to go to Aunt Margaret's just before dark. Peter fired up the evaporator for the first time in 2010.

The Rhoades's sugarhouse was about thirty feet from a brook that ran hard in the spring and trickled in the summer. It was close enough so they could wash equipment in it. The sugarhouse sat up against a bank into which a stonewall had been built—probably in the 1870s, Peter thought, after evaporating pans came into use. The placement against the bank allowed them to back a truck or tractor—in the old days a sled or a wagon—up to a sap tank that was on a level above the evaporator so the sap could easily flow down to the pan. There are still, after all the years, indentations in the ground in front of the sugarhouse from when the horses, before them the oxen, came down the hill and looped back around to the road. Where the narrow road to the sugarhouse joined the road that ran from Aunt Margaret's to Peter's mother's house was a parking space, a 6000-gallon tank, and a shed that housed a vacuum pump and wiring. They were at the bottom of a ravine, and you would never find this place unless you knew exactly how to get there.

The sugarhouse itself is made of castaway boards and timbers. The support beams by the door are notched barn beams that were in a dance pavilion in Alstead before they came to the sugarhouse "and had probably been somewhere else before that," Peter said. There aren't many straight lines in the place. There had been fires there, roofs repaired—so many repairs that not much remained from the original structure. "It's like George Washington's axe," Peter said, "with three new heads and five new handles." There is a small window that looks out onto the brook. The door, made of plywood and braced with timber slabs, has old-fashioned metal latches that flip up to the touch and clink and that were part of the original structure. Inside is a bench along one wall and under the window. It is the only place to sit and where, at the end of the window, Peter and Deb filter their syrup and pour it into containers.

At the end, near the firebox door of the evaporator, they stack wood, mostly pine and hemlock because it's a good use for those woods and because they burn fast and hot. Peter keeps two piles in a field up the road, tall and narrow stacks, nine feet high and thirty feet long, that Peter props up with poles so the wood can catch the wind and sunlight and be dry to burn.

On the far side from the window, and by far I mean eight feet away, is a short set of stairs going up to the sap tanks. It's a good place to get away from the heat of the evaporator; Petey liked to climb up there.

In the center of the room is the evaporator, a Grimm model manufactured in the late 1930s, a duplicate of the Grimm Peter's grandfather bought in the late 1930s. It is a traditional wood-fired model, three feet wide and ten feet long, with a seven-foot fluted flue pan and a three-foot finishing pan, through which the syrup travels on the gradient path until it's drawn off through a pipe and valve outside the pan near the firebox doors.

Peter said of the sugarhouse, "It's totally inefficient, but as long as the building doesn't fall down, we'll use it. We're here because of the history."

He described how it looks during the boiling time, at night: "When you walk up that road, and it's totally dark and cold, and then you see the light through the planks, and come in here and it's all rosy and warm." He spoke those words, and I hoped to see that someday.

Like so many sugarhouses, for that brief period of the year it is a social place. Peter talked about how, when he's boiling, friends will drop by to get some syrup or just to watch the boil. "It's the time for seeing each other and for catching up."

It was the same when Peter's grandmother boiled there. "She boiled for her generation," Peter said. And when he was in school, walking down the road toward home after school, he would stop in to see her, with his sisters, during the sugar season.

Peter lit the fire in the evaporator as the sky was growing dark.

"There," he said, "off and running." Petey left to stay with Aunt Margaret until his mother picked him up. The room filled with steam that hung in the air. Steam flowed out of the vents in the roof, floated down the rooflines, and disappeared. Drops condensed on the ceiling and dripped on our heads. A couple from Walpole came by to talk to Peter; they had just built a sugarhouse. I left and walked down the dark road by the brook to my car.

I RETURNED ON the weekend with my wife. Peter and Deb were just starting the fire when we arrived. Soon it was roaring, and the sap was frothing.

The season was underway throughout the region. On the way over, driving to Peter and Deb's, we had passed sugarhouses and seen the smoke trails coming from their stacks.

Peter and Deb usually tapped in late February and began boiling at the beginning of March, give or take a few days, depending on the flow. Good runs tended to come around the third week of March, Peter had observed. "For years and years the best run was always between March twenty-three and twenty-five," he said, especially after rainy nights. Usually they boiled into the first week of April or a little longer.

From their 5000-tap operation that yielded about 70,000 to 80,000 gallons of sap, the Rhoades kept about 5000 gallons to make syrup, boiling by the traditional method. They didn't use a reverse-osmosis machine, which meant longer boils. They made about one hundred gallons a year, sold it to friends and family, shipped some by mail, or sold it to those customers who visited the sugarhouse. There was a group of those, loyal customers, who came by specifically to taste the syrup right after it was made and leave with some still hot in the container. After this day we would become one of those.

Peter and Deb took turns stoking the fire, keeping it as hot as they could. They said they had different methods of tending the fire, and Peter did seem to jab and stoke the wood more often with the stick they used than Deb did. But the procedure was the same, basically: feed wood to the fire from the pile nearby and keep it blazing.

While he worked Peter talked about the sugarhouse and its iterations. The room was rebuilt in 1947; there was a fire on the roof, and they used the sugarhouse for a few years before repairing it.

When Peter's grandmother boiled there was no floor. "She would put down some boards," Peter said. "Sometimes the brook would overflow, and a rivulet would come right through our sugarhouse."

"Peter's grandmother was a tiny woman," Deb said. "Really tiny."

"Yeah, but she climbed Mount Monadnock at eighty. She worked every day of her life," Peter said.

Peter talked about how, when his grandmother made syrup, she determined when it was finished by taking a temperature reading—syrup boils at a higher temperature than water. "She would measure by degrees, pour it out into a tin, and put a drop of the syrup on top of the tin. That would be how she could tell the color of the syrup."

It was so elemental, this—fire and water, wood and tree sap, steam and smoke. That had to be part of the appeal, this atavistic act of boiling over a wood fire for hours. Deb checked the syrup at the front of the pan now and then with a hydrometer, to measure density, and with a thermometer. Peter checked by lifting the syrup with a scoop and watching how it sheeted off the edges. He watched the bubbles to see how they held together—when they seemed to stick to one another the syrup was getting close.

As I watched I said something about the King Lot and the trees, what a fine few hours I had experienced there. A couple of weeks ago I went along with Peter and Deb while they tapped trees. We walked through a dark glade of hemlocks to what looked like a clearing but was actually a stand of maples—a sugar orchard Peter called it, the first time I had heard that term. The King Lot covered twelve acres and ran down toward the brook near the sugarhouse. The trees were like tall columns, eighty to ninety feet high, and they were 150 to 200 hundred years old, Peter thought. In recent years the trees hadn't been used for sap production. Peter managed them for timber, which was why they were so tall and straight—"Long, straight stems with high crowns," he said, "which is what you want for timber." During the syrup shortage in 2008, when payment for sap went from 21 to 32 cents a gallon, Peter cleared the underbrush and strung tubing, and so returned the trees to their use of 50 to 100 years ago. I kept looking up at them. "This is one of our favorites," he said. "It's nice to look up at the blue sky above them when the leaves are out." Peter thought that people don't look up at the crowns of the trees often enough when they are in the woods. They worked through the morning, and on the way back Peter pointed out a foundation for an arch that was used to make syrup in this sugar orchard before the time of evaporators and sugarhouses. He said he knew of at least a dozen other arches nearby. They valued the history in their woods. They hoped someone in their family would be interested in taking them over someday. Not just in owning them, but in continuing the tradition.

At the King Lot Peter said, "We hope that the grandkids come along with enough interest to take over when we're too weak to come out here."

"Petey seems to be very interested now," Deb said. "He wants to come down here all the time, to the sugarhouse."

Peter talked about how when he was a boy he thought he would be a dairy farmer, but it became clear by the time he was ten that dairying wasn't the best choice. He decided in his teens to go into forestry. Now he was a forester for several towns around here, had a private clientele and this, the sugaring operations at the center of a sizeable managed forest, with its various orchards named according to the previous owners.

"After I finished college, when I was back here at home and spent a day in the woods, I would come home and talk to my dad and granddad about what I did that day, and they knew every tree I was talking about. After they died no one was interested in what I had done that day. They gave me validity."

That would have worked both ways, I suppose, in that he would have given validity to them too. And validity seemed to be what he was passing on, or hoped to do. That could be a mutual gift.

Bruce was looking at a similar challenge, but with a very different set of conditions. His too was a forestry operation looking at another generation.

Bruce's name came up that day as we talked about taste. The syrup that the two old friends produced was markedly different in character. Sometimes when Peter and Deb stoked the fire, smoke came into the air. Some people claimed that smoke was a component in the flavor of this type of syrup. When Bruce and Peter used to visit Peter's sugarhouse, he teased him about the wood smoke getting into the syrup and said he should try to find a way to filter that out.

This was a part of the discussion about the difference in flavor between the modern method—filtered and flash cooked—and the traditional wood-fired approach, with its lengthy boil. Often the word used to describe this kind of syrup, cooked for a long time over a hot fire, was caramelization. Bruce himself claimed that the caramelization of sugars was the difference between the new and the old.

The description of taste and flavor in maple syrup could go much farther. Vanilla was the most common word used, after the maple flavor itself. Creamy and chocolate were other descriptors. Some aficionados claimed that terroir, the influence of geology and geography, played an important role—the granite soils of New Hampshire or the limestone and shale soils of Vermont. The Canadian agriculture department created a flavor wheel for identifying the flavors of maple for the purpose of developing accomplished tasters who would wield all sorts of descriptive words, such as marshmallow, dark brown sugar, brown coffee bean, or even roasted dandelion root, coconut, mango, or baking apple. Or even hay, which I had yet to experience.

This syrup would be darker in color. Between this day and the time five days ago, when I checked tubing with Peter and he made the first fire of the season, there was some 50° weather. "Because of the two fifty-degree days we had this week, the syrup is going to be B grade," Deb said.

That was okay with us. We liked B grade best of all. I had talked to one sugarmaker who sold to a diner in Boston, and the waitresses told him they got better tips when they served B grade. They thought it had more flavor.

"The sap and the syrup is always changing over the course of the season," Deb said. "Sometimes it will get dark and then lighten again."

When some of the syrup was ready—219° by the thermometer, sixty-seven percent sugar by the hydrometer, sheeting off the spoon the way Peter liked—they took off a gallon and a half. They boiled two hours to get that gallon and a half.

After opening the draw-off valve and pouring syrup into a stainless-steel bucket, Peter poured the syrup through two filter cloths, one a bit finer than the other, into a cream pan. We tasted some: exquisite.

Peter then poured a sample into a jar and placed it into a grading set, matching it to other samples. This syrup was not actually B grade but rather a notch lighter, an A dark. Third on the scale of color: A light, A medium, A dark, then B, and even a darker C grade, all according to light transmittance.

Deb poured the syrup into containers, plastic jugs, labeled them, and we left with a gallon. Its flavor—maple, vanilla, maybe a note of chocolate, and something else, some as-of-yet-unnamable quality.

A WEEK LATER in that 2010 season, when we visited again, on March 20, the first day of spring, their season was over.

"This is the earliest we've ever shut down," Peter said. "The trees want to run. It just won't freeze."

"We've been making C grade all week," Deb said.

When we arrived on this bright March day, Peter was on his tractor gathering water. He was going to use it to cool the evaporator and to clean it. Deb was in the sugarhouse, doing the last boil. They would make a few gallons at the sugar-house, take what boiled down sap was left over, and finish it off at their house.

The 2010 season turned warm during the second week of March, right after Town Meeting Day. The temperatures started to rise into the forties and fifties by day and settle around the freezing point at night, or even a few degrees below at Bascom's, but not enough to give the trees the charge they needed to run. During that week I had been at Bascom's and gone to check tubing with Jeremy Bushway, a member of the tapping crew at the Cole's Lot, one of the colder places among Bruce's sugar lots. There we tromped along on snow-shoes following the mainlines and looking for leaks, and we were on the way back toward the road when Jeremy said it was going to be a "quick season." I didn't know what he meant and wasn't sure I believed him—there was so much snow on the ground—but I knew the run had slowed in the last couple of days. Kevin told me the sap had run all through the night—good for gathering but not a good omen for the season. Jeremy said the forecast for the next five days called for temperatures above freezing at night. He told me that people on gravity were cleaning up their equipment. Jeremy would work one more day checking tubing and then be finished for the season.

They were saying that the sugarmakers farther north were doing better, that the temperatures were fluctuating between midtwenties and midforties, and they did keep going longer. But later that year, when Timothy Prescott, of the Proctor Maple Research Center, gave talks at maple meetings, he would say that 2010 "was a strange year, a short season with few freeze events. Between March ten and March twenty-seven there was no freeze at all." There were only three major freeze events during the 2010 season throughout Vermont and New Hampshire, Prescott said. Normally the season would have gone to mid-April in the northern part of Vermont. "We lost about two weeks," he said. "This was a good year for vacuum, not for buckets."

The warm period came before New Hampshire's Maple Weekend, when sugarmakers opened up their sugarhouses to the public. Some sugarmakers called Bruce, asking if they could buy some sap to boil, but Bruce told them he didn't sell sap; he bought it. Some sugarmakers boiled water that weekend just to have the evaporators running, out of custom. As a result of the 2010 short season the date for Maple Weekend was moved to an earlier date, from the fourth weekend in March to the third.

As Tim Prescott said, 2010 was a good year for vacuum but not for buckets. Bascom's held on as though they were a hundred miles further to the north, with their high vacuum and tight tubing systems and their colder lots. Unlike many others, Bascom's didn't shut their vacuum pumps off at all during the season, which made the trees produce for a longer period. Bascom's boiled until April 3.

On March 20, when Peter shut down, he was quick to say that every season is different and told me, when I talked about the character of the 2010 season, that "in 1925 my grandfather and his brothers made all their syrup in February."

But Peter worried about climate change and the effect it would have on maple syrup production. He had been to a conference on climate change a few years ago, where he heard that at present trends there would be no maple syrup production in southern New Hampshire by the end of the century "and possibly within the next fifty years. It seems to be accelerating."

In 2009 the State of New Hampshire issued a "Climate Action Plan," which contained some dire warnings:

> Changes are already occurring to New England's climate, including warmer winters, reduced snowfall and snow-on-ground days, increased rainfall, rising sea level, and more severe weather events that result in increased risk of flooding. These changes are projected to grow in severity and could include other impacts such as a decrease in the abundance of sugar maples, stresses on our fisheries, more widespread occurrence of insect-borne diseases, and an increase of heat-related illnesses. Although the extent and timing of these potential impacts is uncertain, the costs of inaction could be large. The Stern Review found that failure to take actions to avoid the worst effects of climate change could de-

press global gross domestic product (GDP) by as much as 20 percent below what it otherwise might have been. On the other hand, avoiding the most severe impacts of climate change would require the investment of just 1 percent of global GDP per year. As a small state, New Hampshire is responsible for only a minor fraction of emissions contributing to global climate change. However, the actions identified in this plan will enable New Hampshire to continue to do its part to reduce emissions of greenhouse gases and prepare for a changing climate.

Another paragraph stated, "On a regional scale, the 2007 Northeast Climate Impacts Assessment (NECIA) concludes that if greenhouse gas emissions continue to increase at current rates, by late in this century New Hampshire's climate will more closely resemble that of North Carolina."

Such a change would reduce the viability of New Hampshire's ski areas, a $650 million industry in the state; kill the snowmobiling economy—already almost eliminated in southern areas due to lack of snowfall; increase the frequency and severity of heavy, damaging rainfall events; increase the frequency of summer droughts; increase coastal flooding and property damage from an estimated rise in sea level; increase human health problems due to extreme heat; and bring change in forest species and extinctions.

Peter Rhoades, as the chairman of the planning board in Alstead, already knew of the danger of heavy damaging rainfall events. In 2005, when ten inches of rain fell in a single day, the Cold River flooded, taking out bridges, washing away homes, and killing five people. A photograph of one of the destroyed bridges appeared in the New Hampshire

Action Plan on the opening page of chapter 3, "Adapting to Climate Change," which included this statement: "In 2005, forest-based manufacturing and forest-related recreation and tourism in the state contributed over $2.3 billion. These industries will face significant challenges as the climate continues to change. Climate models project decreases in the number of frost days, where temperatures dip below freezing, and increases in the length of frost-free growing seasons. Tree species composition is likely to change. . . . The eventual changes in forest composition and function could profoundly alter the scenery and character of New Hampshire, as well as the ecosystem services our forests provide."

"A climate like North Carolina?" I said of what seemed the strangest detail in the report.

To which Peter responded, "We want to give this to our grandchildren, but we can't give them something that isn't there."

But the feeling that day was only that the season was coming to an end, not the industry. Peter was the welcoming host, as was Deb. It was a beautiful spring day in March: the brook was flowing, the sugarhouse was running, even if it was a quick season, and all seasons are different—1925 was a quick year. Deb took off some syrup—this was dark and chocolaty with an orange hue and richly flavored, not something you'd see in a pancake restaurant or even on a grocery store shelf but instead something almost enchanting for home use, especially if you knew where it came from and how it was made.

We left them to finish up. Later Peter ran water through the evaporator and a cleaner to take off the burnt sugar and the niter—or sugar sand, the crystallized potassium nitrate.

Getting that off was essential. Then he took down the smokestack. He closed the windows and then turned it over to the squirrels and mice.

A YEAR LATER on a Saturday night in 2011 my wife and I walked along the road to Peter's sugarhouse, lighting our way with a flashlight. It was a cloudy and dark night, about 8:00 on March 12, a few days after the big ice storm at Bascom's. A cold winter. When we got close I turned off the flashlight because we wanted to see what the sugarhouse looked like. The snow was piled high around this opening in the woods, and the trees rose all around us while the brook roared from down below. Then a cascade of sparks rose from the stack, shooting high as the treetops. Peter was stoking the fire and tossing more wood on. We could see the steam billowing through the vent windows and hanging over the roof, and we could smell the scent of maple sugar.

Peter was alone inside, making the first boil of the year. Deb boiled earlier in the day, and Peter took over for her after dinner. They hadn't poured off any syrup yet. The first boil was often slow, Peter said, and it was made even slower by the low sugar content in the sap.

This was a delayed season, 2011. Peter's trees were still relatively frozen. "The sap's not really running," Peter said. "Blah weather. Temperatures in the high thirties. Cloudy."

"Some sunlight is needed?"

"Not just sunlight, but a change." Something to trigger the run. That would happen fairly soon. In the end Peter and Deb would have their best year, making 150 gallons.

We stayed about two hours, talking to Peter and watching the boil. The steam hung sometimes around the waist, sometimes above the head. We left before Peter poured the syrup off, unfortunately. He said that a half hour later he poured off five gallons. When we walked out we did the same as when coming—turning off the flashlight to watch the sparks fly in the air and see the rosy glow inside the sugarhouse.

On Sunday afternoon I returned again, and this time I meant to stay until they poured off the syrup.

Petey was at the sugarhouse on this day along with Peter. Deb was off running errands. Petey had brought a stuffed animal, a dragon, and placed it on the stairway above the evaporator. The dragon was on loan from his school, here to help him write a story about his adventures over the weekend. Petey figured he would get two pages out of today.

Peter was bringing him along slowly, teaching a bit at a time. When maple syrup boils it builds up foam, and sugarmakers use a defoamer—usually canola oil, a few drops at a time—to settle the foam down. By some mysterious process three or four small drops of oil break the surface tension of foam over the entire boil, and the chatter of the bubbles settles down immediately.

"Why is foam bad?" Petey asked.

"It is when it comes up over the side. Otherwise it's not," Peter answered.

After an hour Peter's mother, Ellie Rhoades, stopped by. She lived at the end of Rhoades Road in the house where Peter grew up. She had done the boiling in this sugarhouse in 1948, she said, when Peter's grandmother was away tending to a sick relative. She and Peter's father gathered sap on weekends and at night.

After Peter's mother left, a friend named Anton Elbers dropped by with two of his friends. He said he wanted to show them a real sugarhouse. Elbers was an original back-to-the-lander, a member of a commune that settled in this area in 1971. A local farmer helped them begin, and for years he and Anton sugared together. They ran a sugarhouse in partnership and got up to 3000 buckets. Anton still did some sugaring on a small scale, he said, but it was impossible to continue at that level because you had to commit four weeks full time to it. He wasn't a fan of plastic tubing. "I wouldn't do tubing," Anton said. "I just wouldn't go there. I couldn't see putting tubing in the woods. I couldn't do it."

"I couldn't see going back to buckets," Peter said, laughing.

Anton explained the evaporation process to his friends, and Peter told them about sugar content and the Rule of 86. Peter said he boiled an average of fifty-seven gallons of sap to get a gallon of syrup. Anton explained the reverse-osmosis process, how it was possible to filter out eighty percent of the water so that a sugarmaker only had to boil four gallons. Which was something Peter didn't do here. As a result his was a slower process. Anton teased Peter about the syrup not being ready for his friends.

Good things come from waiting. They left as I had the night before, a half hour before the syrup was ready. Peter poured a few gallons into a steel bucket. He asked Petey to watch the float level while he tended to the syrup. The float level showed the amount of syrup in the flue pan, and Petey kept an eye on it, at one point opening the valve to let a little more sap flow in.

Peter brought the syrup to the bench near the window and poured it through the layers of felt cloth. He then poured it into plastic jugs. A one-gallon container, a half-gallon container, seven quarts, a pint—almost four gallons altogether. He set the jugs on their sides to cool.

Peter poured some of the syrup into tea cups and set one on a shelf by me. "Try some when it's cooled a bit," he said.

He poured some into the grading set and compared. An A-medium, he said. Peter labeled the jugs, putting the date on them and the grade. He then stoked the fire, and the boil roared up again.

Peter asked me if I ever heard of a man named Hemon Chase. He was a surveyor and wrote a couple of books about his life. "He was the person in the oldest generation I admired most," Peter said. "He and Ben Porter. Ben Porter was a surveyor too." And a sugarmaker, I heard, someone who also refused to use tubing, declaring he would never suck sap out of his trees.

Peter admired their honesty. "I don't know if it was their character that made them surveyors or whether it was surveying that made them who they were. Maybe it was being out in the woods all day. I suppose that today surveyors don't even have to go into the woods."

"Thoreau was a surveyor," I said. "Henry David Thoreau, who wrote *Walden*."

"Hemon used to drink a shot glass of maple syrup every day. I used to bring him a quart now and then."

I had been and would go into the woods with Peter on occasion, and I had wondered how his life in the woods influenced his development. Peter was known as an ethical forester. ("I hope so," he said, when I brought it up one time.) Mostly I liked hearing his perspective as I watched him work and listened to him talk about trees. I watched him make choices as to which trees to cut and which to leave in a town forest in nearby Walpole—he was making decisions that would bear out long after his lifetime, such as when he selected an oak tree that would bear acorns, that would produce other oaks, that would also bear acorns, that would feed wildlife that would find that particular spot a favorable place to be 150 years from now. It seemed to me that the mentality of ethical forest management was similar to the mentality needed to reduce the human effect—the mentality for effective forest management could be a guide for reducing climate change. The long view, 150 years from now.

Peter stoked the fire and it roared again, another stream of sparks soaring up the stack. I picked up the teacup and sipped. My words: "Oh my, this is amazing. Never have I tasted anything like this."

How to describe it? I couldn't stop sipping, light sips.

"I hope I don't get sick drinking so much of this," I said.

"You won't," Peter answered.

Just then Aunt Margaret came to get Petey, as it was getting dark. Peter's Aunt Margaret was a teacher in Baltimore before she moved back to Acworth to take care of her parents, and she lived in the old farmhouse atop the hill above the sugarhouse. Peter handed her a teacup.

I said something that included the word amazing about the taste.

"The best," she said.

Petey took his dragon off the stairs and walked out, but Peter called him back. "Here, take a quart of syrup for Aunt Margaret," he said.

I soon left with a gallon of my own, enough to last a few months. I stopped to look at the sugarhouse again, the steam still rising, clouding actually, as it rolled down the roof. I saw sparks shoot up through the chimney. So elemental, all of it. I walked along the brook, passing through a pocket of cool air, carrying the jug that was so hot I had to keep switching hands.

When I got home I told Kathy she should taste some while it was still warm. She made some toast. I opened the jug, and she bent down to it.

"It has the scent of the sugarhouse," she said.

I bent to take a whiff of the vapors. "You're right. It's not just the maple scent, but the sugarhouse itself."

"Yes," she said.

"It has the scent of the wood, the woodpile, doesn't it?"

"Yes."

That was it, the magic of this. Under the right conditions the sweetness of the sap, the taste of the tree, and also the character of the place where it was made. It seemed so, on this particular day.

10

THE SUGAR MACHINE

BRUCE LEFT A PHONE MESSAGE and then sent an e-mail, asking whether I had seen the new sugar machine. This was a surprise to me because the sugar-making operation had always been off-limits. "Top secret," Bruce said back in 2010. He even said this to the woman in Brattleboro who sold the granulated and powdered maple sugar; Cindy Finck was her name. You couldn't help wonder what was going on in the sugar plant. Sometimes they ran three shifts, making sugar day and night in that room with the closed doors beyond the Cooler.

Occasionally I talked with the man who was making the sugar, Joe James. This always happened when I was in the Cooler by the scales, when Joe came out of the room, dusted in powdery white. To me Joe had the look of an Iroquois warrior—tall, fierce, and sensitive, with a shaved head and a goatee. He was a chef by trade, one who now made sugar. Joe was quick to say that he was not a sugarmaker. "I make sugar," he would say. And lots of it. Day by day Joe was probably making more maple sugar than anyone else in the world. Leading up to the changeover to the new machine, Joe was putting in serious hours building up a surplus of granulated and powdered maple sugar, just in case there was some sort of malfunction.

Ken Bascom would have liked Joe James, maybe, for the eighty-hour weeks he put in. Doing the work of two or three men, Joe got ahead of the orders and had accumulated 500 barrels of sugar. The barrels were stacked two high and spread wide in a corner of the Cooler. As the stacks accumulated, Joe increasingly spent more time there. Once he said to me of the surplus, "I guard it like it's my kid. Why? Because I made it."

Those 500 barrels represented a significant investment. It took fifty gallons of syrup to make a barrel of sugar, which weighed about 350 pounds. Therefore, Joe James's 500 barrels represented 25,000 gallons of maple syrup, about one-fourth of the average New Hampshire crop, about $750,000 worth of syrup wholesale and $1,375,000 retail. But the sugar was worth much more than that. I paid $14 for a one-pound bag. Multiplied out by that figure, the retail value of Joe's surplus would be about $2.45 million.

Though expensive, granulated maple sugar was a fun product to use. I did a little experimenting with my pound and sprinkled some on French toast (very nice), made bread pudding (perfect for that), spooned some on oatmeal (no better way to add maple flavor), and stirred it into coffee. I heard that chocolatiers were becoming interested because of the smooth consistency maple sugar brought to a chocolate sauce, and I tried that—possibly the best use of all.

The biggest customer for Bascom's sugar was a Japanese man named Takashi Oshio. He had attended the University of Vermont, discovered maple syrup, and formed a company to export it to Japan. Though Oshio was promoting syrup, the majority of his sales were in maple sugar. He sold it to bakeries and other food manufacturers. Bruce told me that Oshio's most enthusiastic customers were Japanese girls, who ate the sugar like candy out of small plastic bags. Bascom's shipped a truckload a month to Japan, sometimes two. A truckload consisted of about 147 barrels—about twenty-five tons of sugar.

I met Takashi Oshio for an entertaining couple of hours during one of his periodic visits. He brought gift bags with samples of products in development—instant maple cappuccino, maple cookies, maple cereal. He held a tasting session and asked for comments. Most tended to be "Very good." The main event, mostly tongue-in-cheek on Mr. Oshio's part, was his performance of "Home on the Range" on a musical saw, an actual handsaw played with a violin bow. Bruce and David took the performance seriously, however. They printed up lyrics and assembled in the lunchroom all the workers they could gather. The woods crew was there, in boots and jackets. The bottling crew in white shirts and hairnets. Bruce, David, Sam Bascom (David's son, who worked in the equipment store). A couple of the women from upstairs in the offices. Before Mr. Oshio began, Bruce and David presented him with another handsaw, not musical but painted, with scenes from Bascom's. Mr. Oshio made a couple of false starts but then to that weird metallic vibrato everyone sang, "Give me a home, where the buffalo roam, and the deer and the antelope play . . ." Even Bruce sang, or seemed to. There was a round of applause and then a friend of Bruce's, a sugarmaker and metal fabricator named Gardner Stetson, who was also a church organist, bowed his way through a tune. Judging by the expressions on both Mr. Oshio's and Mr.

Stetson's faces, fleeting moments of pain—the saw was a fun but unruly instrument to play.

All these weeks and months Joe James had been working on and had adapted to the old machine that Bruce had bought at auction after a maple company folded. Joe made a barrel of sugar—one barrel at a time with each batch—like he might make a bouillabaisse. As the syrup was cooking and approaching the crystallization stage, he sniffed the air—a smell like cider was good. Joe also felt the air upon his skin. If it felt too sharp and acidic, it might be time to adjust. Depending on what he sensed, Joe might dump another barrel into the mixing tank, and this is where it got tricky; this is where Joe's skills as a man who made sugar came into play.

The leaves on a maple tree produce carbohydrates through the process of photosynthesis. When the trees thaw in late winter or early spring they convert those carbohydrates into sucrose. When sugarmakers extract the sap from the trees, that first run contains nearly pure sucrose. People who make maple candy prefer syrup made on the second run, after the tubing lines have cleaned out during the first run.

From then on, as bacteria and yeasts grow and act upon the sap, some of that sucrose is converted into other sugars, such as glucose and fructose. In technical terms the twelve-carbon-atom sugar of sucrose is converted into the six-carbon atom of glucose and fructose—essentially the microorganisms split the molecules. The sugars are inverted, as they say. As the temperature warms and the season progresses, the amounts of inverted sugar in the sap and syrup increase.

Some inverted sugar is essential for making granulated sugar and other maple confections, but generally a low invert level is preferred. The higher the level of inverted sugar, the more difficult it becomes for the larger sucrose molecules to bond and crystallize. When people like Joe James are making sugar, they test the syrup and select barrels with a range of invert levels. Those barrels, in a sense, become Joe's pantry. When he is making syrup—smelling the air or looking at the color of the sugar in his batches—Joe adds barrels with different invert levels according to his judgment—a two or seven percent or even twelve percent invert (about as high as he could go with the old machine). If the sugar was coming out too light, Joe might add a high-invert syrup to his mixing tank to darken the batch.

The limitation of making maple sugar was that the invert level had to be relatively low, and this limited the kind of syrup a sugarmaker could use, sometimes severely. Joe, through practice and with Bruce's help, was able to push the boundaries and use higher inverts—use the darker, more late-in-the-season kinds of syrup. Though sometimes, for some strange reason, light syrup could be high invert and dark syrup could be low—one never could truly tell going strictly by color. If the choice of the syrup going into the mixing tank was wrong, the sugar could go awry too. Joe once walked out of the sugar room with a batch of softballs to show the guys what he had made. The process could strain the machine while the sugar crystallized inside; Joe often watched the electric meter surge when crystallization was occurring. There had been times when Joe crawled inside the machine with a hammer and chisel to break up some solidified mass of sugar. Freak batches aside, Joe kept producing—thirty-five batches a week sometimes—working seven days a week, accumulating his stacks of surplus, his sugar babies.

In March 2012, however, Joe was told to slow down, that he was getting too far ahead. He went back to working a forty-hour week, which seemed like nothing. But Joe lay awake at night thinking about his diminishing stockpile. When it got down to 150,000 pounds in those barrels, he thought, there would be only seventy-five tons left. An order from Oshio could wipe out a third of that.

Bruce was well aware of the whole process and the limitations of invert levels in syrup. His goal in developing the new machine and in making sugar in general was to further push the boundaries of the types of syrup he could use. Bruce wanted to be able to use syrup with any invert level, to use B grade, C grade, or even Commercial syrup with invert levels that got up to twenty percent. It was also possible even to use buddy syrup, that late-season syrup with a taste of the leaf, because when all the water was burned off the leafy taste departed too. As one maple syrup producer told me, Bruce had pioneered the use of darker syrups for making granulated maple sugar. The new machine would be the only one of its kind in North America. The only one in the world, Joe James said, and this was probably true, as North America was the only place maple sugar was made at this level.

For Joe James the new machine meant another change. In March 2012, when Bruce and I stood in the parking lot with Peter Gregg, the editor of *Maple News,* who happened to have stopped by for the day, Bruce pointed to the building where the sugar machine was housed and said, "That's top secret." Then he broke the secret and told Gregg that with the new machine they would be able to make granulated sugar from any kind of syrup, that it would be only a matter of turning dials. Like John Henry driving steel, Joe would no longer need to smell the air or feel the acidity on his skin. He would be using a touch screen, becoming less of a chef and more of an operator, a button pusher.

I THINK BRUCE wanted to show me the new sugar machine simply because he was proud of it, because after several years of development here it was, designed in the United States, engineered in Germany, shipped to Acworth, and almost ready to begin production in such a way to capture the market. Secrecy would always be part of the program, but for now Bruce was opening up the doors and letting a few people see what he'd done.

"Tell me if this is interesting," he said when we walked over to look at it. "I think it's interesting, but I want to know what you think."

A few words about the geography here. The Cooler, what was once called Bruce's Playroom, had expanded in two directions. Most of the expansion was to the east, toward Ken's Lot. The Middle Cooler was attached to the original Cooler, and above it was the warehouse for used and new equipment. On the east end of the Middle Cooler was grafted the new building, with the New Cooler, above which was the warehouse and bottling plant.

To the opposite side of the Cooler, to the westward, was the sugar room. A new building had been grafted on to that, not so large, approximately thirty feet by thirty feet. This new addition was defined by its verticality. It had a deep basement and two floors. When it arrived the sugar machine was dropped down into this structure with a crane.

Bruce and I rounded the corner of this new building and surprised two construction workers who were throwing snowballs made of the fresh snow. "Working hard or hardly working?" Bruce asked as we passed by.

We climbed the stairs and entered a new kitchen and coatroom, then passed into an open space where another set of stairs led to a room on the top floor. These stairs were industrial, bright aluminum with handrails and well crafted.

"It's like something on a ship, isn't it?" Bruce said as we climbed up.

Here on this uppermost level, surrounded by a gangway, was a capsule-shaped chamber made of thick stainless steel with many huge bolts and fastenings, with a hatch on top and rounded ends that made it look like a miniature submarine. There were hoses and pipes feeding into it. And, importantly, attached near one end was a panel with a touchscreen.

Bruce lifted up the hatch, which was at about head height, and I stretched up to peer inside. There, to churn the syrup as it went through the crystallization process, was a large screw running the length of the capsule, a magnified version of a flour grinder or meat grinder. "The syrup will be cooked with steam," Bruce said, "but a vacuum pump will reduce the temperature to a hundred and ninety degrees so the sugar doesn't caramelize." That seemed clever, that you could use vacuum to reduce a boiling temperature. The room would be air conditioned, Bruce said, so there would be no condensation building on the metal parts. That was another new development for Joe James, who would no longer have to work in 80° to 90° heat.

We went down a stairway to the second, or middle, floor. Here was another capsule, as large as the one above and with as many oversized nuts and bolts, but this one had a chute on top instead of a hatch. Through the chute the cooked sugar would drop down and be mixed with paddles. On the outside of this capsule were sensors, attached to and guiding the paddles. In this unit the sugar was cooled by means of a stack of refrigeration units placed outdoors.

A testing period would soon begin, which was the reason Joe was building up that surplus. No telling how long it would last. Bruce said, "David and I both think there's a hundred thousand dollar mistake in here somewhere."

Another stairway led down to the basement of the building to the sifter. This unit had conveyer belts with screens that would move rapidly and separate the sugar into powder and grain. The finished sugar would drop from the sifter into barrels.

In the next room the old sugar machine was cranking away, and Bruce said that the interior wall between the two rooms would soon be taken down. I looked through the window and saw the old sifter vibrating, like a cement mixer on springs.

We climbed back to the top floor and stopped by the cooking capsule again. "With this," Bruce said, "we will be able to make all the sugar America needs for a very long time."

A lofty goal. It was weird to think that this product, dry sugar, was made by Indians and by the sugarmakers of 150 years ago during the Civil War, during the no-sugar-made-by-slaves era, and that 50 years later folks around here had been making it in pans in their kitchen.

"It's impressive," I said to Bruce in response to his question earlier. This was another huge project, especially considering the cooler down at the other end of all these buildings. "You've grown so much in the past two years."

"We're now at the point where I can't run everything on my own. I could run the warehouses and all that goes on there if I focused just on that. But I can't focus just on that. I've got too many other things to do."

He said more quietly, "It's not easy to motivate tiers of people to make everything run smoothly."

"Could someone like Tom Zaffis run this for you?" I asked. Bruce had mentioned Zaffis, saying it seemed less likely he would come.

"We'd need two people, two managers." He chuckled and said, "We've gotten big."

"You already were big."

"If I die, no telling what will happen. They'll have to sell out parts of it."

He was thinking about the possibility of getting several part-owners involved, giving stock to several people "and then letting them fight it out."

When we left the building Bruce heard a sound, the banging of steel barrels. The noise was coming from the area on the other side of his house, a flat open space where they stored barrels. "Let's go over there and see what's going on," he said.

As we walked by his house Bruce said, "Barrel organization is a problem. We're going to have to devote someone to it full time someday."

The area was large enough for a trailer truck to turn around, and along the edges were stacks of barrels of a multitude of origins. There were barrels with embossed lids that read American Maple, R.C. Coombs, Jacques & Bureau, Carey Maple (the forerunner of Maple Grove), and dozens of contemporary sugarmakers from the United States and Canada.

Three men were loading barrels from one of the stacks, tossing them into a long trailer. The three worked in the coolers—Dave St. Aubin, the cooler manager; Greg Minard, who worked with him; and Brooke Adams, who spent all of his time cleaning or moving barrels. Brooke had done other jobs at Bascom's, but he preferred steam cleaning barrels and took a philosophical approach to it. "I do barrels," he said with a note of importance to its utmost necessity at the base of the business. "The only guy who can make a career out of steaming barrels," Bruce had said to him once. Brooke thought about barrels and even talked to his barrels. He could—I saw him do it—walk along and roll two barrels on their edges at one time. Brooke cleaned 100 barrels a day, 500 a week, 2000 a month, 24,000 barrels a year.

We watched them work for a while for the fun of it. Greg Minard, who was a football player a few years ago, tended to pick them up and throw them with a chest pass. Brooke, leaner and longer, had a way of putting his body into it, with a turn, twist, and toss.

These barrels were headed to Moravia, New York, to a man named Dan Weed, who was one of Bruce's sub-buyers, his agents. Bruce controlled seventy-five percent of the bulk market in New York through the efforts of people like Weed.

I had met him two months ago when I traveled with Bruce to the annual maple conference in Verona, New York. Weed had a booth there. He told me he got into making maple syrup in the mid-1990s after his daughter received a gift of maple spouts from her grandparents. He helped her tap some trees and boil the sap. Now Weed owned a sizeable sugarhouse and worked in partnership with his son, buying syrup and selling it to Bruce. Weed also told me in Verona that his brother was involved too, that he made pancake mixes.

"And you can't get a closer relationship than that," Weed said. It was probably true, though you had to think about those other relationships on the table, about cream and coffee, bacon and eggs, vanilla and chocolate, cheese and hamburger, lettuce and tomato, peanut butter and jelly, you could go on and on—but this effort here, this was all about that special relationship with the pancake.

Sugar was a different story, though, an old timer now a newcomer on the market. In further news Bruce soon told me that Gold Coast had made an order for 50,000 pounds of maple sugar in six-ounce bags. Joe James started working overtime again.

11

YOU NEED

A MOUNTAIN

INSIDE THE STORE on the whiteboard were the words, "We made 5000 gallons!" Kevin boiled on February 29, the only boil in that ten-day interval after the big run. The boil was after two days of what he called "a light run" on the chart, but it was a substantial day, when he made 1022 gallons, and it moved the total 2012 production up to 5040 gallons. And so the announcement on this Saturday, March 3.

A snowstorm had passed through, large enough for moderate rejoicing. Eight inches fell on March 1, an inch on Friday, March 2, and another inch was coming down on that Saturday we spent in the store.

Bruce's neighbor Alvin Clark, an eighty-year-old sugarmaker, was one of those rejoicing. After the snowstorm Alvin gathered up his flat pans, went to his backyard, filled them with snow, and put them in his freezer. Alvin even froze some icicles and snowballs, thinking he might use them in July.

On that Saturday morning a man came up to the counter with a stack of books and said he drove 145 miles, all the way from Connecticut. He had tapped the four giant maples on his property that spring and hung eleven buckets. He said he was collecting twenty-five gallons of sap a day. "It's flowing so hard you don't hardly hear any breaks between drops," he said. He felt that because he was harvesting the sap from his trees, he had a responsibility to do something with it.

"I came all the way up here for these books," he said to Bruce, who got up from his stool, looked at the stack, and said he liked the manual from Ohio State University. The man said he had made two gallons of syrup so far, boiling in a turkey cooker. It was a very light syrup, much lighter than the syrup in the display bottles on the shelf over by the wall.

"That syrup in those bottles is all Fancy grade," Bruce said. Fancy being the Vermont term for the highest and lightest grade of syrup—you couldn't make syrup unless you could make fancy, I heard Vermonters say. "Some of the bottles are larger than the others, and the syrup looks darker because of that."

The man from Connecticut wanted to know how to improve. Should he buy an evaporator? Another customer who was standing nearby said he lived in Connecticut too, but he grew up in New Hampshire. He offered some advice, then they traded phone numbers and went to look at the new evaporators.

While Bruce worked out a deal on some used equipment outdoors at the back of a pickup truck, I went into the Cooler to see what was happening there. Business at the Cooler was slow so far this year, unlike 2011 when the trucks had lined up at the door, and lately Dave St. Aubin had been relegated to the store, bagging spouts. Though there were some busy days. Bruce bought several truckloads of commercial syrup and Dave was organizing those, and Bruce was buying lots of 2011 syrup that some producers had been holding onto in case of a shortage but were now unloading. A truckload of syrup had come in from Pennsylvania Amish country via Henry Brennaman after a good start there. On this Saturday Dave was weighing syrup brought in by a Vermont sugarmaker, Jed Wheeler, who lived in the part of the state they call the Northeast Kingdom, near the Canadian border. His company was called Jed's Maple Products, and among their products was a line of mustards sold at Whole Foods supermarkets. Wheeler was an engineer before returning to where he grew up to run a maple business with his wife and family. There was snowfall in the Northeast Kingdom too, nearly three feet of snow. "We're about four inches away from going out on snowshoes to clear snow from under the mainlines," he said. The sap hadn't run yet in the Northeast Kingdom.

As we talked, someone appeared in the doorway—the man from Connecticut. He wanted to know where to find the used equipment. Next door, Dave St. Aubin said, in the next warehouse. Off he went, the newest, most earnest sugarmaker.

THE SAP RAN SLOWLY during that first March weekend, but Kevin boiled on Monday, managing to make 279 gallons. The temperatures on Monday and Tuesday were too cold for a run—5° on Tuesday, March 6, not getting above freezing in the afternoon.

Things were about to change however, according to the new forecast. Wednesday called for temperatures in the high fifties. On Thursday, March 8, temperatures were supposed to reach 60°.

Of that Bruce said, "We'll be making grade A-dark with sixty-degree weather. Up north everything will let loose."

He told me he made a trip to northern Vermont, making the rounds of the maple supply companies in the northwest corner of the state. He visited Dominion & Grimm, CDL, LaPierre, and Leader. They had good news.

"Biggest tubing sales ever," Bruce said. "A million new taps, that's the estimate." He meant a million in the United States.

That seemed an exaggeration, given that the USDA estimate for the United States was an increase of 191,000 taps in 2012, for a figure of 9,771,000 taps in all. The USDA, however, had reported an increase of nearly a half-million taps since 2010. Bruce thought the USDA figures were underreported, that there was too much diverse and hidden activity to assess accurately.

During a lull in the store Bruce called out to me, "There's a sugarhouse you should visit." He stopped there on his trip to talk about buying syrup. "Georgia Mountain Maples. This sugarhouse cost several thousands of dollars to build."

I asked if it was a tax write-off.

"No, these people make money, they don't lose it. This sugarhouse was built by the Harrison family. They have a very successful concrete business."

He described the place. The floor was made of black concrete buffed to look like marble. At the entryway hung a chandelier made of copper maple leafs. Etched into the concrete below the chandelier was a copper-colored maple leaf. The building was a post-and-beam structure, very smartly done, nothing wasteful. A red roof made it stand out from a distance.

"They have about twenty-five thousand taps and will put in another thirty thousand next year. The want to get up to a hundred thousand." Bruce smiled and said, "They were embarrassed to tell me that they only have twenty-five thousand taps."

There was a greater point to this bold construction. "This is an example of people with money getting into the maple business." The industry was promising enough now to make big investments, and banks were lending. Bruce said the new generation didn't have to do it the way he had, developing slowly by reinvesting profits each year, edging ahead with an eye on the syrup price.

I had a couple of free days ahead, and they happened to be on March 7 and 8, when the forecast was for high temperatures. When everything would let loose up north, if Bruce was right.

I DROVE THREE HOURS traversing Vermont before heading along a back road through Milton. When I reached Georgia Mountain and stopped and saw the red roof, I understood Bruce's enthusiasm. The building sat up on the slope, near enough to be accessible but high enough for a lofty view.

I drove up the hill and parked by a truck, found a side door, and went inside. The room seemed enormous, like a dance floor, except for the supersized evaporator near the other end. A man wearing a baseball cap came into the room. His name was Marty Rabtoy. He was one of the three owners of Georgia Mountain Maples. His brother-in-law Kevin Harrison, president of Harrison Concrete, was also a part-owner. Another brother-in-law, Rick Fielding, who worked in construction and built the sugarhouse, was a third owner.

Marty worked for Harrison Concrete, but for now he was running the evaporator. The timing of the sugar season was perfect for him because concrete work was slow in the changeover from ice to mud. Marty was thirty or so, of average height and build, with large, thick hands. I asked him how all this came to be.

"We're Vermonters," he said. "We're all into this sugaring a little bit. I used to gather buckets with a guy down the road when I was a kid, but that's a little different."

He said there were lots of visitors. "From everywhere, even from Canada. They see the big red roof from Route 7, figure it's a sugarhouse, and decide to go see it." US Route 7 was two miles away across a valley.

"We're a typical Vermont sugarhouse," he said, "with an edge."

I took "edge" to mean what Bruce talked about, that they went at this pursuit all out, right from the beginning.

"Edge" may have also meant Franklin County, Vermont. Franklin County, in the uppermost northwestern part of the state, produced a third of the Vermont maple syrup crop and ten percent of the maple syrup crop in the entire United States. In Franklin Country were several sugarhouses with tap counts equal to or greater than Bascom's. On one road that ran from Fletcher to Fairfield, I had been told, there were more than 500,000 taps among the many sugarhouses, with names such as J. R. Sloan, who boiled from more than 90,000 taps, Matt and Rex Gillian, the Minors, the Sweets (could you ask for a better name?), Rick Mayotte, Gary Corey (who also made tubing installations), Geoff Corey, four Branon families (a family with a long history of sugarmaking), six Howrigan families (sugarmakers in their sixth generation), the Tiffany brothers, the Dubie family, the Ryan brothers, and the Boisenaults. All were over 10,000 taps and several were over 50,000. Georgia Mountain was the newest entry into the Franklin County pantheon.

The Harrisons owned a sizeable section of Georgia Mountain and had used it primarily for hunting. Over the past few years, since the price of maple syrup had gone up, people were telling Kevin Harrison that he should think about getting into maple. He decided to investigate. Kevin, Marty, and Rick walked through the woods in the fall of 2010 and brought sugarmakers along. They toured sugarhouses and asked questions. One common theme, they noticed, was that everyone talked about adding on.

Marty told me, "Kevin said, 'If we do it, we're not going to add on.' Kevin looked at the figures and decided to go ahead. Kevin makes decisions and we stand by them. He's made a lot of good decisions."

They walked the woods, did further planning. In April they poured the foundation for the building, 100 feet long and 50 feet wide. They hired a sugarmaker and logger named Doug Edwards to thin the woods and supervise the tubing installation. They strung mainlines and tubing for 23,000 taps. Doug Edwards told me that the cost of installing tubing was $15 to $20 per tap, including mainlines, which meant a cost during this phase of $345,000, at the low end.

They put a similar amount into the sugarhouse and hired a plumber, Nick Lemieux, to oversee the pumps and lines.

"Last April it was just a little goat path," Marty said.

Marty took me to what he called the tank room, where I climbed a ladder to a platform and where I saw the evidence of what you could do if you had a concrete company at your disposal. Below were six tanks for storing sap or concentrate, each tank with a capacity of 9000 gallons. They looked like small swimming pools. "The first thing we did," Marty said. "All built in-house, with our mechanics. Like potable water tanks."

He told me they built another set of tanks just like these on a hill three miles away, where Kevin Harrison owned another 300 acres of maple woods. "Some of the best maples I've ever seen," Marty said. They built a hunting cabin above the tanks. They ran a set of mainlines over Georgia Mountain, up and over a 500-foot incline, and would use high-powered pumps to pull the sap from those faraway woods to this sugarhouse. That was sugaring with an edge, for sure.

MARTY WAS WAITING for some technicians to arrive from the CDL company to adjust his evaporator, so I went outside to have a look around. It was noon by then, and the temperature was 57°, so warm that I felt I had to take a walk up the road into the sugarbush.

Though no one ever told me this, it seemed that there was something iconic or heroic about owning a mountain or even working on one to make maple syrup. At least it felt that way when I was at Bascom's or later walked on David Marvin's mountain and when, on a tour of sugarhouses a year ago, the bus driver stopped so that a young sugarmaker could tell the tale of the mountain he was leasing and had thinned, that he was stringing with tubing and at the bottom of which he would build a new sugarhouse. Maybe it was just my regard of mountains, which I thought had a story within themselves, with their ascents, peaks, and descents, but there seemed to be a kind of special status for the sugarmakers who inhabited mountains. It was like you needed a mountain to do it up right.

The sugarbush on Georgia Mountain was brand new, and clean, as they say, but to my untrained eye it seemed just a little overmanaged. All the ground seemed to have been worked, and the trees that had been removed were plucked from the ground by a mechanical harvester—it was like a haircut too close to the skin, in a way. But I could see the plan. The young maples were mostly in the four- to six-inch category in diameter. The other trees had been removed to give them room to grow. When I had watched George Hodskins at Bascom's remove hemlock trees from a new lot so as to reduce shade, he told me he was "punching holes in the sky." It was a bold term. Peter Rhoades used the standard forestry term, saying he was "releasing" trees—I loved this term, in the idea that you made some room above and the chosen trees shot up to inhabit it, filling the space with their crowns. The term had the concept of dignity, of ascension. These woods, I could see, would soon have ferns covering the ground, and the green light of the leaves would be shining down upon them.

The road curved up the mountain and passed by a beaver pond, an open and untended space. I wondered about the beaver, whose options seemed to have been limited severely. I walked by a high point on the trail, to a rocky knob that had been blasted and crushed to make the road, which was a mile and half long and a flat, workable surface. Roads are everywhere, but what a thing it seemed to make this road so quickly, as an accessory to the woods.

Coming down the mountain on the western slope I caught a glimpse of Lake Champlain, a faraway silver sliver of water. The sun was shining, it was a beautiful day and easy to forget it was winter. The temperature had hit 60°, and I took off my jacket.

THE FLOW WAS UNDERWAY, and the sap was gushing from the mainlines into the pump room. Doug Edwards arrived and took a reading of the sap—the sugar content was at 2.3 percent, a very good level.

Doug Edwards was a burly, bearded man, a professional logger and sugarmaker with 43,000 taps of his own and about to increase by a few thousand more. He was at the sugarhouse to advise and help out as needed.

Kevin Harrison arrived soon after Edwards. They referred to Kevin as the brains of the operation. He had a small office up on the second floor with a window that looked out over the sugarhouse floor, but Kevin stood near the evaporator and by the R.O. room and watched things closely that afternoon. He was wearing a heavy jacket and a baseball hat and had a dark beard. Kevin was a quiet man, even shy, I thought. Clearly he had concerns about the weather on this day, with the temperature at twenty degrees above average. Adding to his concern was the new weather forecast, calling for an entire week of 60° weather.

He and Doug Edwards stood together talking about this.

"I usually have thirty boils a year," Doug said.

"How many have you made this year?"

"Five. If it gets into the fifties next week it could slow things down."

"I'm going on a ten-year average. I can take a bad year this year. Just don't give me two bad years in a row."

Of course Doug had nothing of that sort to give. All he could offer was advice and information. Marty had also made five boils, the first on February 2 during that heat wave and the last on March 3, four days ago.

Two men arrived from the CDL company. One I noticed was Daniel Lalanne, one of the owners of CDL and a French Canadian. CDL is a Canadian company. Bruce had introduced me to Lalanne on one of his trips north when we stopped at the equipment companies. Bruce thought of CDL as an aggressive company on the move.

Georgia Mountain Maples had bought the top-model evaporator produced by CDL, the "Tornade" (the French word for tornado), which ran for about $60,000 with all the bells and whistles, Lalanne soon told me.

Marty was having some problems with the oil burner. The technician opened a front panel, worked for a few minutes making adjustments, and then, with a whoosh, the Tornade shuddered into being. Lalanne and the technician went into the pump room to confer on the equipment there. They stayed for a couple of hours, going back and forth from the pump room to the evaporator.

I waited for the opportunity to talk to Lalanne because I wanted to know his thoughts on the expansion of the US industry. Bruce talked about it often, how in this new era the production on the American side of the border was growing. Actually that was why I was here on this day: Georgia Mountain Maples was a premier example of the expansion. People with money getting into the maple business.

When I saw Lalanne standing alone away from the evaporator, I walked over and reintroduced myself. Almost immediately we began talking about the Federation. You couldn't talk about American expansion for long without talking about the Federation, and you couldn't talk about the Federation without talking about the surplus, the Global Strategic Reserve.

The Global Strategic Reserve was more commonly called simply "the surplus," which was a supply kept in reserve in case of a shortage. The surplus had been established in 2002 by vote of the Quebec producers who were members of the Federation. At the same time a provision called "sales agency" was established, after which all bulk sales of Quebec syrup were channeled through the Federation. By 2004 the Global Strategic Reserve had grown to be as large as an entire year's crop, and the Federation established production quotas for its members. These measures were controversial and brought on a difficult time—plainclothes policemen attended Federation meetings, leaders received threats, and the president's sugarhouse was burned down. The leadership assured its members they were being visionary for making the changes, and this proved true after four consecutive poor crops between 2005 and 2008 due to prolonged winters. Prices went from $2.50 to as much as $4.25 a pound, and in US stores there was a twenty-five percent loss of shelf space—for every four quarts on the shelves there were now three. The Federation surplus, depleted during that time, prevented much greater losses. Arnold Coombs was still working in 2012 to put that fourth quart back on the shelf.

"The Americans have the best of both worlds," Lalanne said. "They get the Federation price and no production limits. I think the Americans should support the surplus. But that will never happen. The Federation has thirty-something million pounds in storage now. It's protecting the industry if there's a shortage."

I mentioned a prediction Bruce had made, that with continuing increase on the American side, by the end of the decade the US crop would be 50 million pounds, half the production of Quebec.

Lalanne's prediction went way beyond Bruce's. "I see the US out-producing Canada in five to six years," he said. It sounded so outrageous that I stepped back to get a better look at him.

He had warnings about rapid US growth. "I think the expansion will continue for at least another four or five years, but eventually there will be a bad year. It won't be like this forever. I tell all the sugarmakers: be able to live with two-dollar syrup."

The best of both worlds, Lalanne said. One thing that seemed ironic was that the Federation, with its price support and surplus, brought the stability that allowed Kevin Harrison to place a fairly safe bet on Georgia Mountain Maples.

As for catching up in four or five years, that seemed unlikely. Even if Bruce was correct in saying there had been an increase of a million taps in 2012, that would only put the US tap count at just under 11 million. There were about 45 million taps in Quebec. The United States would have to increase its tap count by 10 million a year for the next five years in order to equal Quebec.

Marty boiled through that afternoon, sending his syrup to the room with the filter presses, where other workers, concrete workers too, grappled with those machines. Everyone seemed to be in the tenderfoot status, though I had the feeling, just like with that road on top of the mountain, that things would be smooth and workable before long.

People came, watched, talked about sugaring. Some brought beer toward the end of the day. One offered a beer to Kevin, but he didn't accept. Other workers from Harrison Concrete came by. Some had worked in the woods that day and put up 400 more taps. Some had shoulder-length hair and thick beards, others had hair cut short, but all had powerful physiques. I possessed a built-in respect for concrete workers, having gone to school with a boy whose father owned a cement block factory and who came a few inches within winning the state shot-put championship.

As it grew dark Kathy Harrison arrived with her and Marty's kids, who were soon running around and sliding on the floor. Kathy's mother came along with pizza. Kevin Harrison left the scene of the work and went over to join them, not eating but standing near the table.

I walked over to Kevin before I left. I told him I walked on the road and saw the mainlines running between the sugarhouse and the woods three miles away. He said that not many places pumped everything directly into the sugarhouse. I wanted to know about something Marty had said about Kevin and decision making. I wanted to know how he came to the decision to build this sugarhouse, how he agreed to take the leap. Maybe that was too complicated or too personal a question. His answer was that the decision provided a way to keep people working.

"I would have had to lay off fifteen guys," Kevin said.

He brought a large scale to his venture, brought an edge, but it seemed to me in that moment his place was like almost any other sugarhouse. The visitors, the friends stopping by, the kids playing, and the family enjoying themselves at the end of the day. I suspected that was part of Kevin's thinking too.

When I arrived at the hotel in Burlington that night the warmth had held. At 8:00 it was 53°. The next morning it was a degree warmer, at 54° when at 8:00 I left for Johnson and Butternut Mountain. Rare is the night in Vermont in early March when the temperature rises.

12

WHY BE COMPETITORS

WHEN YOU CAN BE

COOPERATORS?

WHEN JAMES MARVIN went looking for a piece of land capable of sugarmaking in the late 1940s, he settled upon a farm in Johnson, Vermont, a few miles away from downtown, along a back road that coursed uphill to a place called Butternut Mountain. An old farmhouse was part of the property at the base of the hill, but Marvin and his wife didn't move there. They remained in South Burlington near the University of Vermont, where Marvin was a professor of botany. He didn't intend to produce maple syrup himself there, only to be a steward of the land.

Not that James Marvin wasn't occupied with maple syrup production. He had begun conducting research on the biology of the sugar maple tree after joining the faculty at the university in 1936. After a decade of work he was convinced that the university needed its own facility. With another professor and maple researcher, Dr. Fred Taylor, Marvin persuaded the governor, Mortimer Proctor, to buy a farm on a hillside in the town of Underhill. In 1946 they established the Proctor Maple Farm, later the Proctor Maple Research Center.

James Marvin and Fred Taylor were continuing research that began in Vermont at the beginning of the twentieth century when an important bulletin was published in 1903 based on research by Charles Jones and others. In "The Maple Sap Flow" they revealed, among other things, that the mystery of the sap flow was based on the fluctuation of temperatures between freezing and thawing.

James Marvin also studied maple sap flow, published papers, and became the leading authority of his time. With Fred Taylor they discovered that the higher the sugar content in a tree, the greater the sap volume, and that the sweetest trees are sweetest every year. Marvin and his students closely observed a few select maples as they progressed through each season, taking daily measurements of temperature, internal pressure, sap volume, and sugar content. They spent summers correlating their data and recording it on large charts.

Based on this and other observations, Marvin devised a scientific equation that approached poetry in form and the mystery it conveyed: *The extent of the shock is equivalent to the rate of the flow.* As I stated at the beginning, what this means to me is that the thermodynamic energy of the sun, in the form of light or wind or weather, has a precise corresponding effect on the sap flow. Marvin's formula had a beautiful symmetry—*the extent of the shock* on one side of the fulcrum "equivalent" and *the rate of the flow* on the other. It seemed to mean that sunlight is equivalent to sap in the maple tree.

Marvin and Taylor also discovered that the maple tree exerted back pressure during the freeze phase and would pull sap back into the tree. This brought bacterial contamination into the taphole, to which the tree responded by sealing the freshly cut wood fibers, and this reduced the sap flow and ultimately brought an end to the run. Marvin came up with the idea that a standing column of liquid of eighteen inches would be enough to prevent backflow of sap into the tree, and so he created the "dropline," a loop of tubing at the end of the spout filled with sap and functioning as that standing column of water. It was a simple innovation that changed the industry by making tubing more productive than buckets.

James Marvin's son David was born the year after the Proctor Farm opened. As a boy David often came to the maple farm, spending time by the heater in the shed that served as an office. Fred Taylor kept a jar of jellybeans, and James Marvin had replaced an addiction to tobacco with an addiction to chocolate, which meant the shed was a good place for a kid to be. As was the sugarhouse. They kept a coffee cup near the evaporator and filled it with hot, fresh syrup. The first cup went down easily, the second with some difficulty. David played on the bulldozer his father purchased for the farm and rode on the sled when they went to gather sap from buckets.

David was someone who thought about ways of making money, a trait he felt he may have inherited from his grandfather, who ran a feed and grain store on the docks in Norwalk, Connecticut. At the age of ten he came up with the idea of raising a flock of chickens in the basement of their home, but his parents wouldn't sign on—maybe that was for the best, he thought later. He also wanted to make maple syrup of his own and bugged his father so much that James set up a garbage can for David to boil sap in. James wouldn't allow him to tap the big shade maples in the front yard, out of concern for their health, so David trekked into the woods, for quite a ways, and tapped other maple trees. The next year James went to Leader Evaporator, bought a flat pan with a draw-off spout, and placed it outdoors on cement blocks—a real evaporator! David still owns it.

As college approached he struggled with the question of how to make a contribution to society that was compatible with how he wanted to live. His parents were academics and avid readers, and he thought at first that he should get an academic degree. After two miserable years at the University of Pennsylvania he did what he wanted to do, and enrolled in the forestry school at the University of Vermont. David thought his parents would be disappointed but realized that, like most parents, they wanted their son to be happy. They only worried about his chances of finding a place in his chosen profession.

David had to hold his tongue in forestry school, and sometimes he couldn't, when encountering the standard practice of clear-cutting forests and reproducing them with hardwoods block by block—the even-management plan, considered to be the best way to get the most fiber per acre. David wasn't the only student who questioned even-management. The 1960s were a time of change in forestry too, and David's classmates also believed there were better ways to manage woods. David thought that if you owned a small piece of forest and cut everything, that would be the end of those woods for you, your kids, and your grandkids.

They argued for single tree management, for practicing forestry by assessing trees individually whenever possible.

When David began to practice forestry, working for private clients, the Forest Service silvicultural (the growing of trees) guidelines required even-age management when writing current-use plans to have land appraised according to forestry value. In his first plans David gave a wink to even-age management but actually managed by the individual-tree approach.

Thinking like a forester and a sugarmaker, he grew to believe that maple syrup production was the best possible approach to stewardship of the woods because sugaring was all about single-tree management. As a sugarmaker you could take a piece of land depleted by previous logging operations, designate it as a sugarbush, and the silvicultural guidelines went out the window. You could take timber off the land, but you did it by selecting individual trees. You left the maples, most of them, and you also left nonmaples that were good trees and that you could watch as they developed. Maybe you cut them later, maybe you didn't, but that wasn't the goal, only a possibility in a sugarbush.

As a proponent of individual-tree management, David was excited by the idea that when managing a sugarbush you had a much closer relationship with the forest than almost anyone working in the woods, past or present. The settlers came primarily to cut the trees down. As a commercial forester you normally visited a tree two or three times—when you planted it, maybe when you released it, and finally when you marked the tree for cutting, before losing it to a chainsaw. As a maple syrup producer you might visit a tree eight or ten times in a single year. What sugarmakers did was more akin to agriculture, where you intensely knew fields or animals. For David maple production was a way to farm without working with animals, and importantly, there was a preservation ethic embedded in maple production. You could take a run-down piece of abused forestland and make something of it financially over time with a sugar-bush—a sustainable effort with an intimate connection to the trees and land.

David felt that he had inherited more from his father in the way of preservation than in the biology of maple trees. James Marvin established the first Nature Conservancy chapter in Vermont; the first meetings were held in the Marvin kitchen. His father was on the first board of what was called Act 250, a legislative effort to control statewide planning, and which resulted in the statewide billboard ban. James Marvin was one of the founders of the Vermont Natural Resources Council, which recognized that the environmental health of Vermont was also an economic driver. When James left the board after ten years the Vermont Sugarmakers Association elected David to it. He became chair of the VNRC the year James Marvin died, in 1977.

After finishing college David held a job for a few years, working for the Forest Service as a technician. Under the supervision of two scientists, he was the maple specialist in a study of the economics of the maple industry. David traveled and looked closely at the impact of the losses resulting from the blend syrup market, as companies began to add corn syrup and then artificial flavor as they further reduced the presence of maple syrup. He talked to people at General Foods and Quaker Oats, looked at Aunt Jemima, Mrs. Butterworth, and Log Cabin. Blended syrup went from fifteen percent maple syrup down to two percent. Then one brand came out with all artificial and gained market share. Even at two percent, the blend syrup market was a substantial market for maple syrup producers. He wrote a research report about this devastating time for the industry.

Through his college years he worked at the Proctor Farm, first for free and then on the payroll. For ethical reasons his father wouldn't hire him, but Fred Taylor did. David boiled and worked in the woods. After college he wanted to make a go of it as a sugarmaker but didn't have enough money. He saved for three years before leaving his job. James advised against this, saying it was too hard to make money in the maple business (he was right, David would later say). James thought David should stay in the Forest Service, let them pay for a master's degree, and do sugaring full time in his retirement. By then David was beyond being influenced by that.

He put up tubing and 4000 taps on Butternut Mountain and boiled in the sugarhouse he built on a barn foundation using a chainsaw, making a crop of 990 gallons in 1973. That wasn't enough to live on, but he made money in other ways in those woods by harvesting timber and cutting firewood. One winter he cut 500 cords—in all a stack of wood three-quarters of a mile long. He sold balsam branches used to weave carpets for graves. He sold brush for making wreaths at $2 a bundle. Occasionally he cut a pickup load of ash, took it to a plant that made hockey sticks, and was paid $200. He sold pulpwood to a company that made cardboard holders used for hot dogs purchased in baseball parks—an opportunity that fell away during a baseball strike and that made him think about the interconnectedness of the economy.

After he had two bad crop years, one right after the other, in 1986 and 1987—1800 gallons and 1300 gallons—everything changed for David. He had to sell a second farm he had bought for sugarmaking. To meet his accounts he borrowed everything he could and bought all the syrup he could find. Syrup was scarce in 1987, and he paid an exorbitant price for it, $3 a pound, crazy high. But he discovered something: if you are the only one with product and people want it, you will sell it. He developed markets that year.

The producers he bought syrup from in 1987 in northern Vermont, many in Franklin County, asked whether he would continue to provide a home for their syrup. That next year David became a buyer for Maple Grove and made a deal for a large supply, but then Maple Grove backed out of the deal. In trouble, in possession of a buying base that had suddenly become outsized, he scrambled to sell the syrup and make a profit.

"And that's how I got into the packing business," he said.

ON MARCH 8, the day after I visited Georgia Mountain Maples, I stopped at the Butternut Mountain Farms plant in an industrial park in the town of Morrisville. Butternut Mountain Farms is about the same size as Bascom Maple Farms. Both employed sixty to seventy people full time, and both ran a sugarbush, though Bruce's was substantially larger. Bruce Bascom and David Marvin both purchased in the neighborhood of 10 million pounds of syrup each year. Both inhabited the second tier of the industry. Actually, I realized, Marvin and Bascom *were* the second tier of the industry in the United States. Butternut Mountain Farms was also the only other company that made granulated maple sugar in substantial quantity.

The plant in Morrisville was housed in a single building—offices, bottling plant, sugarmaking, candy making, shipping, and storage. But that was about to change. Ground preparation was underway for a new large facility that would be used for syrup storage and warehousing. It would be a new building much like Bruce's, with some variations: Marvin's building would have solar panels on the roof, offsetting the energy costs for both buildings.

They had known each other since college, seeing one another at maple meetings. Bruce competed with Marvin, but he also consulted with him on all sorts of things. Bruce talked frequently with Marvin when planning his building, bouncing questions off him, including the problem of whether to erect the building on Mount Kingsbury or place it in an industrial park a few miles away in Charlestown. Building it on the mountain would forever alter the farm, but Bruce wanted to be able to walk to the place from his house. Marvin told him he should do it if that's what he wanted.

From the very beginning of my visits to Bascom's, Bruce talked about Marvin and suggested I visit him. It seemed a generous gesture to me, sending a writer off to talk with your primary competitor, someone who had taken accounts away—someone who was, Bruce told me, the only person in the industry he envied. Marvin spoke well, he said, like a writer. And he was, Bruce thought, as shrewd a businessman as any, despite his professorial appearance. I first met David when I traveled with Bruce to Leader Evaporator for the panel discussion when the two talked to bankers about how to lend to the maple industry. I saw him again at the Maple Hall of Fame when Bruce was inducted—David was already a member, and the two were the youngest members of the

Hall of Fame. With their fathers, who were also members, they formed two of the three father-and-son pairs at the Hall.

In the summer of 2010 I took Bruce's advice and visited David in Morrisville, and we had lunch at the sugarhouse at Butternut Mountain. When I expressed interest in the trees, he told me that he would be happy to walk in his woods with me—no one came by who was interested in the woods, he said. We walked a few months later in the peak of fall, when the leaves were yellow and the ferns on the ground were still green. Because David seemed to enjoy the walk so much ("It's always good," he said at the end), I invited myself back and we took several more.

If I came to believe that mountainsides managed by sugarmakers reflected the narratives of their lives, Butternut Mountain was where I hatched that notion. On that first walk we covered most of the five miles of roads in David's sugarbush. He had made the first of those roads in the early 1970s using a bulldozer. We passed by some of the fifteen stone foundation sites that he kept clean and intact—he thought maybe he was overstating their case in Vermont, where there were so many, but the foundations, from the time when people lived by subsistence farming on this mountain, seemed like archaeological sites, and he wanted to keep them for future generations. We passed by Horse Barn Bank, site of a logging operation before World War II, when they cut the spruces down, when loggers and horses lived in the same barn, separated by a curtain, sharing heat. We passed by the 83-Woods, named for the year their son Ira was born, after passing by the 82-Woods, named for the year when David and Lucy had an infant child under intensive care in a hospital in Boston, when David got to know the roads to Boston really well during the six months she lived, when he cut heavily to pay medical bills. We passed by the Glade, and the Glade Landing, and Belvidere, near the top of the mountain, near where the Butternut Mountain Sugarbush came within a few feet of Vermont's Long Trail and where the trees once looked like a park until the tops broke off in the ice storm of 1998. David couldn't look up at them, even now; he hired a plane to fly over the area, then took Lucy and the kids on a tour into Canada, where he talked to a sugarmaker who said he was finished—"*fini,*" he said; twelve years later he was sugaring again. We stood on a place called Hard Rock, an outcrop with a view beyond Mount Mansfield to Lake Champlain. David had always lived with a view of Vermont's grandest mountain. We walked by a brook; he pointed out that the spring where the brook began was further up the hill and that the brook emptied into the St. Lawrence, which emptied into the Atlantic, and said that you had to think about the implications of messing around with a mountain. We walked along Ira's Road, the new road David's son was building in a part of the woods David tapped in the 1970s, and beyond that we came to what they called the Park. It truly did look like a park, with stands of tall, mature maples 150 years old or more, and other mature full-growth trees. At another stand, much newer, David said it would take 100 years "to get an expression." He said of maples, "During the history of the white man on this continent we haven't been through two rotations of maple forest. We can't know what that means for forest planning."

WHILE WE DROVE to the sugarbush at Butternut Mountain I asked what had been going on, aside from the weather. He answered, "You said 'aside from the weather.' But I think it's all about the weather." With a week of 50° days in the forecast, he wanted to know if they could maintain a sap run on the pressure differential between 35° and 55°.

We passed through Johnson, where David owned a small store he opened in 1985 where they sold syrup and other Butternut Mountain products, and equipment for sugaring. Over the years some of James Marvin's students had stopped by after they saw the name. We headed out of town, by Vermont Studio Center, an artist's colony, and by the state college, uphill by pastures and fields, through some scraggly woods, along an unpaved road, and up a steeper hill. In a hollow was the sugarhouse, painted a light shade of gray. A road from the sugarhouse led up the hill. Mainlines ran parallel to that road and coursed into the upper story of the building.

The sugarhouse at Butternut Mountain Farms was of a modest size, capable of handling about 14,000 taps. The sugarbush was of a size that two people could manage, and one person could manage the sugarhouse. They decided for the time being not to increase their tap count substantially, as doing so would require another full-time worker. David's son Ira, who was twenty-nine then, had taken over management of the sugarbush, and David was training him to eventually manage the business. David's daughter Emma was involved in management too, working at the plant on the marketing end of things. On this day Emma was at a food products convention. Ira normally would have been here, but instead he was at the plant working on the plans for the new building. He had been writing grant applications. David said, "I've done to Ira what I've done all of his life, which is to put him in charge of something over his head."

Inside the sugarhouse doing the boiling was a man named Steve Wilbur. He was a former baseball player with broad shoulders and an athletic physique who wore a frayed wool jacket and coveralls. Steve was in his sixties and had worked for David for many years and, before that, for James Marvin. Steve spent his time working in the sugarhouse and sugar-bush, checking tubing lines, installing tubing, or doing forestry work. Checking tubing during the season was some-thing he shared with David's wife, Lucy, who liked walking the lines and sometimes took friends along; checking tubing was also somewhat easier in the Marvin sugarbush than other places, as they had placed pressure gauges at key points and could narrow down the areas where the leaks occurred.

They were making their third boil of the year. The second had been yesterday, March 7. It was a normal time to start the season in northern Vermont, but there was that problem of the temperature getting into the high fifties. David asked Steve the question he posed earlier.

"I wonder if we can maintain on a twenty-degree differ-ential. What do you think, Steve? Can we manage between thirty-five and fifty-five degrees? Will it be enough?"

Steve thought they could, with vacuum. "If you have high enough vacuum, you can keep getting sap," he said. This was the new truth in sugarmaking, with these pulses of warm weather in spring. Vacuum was a way of coping with a changing climate.

This sugarhouse was neat, tight, and shipshape, a model of David's thinking. And with backup systems, two of every-thing—like Noah's ark, David said. A smallish sugarhouse with a substantial reverse-osmosis system. With R.O. they could manage 13,000 taps here; without, about 2000.

The tubing systems traveled through the various zones and over the two miles to the upper reach of the sugarbush, up in the area called the Glade. The mainlines narrowed down to a final six, and all fed into the releaser on the second floor. Upstairs the lines were labeled according to their origin, such as "Old Woods" and "Big Booster" and "Bottom Feeder." David and I climbed upstairs to watch the releaser, a chamber with valves that separate the sap from the vacuum system. It can be exciting to watch a releaser, to see the sap come crashing out of the chamber and making a sound like an explosive sigh. He timed the releases of the sap, at 5 gallons each, and determined that the sugarbush was producing 390 gallons an hour at this point, before noon. Yesterday the rate got up to 500 gallons per hour.

When we walked out into the spring-like day he said, "Well, we've had best years three years in a row. Why expect four?" They were having a good year in Ohio, he said. "We always say, when they have good years in those places, we don't have them here."

The crop at Butternut Mountain was usually between 4000 and 5000 gallons and was an important part of the business, but similar to Bascom's, they made only a tiny fraction of what they sold. David was already buying syrup in 2012, quite a lot of it. He hadn't yet set a price, however, because he needed to know how large the crop would be. He might have to wait until the season was over before he came up with the price he would pay his producers.

"I haven't set a price because I don't want to go back on my word."

He was advancing money to those who needed it. David said he had received a call from a producer in Ohio who asked for an advance. "I said to him, 'How about ten thousand dollars?' He said that would get him through. I did it because there is no risk."

He told of a producer in southern Vermont whom he advanced money to before the crop came in, and he had been doing it for years to help with payments for fuel and labor. "When he gives me his syrup there might not be anything left to pay. Or sometimes we have set up a monthly payment plan that goes for the rest of the year."

Bruce had said he was better at buying syrup and David was better at selling it. David agreed, though he thought he knew just as much about the business as Bruce did. They used different strategies when it came to buying syrup. Both had suppliers they dealt with every year, the group of producers who were the foundation of their businesses. David understood his markets and tended to buy everything he needed for the entire year. He didn't want to buy syrup on the spot market because he didn't like speculating. Bruce was always on the hunt for good deals, ready to trade, and loved to make profits on swings in the price when he could. He liked to win. David noticed that Bruce used the language of war when it came to buying syrup. He thought Bruce had nerves of steel when it came to buying, and to business in general.

David's supplier base was made up primarily of larger producers. Bruce had told David that he had 3400 suppliers in 2011, a number that included those small producers who came to Bascom's with five-gallon containers. To David that seemed an impossible number. "How do you keep track? I'm very engaged in the agricultural community in Vermont and want to support local agriculture, but I could probably do well with three hundred suppliers, not three thousand."

He bought according to relationships, some that had begun twenty-five years ago when he had to scramble for markets. The majority came from Vermont and many from Franklin County. David had locked up Franklin County long ago and, in a way, all of Vermont, as he controlled fifty percent of the syrup in the state. His supply had at one point become so concentrated in Vermont that he decided to broaden his base and sought out suppliers in other states and in Canada. He and Bruce were the majority buyers in the St. Aurelie region of Maine.

He had a waiting list of producers who wanted to be part of what David referred to as his community. This community was composed not only of him and his suppliers but also, as he saw it, the biological community consisting of the forests and the greater environment. David had written a mission statement to express that idea and worked on the definitions with his family. He rewarded his suppliers for their loyalty with a 10 cent premium per pound, and he extended his loyalty to them. When he took a supplier on, he bought their entire crop, no matter what fortunes the season delivered. With the many millions of taps that fed into his warehouses, he sometimes bought more syrup than he needed. This happened in the bumper year of 2009 and again in 2011. For that reason the short season of 2010 had been a kind of blessing.

"I go by the feeling that if you trust someone they'll trust you back," he said. "And that if you're loyal, you'll get repaid for it. I like the people I deal with. On the producer side there are very few people I don't enjoy working with. We are lucky and can be selective now. I'm not as good at being as selective as I might be, but the people I have been working with and who have been loyal to me, I do a lot for them. We have put our business in jeopardy. In 2009 I bought too much syrup. It was probably a bad idea."

David hadn't set a price yet because if 2012 brought a large crop, he would have more syrup than he needed and would have to price on the low end. A short crop, and he could pay more per pound, use up his inventory, and comfortably buy all the syrup his producers made.

"EVERYONE IS SO ENGAGED with maple," David said as we drove back to Morrisville. "I don't know of any other crop that people respond to in that way. No one comes up to you and asks how your corn crop is going. Or how your second cutting of hay was. But everybody this time of year asks about maple."

If there was one topic that he wanted to emphasize when we were together, I learned, it was the cause of pure maple syrup, a cause that had begun for him when he researched the blend market for the Forest Service.

The market for imitation maple syrup was an estimated $18 billion yearly. Imitation is a key word, because those products came as close as possible to resembling the real thing short of using the word "maple." David would say that in the mind of most consumers, any breakfast syrup poured on pancakes had an association with maple. But those other products—Log Cabin, Vermont Maid, Mrs. Butterworth—contained no maple syrup. The laboratory stuff, Marvin called it, the junk. Their flavor was a derivative of the fenu-greek plant, and the sugar was primarily high-fructose corn syrup, the ubiquitous processed sweetener responsible for major contributions to the obesity epidemic in the United States.

David liked the fact that Vermont syrup had the reputation as being the best and hoped it would continue. But he also argued that sugarmakers should not compete with each other to prove that their brand was better than any other producer's or any region's. There was a better way.

"Only one person can win that battle," he said. "Why spend money trying to convince the Chinese to eat maple syrup, when eighty-five percent of the pancake syrup in this country is artificial? Others in the industry, they think everyone knows about pure maple. They try to differentiate from one another. Why not make the case for pure maple? And everyone wins."

We stopped briefly at a warehouse David was renting for the time being until his new building was completed. "Bruce doesn't know I have this," he said as we walked in. Inside, barrels upon barrels, stacked five high in long rows. It was carryover syrup, his inventory from the 2011 crop. "If it's a short season this year, I'm going to look very smart," he said.

Some of the barrels were from St. Aurelie and other northern points in Maine. I noticed one from a producer in Maine named Scott Wheeler, who sugars north of Jackman in Somerset County, the only county with greater production than Franklin County. A very capable large producer, I heard, who was previously based in Vermont. "I buy almost all of his syrup. He doesn't talk that much. There's so much BS in the business and I get a lot of it, but when you talk to

Wheeler you come to realize he knows what he is talking about."

Back at the plant in Morrisville, he asked if I wanted to take a tour. David had given me a tour on my first visit, and I wanted to check my memory against the present. We went through the employee lunchroom, by the area where candy is made. When we passed by the bottling lines I thought, "Now I know what Bruce means."

Along one part of the line they were bottling jugs for BJ's, the large club supermarket. A little further along David lifted from a box a bottle with a label that read, "McClure's Maple Syrup." In another section, jugs with labels for the Big Y supermarkets in Massachusetts. Then he showed me a case of one-ounce bottles of maple syrup to be used for the restaurant trade. "We bottled some of these for Bruce last week," he said.

He smiled, with what I thought was the pleasure of success.

"Why be competitors when you can be cooperators?"

The Bascom family at the sugarhouse, 1966: Ken, Bruce, Nancy, Brad, and Judy Bascom.

Ken and Bruce Bascom, tapping trees and hanging buckets, 1962.

Ken Bascom and his team, hauling sap, early 1950s.

Ken Bascom emptying buckets near Langdon Woods, early 1950s.

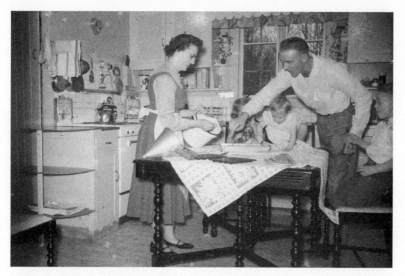

Sunday morning photo shoot for advertisement for sugar parties, 1955. Ruth, Ken, Judy, Nancy, and Bruce Bascom.

Judy and Bruce Bascom placing covers on buckets, 1962.

Bascom's sugarhouse when run by Eric Bascom, Bruce's grandfather, in early 1950s.

BELOW: The Bascom sugarhouse after it was rebuilt in 1959, with Eric Bascom standing near the doorway.

In the Bascom's cooler, barrels from Vermont sugarmaker Mark St. Pierre, open and ready for grading.

A weekend in the 1960s, cars lined up at a Bascom sugar party.

ABOVE: The Bascom sugar-house around 1974, after Bruce returned from college.

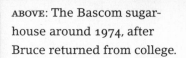

Bascom's logo and sign above the entryway, 2012.

Buckets in the west pasture, looking east to the sugarhouse, 1960s.

The Bascom's steam-powered evaporator, 2012.

The entryway to Bascom's after an early-morning ice storm, 2011.

Peter and Deb Rhoades's sugarhouse during boiling.

The road into David Marvin's sugarbush, with tubing in the woods.

Maple trees with tubing in David Marvin's sugarbush.

13

THE FORECAST

ON MARCH 8 the temperature at Bascom's reached the 60° mark, and Kevin made nearly 1200 gallons of syrup. Bruce had been making deals for syrup, and he told me about one, following my trip to northern Vermont, just after I arrived at the store and he was on his way out to help a customer load barrels.

"I did real well with Mark St. Pierre," he said as we walked. "Held my price, wouldn't budge, said I couldn't go any higher, and he finally said, 'We'll be there Friday morning.'" Bruce had talked about St. Pierre before, after he made his first trip to northern Vermont in 2011 to negotiate for his syrup, about how St. Pierre managed several dairy farms, with somewhere near 3000 cows, how he bought and sold land, and how St. Pierre got into the maple syrup business with the same sort of edge as the guys at Georgia Mountain Maples. Doug Edwards had told me that he also helped St. Pierre set up his sugaring operation. Last year, after Bruce's trip to meet St. Pierre, a stack of 100 brand-new stainless-steel barrels appeared in the Cooler. The same happened today. The St. Pierre truck had just delivered another 100 barrels.

Bruce didn't like to tell anyone how much he paid or would pay for syrup, but he was talking a lot about price lately, almost every time we had a conversation. His major concern now was about the going price in the bulk market and what others would be paying. So I asked him what he paid Mark St. Pierre. With a little smile he said, "You've been traveling around talking about prices." When we reached the truck the customer, a sugarmaker, also asked about the price, not what Bruce had paid St. Pierre but what he would be paying producers like him this season. Bruce didn't give him an answer.

Afterward he wanted to walk up to the new building to see if the jug line was up and running for the first time, and he told me to come along. We stopped by the door, and Bruce looked in through the window to where two workers were packing jugs for a natural food chain in the Midwest. But Bruce had second thoughts about going in because there were no hairnets in the bin or white jackets for us to put on. "We better not," he said. "The other day Lisa told me I was setting a terrible example for the employees by going in there without a hairnet." Lisa Mancussi, he meant, the person in charge of quality control.

So instead we went to the tank room, and Bruce showed me the touchscreen used to move syrup from the silos to the tanks and to the bottling units or used to blend syrup to the desired proportions or grades. On the way out we stopped to look at the boxes that were part of the shipment of granulated sugar going to Gold Coast. Two women were working full time to pack those bags, but now with this new order and the new reality it represented, Bruce had to buy a packing machine. It would cost $68,000. "Scheez," he said of this. The boxes were sealed and he couldn't open one, but there were some empty bags. The bag design had that same appealing art nouveau forest motif as the Gold Coast jugs.

Outdoors I saw one of the sap trucks speeding by, Greg Bascom heading out to pick up another load, and then I saw George Hodskins arriving, moving with greater exertion due to the twelve tons of liquid he was carrying. Greg and George worked fourteen-hour days during the sap run, starting at 7:00 and finishing around 9:00, but sometimes they worked until midnight. I had traveled with both of them on the sap trucks, which could be a grueling ride with a full load of sap sloshing in the tank and jerking the truck side to side while moving over the frost heaves and buckled pavement. While George was unloading I asked him about the sap flow.

"It's not supported after the weekend. After Sunday we've got a whole string of fifty-degree days with no end in sight. The trees like it when it's twenty-five to forty-five. When it's sixty they don't like it. It heats up the bark, even early on when the trees have been frozen for a long time. If there are a couple days of sixty degrees, they don't run."

"You used the word *like*. You said the trees don't *like* something."

"They're alive," George said.

In the store I met a man named Bill Cole from Pomfret, Vermont. I saw a truck outside with lettering that read "Ox Hill Farm" and asked Bill if it was his. He said it was and that he was an oxen trainer, that he went to about fifteen fairs a year and had gone to the Cornish Fair last year. I must have seen him there, I said, because I usually attended the Cornish Fair with a friend who was an oxen trainer and whose oxen I fed during the first two winters I lived in New Hampshire. I enjoyed opening up hay bales for them and breaking the ice in the brook where they drank. I had my first taste of the reality of farm life, however, when the two giant oxen went to Washington, DC, to participate in a Smithsonian exhibition and were led by Vice President Al Gore, with my friend following close behind. This played in the papers in New Hampshire. Unfortunately the big oxen had to pay for the trip to DC and must have fed a lot of people, and I must have flinched when my friend told me. But I didn't tell Bill Cole that tender part.

Cole had 2500 taps in his sugarbush and said that when he increased his tap count he had to buy a larger evaporator, but then he harvested so much sap he had to buy an R.O. to reduce boiling time. Now he had to increase his tap count to keep up with the R.O. He had come to Bascom's to buy barrels, which he now needed more of too. When Liz told him what he owed, he said to put it on his account, that he would pay when he brought his syrup in.

I went to the Cooler with Bill to get his barrels. Dave St. Aubin was occupied at the scale, weighing and grading syrup from a sugarhouse in Shrewsbury, near Rutland. The man who brought the syrup in said they were clearing out the sugarhouse to ready for the weekend. His syrup was in plastic barrels, and one was still hot to the touch. He too wanted to buy some fifty-five-gallon drums, and when Dave finished grading we all walked into the New Cooler where the new barrels were stored.

Along the way we passed by some new and bright stainless-steel drums, a stack two high, five wide, and ten deep. The lids were embossed with the name Mark St. Pierre, en-

suring their return to the owner. The barrels were a significant investment at $240 each, $24,000 in all, merely as containers for the syrup. They were the preferred containers
presently, in a year when the state of Vermont had banned
the use of galvanized barrels. As for the value of the syrup, if
you went by the 2011 average bulk price in New Hampshire
according to the USDA, which was $2.80, and multiplied that
by the 4000 gallons in the drums, the return would be
$123,200. For Bruce that was just one block in the New
Cooler, just one hundred of the thousands.

ON MARCH 11 the forecast for Acworth for the next ten days
predicted daytime temperatures in the fifties and sixties,
with nighttime temperatures in the midthirties and low forties. The warmest day in the forecast was March 16, when
temperatures would range from 43° to 69°. In Burlington,
Vermont, the nighttime temperature would be 49°, higher
than the average daytime temperature. If the forecast
proved true, there would be 240 consecutive hours without a
freeze during the final ten days of winter in the most northern regions of the Northeast.

Kevin didn't boil on Sunday, but the sap trucks were running all day. He came in on Sunday night and built up a supply of 18,000 gallons of sap at ten percent sugar. He slept a
few hours, then returned to the sugarhouse at 4:30 and
boosted the concentrate to eighteen percent. He began boiling at 7:30, and by 11:30 that morning had made 825 gallons.
Kevin kept running fresh sap through the R.O. all day long
as it arrived from the lots.

At 11:30 Bruce emerged from his office, pulled on a hairnet, and said, "This is the worst forecast I've ever seen for maple syrup. You can be sure by this forecast that the crop obviously will be down."

As for what that meant for him, he said, "With a poor crop everybody's evaporator will be big enough. Sales of syrup will be down. With a crop of ten million pounds less, that will be twenty-five million dollars less in the maple industry. Farmers pay their mortgages and loans with that money, and buy equipment."

He continued, "Last year's crop was ten million more than the year before. The increase was all in the bulk market. If you cut off ten million pounds, Marvin, people like me, we'll be out there cleaning up everything we can."

Bruce went to the chart, to the section with bar graphs that marked the yearly crops. He looked at the tall red columns that rose far above all previous others, at the bars representing crops from 2008 to 2011, crops of 22,000 to 24,000 gallons. He put a finger on a line representing 17,000 gallons.

"I'll take ten-to-one odds we're below that level," said this taker of risks.

"That last five thousand gallons is a hundred thousand dollars we don't make," he said of the shortfall. He thought for a moment and multiplied last year's crop—rounded off at 24,000 gallons—by eleven pounds per gallon and by $2.70 per pound, his average price in 2011.

"Last year's crop was worth seven hundred thousand dollars. It will be awfully easy to lose some of that now."

Bruce had barrels scattered all over the Northeast ready to be filled. "But some producers will hold on to their syrup to see what the market will bring," he said. "I can understand that. If I were a big producer, I would never sell in the spring."

He was expecting a truckload of syrup coming in from Georgia Mountain Maples, but said he needed much more Vermont syrup. "I need fifteen to twenty trailer loads of Vermont to fill orders."

He had gotten a call that morning from a Canadian supplier who wanted to sell him some trailer loads at $2.60 a pound. "I have to decide," he said. "Do I buy last year's syrup at a low price, or do I wait for the new? The guy said to me, 'You can buy it cheap. Do you want to buy now?'"

Bruce was concerned about the bulk price and was wondering where David Marvin would set his. He figured Marvin was probably wondering about him too. "Marvin thinks I'm controlling things and setting the price, and I think he is."

Bruce left for lunch.

Kevin was at the evaporator, which was frothing furiously. I asked what he thought of the conditions outdoors. "If it doesn't freeze, the sap run will slow right down," he yelled to me over the mixed sounds. "It takes about a day and a half. Without a freeze we'll keep running because we have vacuum, but people with buckets and gravity will shut right down."

On that day, March 11, Kevin boiled for twelve hours. By 8:00 that night he had made 2023 gallons, breaking the record he set last year. The sugar content of the sap Greg and George gathered ranged from 1.4 to 2.1 percent, averaging about 1.6 percent. Multiplying that out by the Rule of 86, Kevin used 54.75 gallons of sap to make each gallon of syrup.

Multiplying further, he processed 108,736 gallons of sap to make that day's record crop.

14

AREN'T YOU AFRAID,

MR. BUREAU?

ONE OF THE FIRST STORIES Bruce told me about buying was when he stopped by Mr. Bureau's house for lunch one summer.

His name is Real Bureau, but Bruce always referred to him as Mr. Bureau. Mr. Bureau was a maple syrup trader, still is as of this writing actually. He had served as the mayor of St. Evariste, Quebec, and as a math teacher at the local parochial school, and was an accountant. Very good with figures. When Bruce told his story he often mentioned how Mr. Bureau got up early every morning to review his ledger books, written in immaculate penmanship. Mr. Bureau was the person who sold the maple syrup for a lot of producers in his area of Quebec, which is Beauce County in the southeast, their most productive maple syrup region.

When Bruce went to Quebec on a business trip he usually stopped by Mr. Bureau's and would sometimes stay for lunch. On this day, the one Bruce told about in his story, while he was having lunch, "One farm family after another stopped by to get paid for their syrup, and Mr. Bureau wrote out one check after another for hundreds of thousands of dollars."

"Tens of thousands of dollars?" I asked.

"Hundreds of thousands."

Mr. Bureau was Bruce's mentor in the game of buying and selling maple syrup. He had "cleaned my clock" many a time, Bruce said, but that was all part of the game and fair play in Bruce's mind.

Bruce was in his late twenties when he met Mr. Bureau. He and his partner stopped at Bascom's on a trip to New Hampshire and Vermont to promote sales of their syrup. They left St. Evariste at 3:00 A.M. in his Lincoln Continental and made stops at American Maple in Newport, Vermont, McClure's Maple in Littleton, New Hampshire, the Springtree Company in Brattleboro, Vermont, and Bascom's. They were selling bulk syrup on the Canadian dollar. Ken Bascom and Bruce bought a trailer load.

Mr. Bureau was the brain behind Jacques & Bureau. He started his accounting business in the late 1950s in St. Evariste by knocking on doors. Like many of his countrymen he had a passion for maple syrup and ran a small sugarbush. Mr. Bureau bought the first available R.O. in 1974 for $30,000. His neighbors came to look at it and marveled at what it could do. As they grew to know Mr. Bureau, some of the maple syrup producing families around St. Evariste asked if he could sell their syrup for them. He decided to do it. He organized the collection of syrup from his neighbors in the Beauce, and in 1975 he filled seven leased tractor-trailers with barrels of syrup that set off for Vermont. Mr. Bureau was so afraid that something would happen to the syrup that he followed behind the trucks in his car. He sold all seven loads to the American Maple Company in Newport.

Mr. Bureau became what was known as a "barrel-roller" in the days before the Federation and their sales agreement. This meant he contracted with producers, advanced them money or lent them money, sometimes paid interest on syrup that he held for months before he sold it, and, ultimately, paid the families what they were due when the syrup was finally delivered, after deducting his commission. This is what Bruce witnessed when he stopped by for lunch on that summer day.

Mr. Bureau and his methods fascinated Bruce. He had his business degree and enough acumen to believe he could do something similar himself. Older people in the maple business told Bruce he ought to consider getting into the bulk syrup trade. One was the president of American Maple, who gave Bruce a piece of advice that Bruce remembered. He should learn how to let syrup pass him by—other syrup would always be coming his way.

He also told him, "Syrup finds the money."

In the early 1980s Bruce negotiated with a syrup-marketing company in Brattleboro—the Springtree Company it was called, named after the tree of spring. Springtree was successfully developing markets in the big discount supermarkets, selling B grade syrup, much of it Canadian. Bruce arranged to buy $100,000 worth of syrup from Mr. Bureau and made a deal to sell it to Springtree, adding a 10 cents per pound commission. He did this on borrowed money, of course. After the sale Bruce paid off his loan and increased his credit line. Six months later he made another deal with Springtree, this time buying $300,000 worth from Mr. Bureau, again delivering it to Springtree with his 10 cent commission on top. He turned his $30,000 over to his father, who used the money to improve the farm. Things were looking good, Bruce thought. He made another deal, this time for $500,000.

Six months later Bruce asked the bank for a million dollars, and made another deal with Mr. Bureau and the Springtree Company. This time the gross profit was a hundred thousand dollars. The net profit was quite a bit less, after taxes, and warehousing, after deductions for things such as leaking drums, and "things that go bang in the night."

When Bruce visited Mr. Bureau and saw barrels of syrup stacked in his warehouse he thought that the syrup was his. But that was not true. Bruce's syrup was actually sitting at farms in Quebec, and Mr. Bureau had not paid for it yet. Bruce later figured out that Mr. Bureau was borrowing a certain amount of money and multiplying it out on futures contracts—making deals for syrup he didn't yet actually own, sometimes putting deposits down on it, sometimes paying interest on the syrup. He made promises on two fronts—to pay the farmers when the syrup was sold and to deliver syrup to buyers like Bruce Bascom. "He'd buy twenty-five, and then sell one hundred twenty-five," Bruce said.

Bruce began to play a version of the futures game that he learned from Mr. Bureau. He borrowed a million dollars, but contracted for two million dollars worth of syrup, and then he delivered it successfully—for a $200,000 profit. He then thought, why not try for three million? He succeeded again. Bruce ran the numbers up even further until he was selling Springtree $5,000,000 worth of syrup on only a million dollar loan.

"I was overselling by a factor of several hundred percent to Springtree on syrup I didn't own. I would get a contract, then drive to Quebec and get another contract with Mr. Bureau."

During this time Bruce was also working on the farm, cutting wood and making hay and syrup for $185 a week.

"By the sixth or seventh year I got pretty greedy. I was multiplying it even further." Then along came a poor crop year, and syrup became hard to find. "The price went up in the fall, and I still had to deliver syrup to Springtree." Because of the shortage and the price increase, Bruce had to pay Mr. Bureau more for the syrup than he expected.

"In December of that year I had many, many truckloads of syrup going to Brattleboro on which I was losing twenty to forty thousand dollars per load, truckload after truckload."

You play with fire, Bruce said, and sometimes you get burned. He figured he lost ten years' worth of income. He took mortgages to pay for the syrup, using the farm as collateral—essentially he was gambling with the farm. Fortunately for Bruce, two good crop years followed, and he was able to pay off the mortgages fairly quickly. "But I lost my nerve for being out there on the edge." Ken Bascom took the losses philosophically. He didn't ask Bruce to tell him specifically how much money he lost. Instead he asked if the experience cost more than a college education. Much more, Bruce said. "He said to me, 'Then you must have learned a lot more too.'"

OF TRADING SYRUP on the bulk market, Bruce said with some bravado, "You have to know what you're doing. This is not for the faint of heart."

Mr. Bureau was still trading syrup, even at the age of eighty, even with a serious heart condition. I remember that when I first met Real Bureau, on a visit to Canada with Bruce, he trailed along behind us, over to his warehouse, where we watched inspectors from the Federation grade his syrup. After the walk across the street he stood catching his breath, and when I looked at him he shook his head and tapped at his heart. When I visited again a year later on my own to speak with him and his office manager, Carole Rouleau, who translated for us, we cut the interview short so Mr. Bureau could report to the service that monitored his condition. Yet he was still selling, and sometimes still cleaning Bruce's clock. "He's our brain," Carole Rouleau said, and then told me, with an ironic smile, "We tell him to hang in there until we reach retirement age."

Bruce had another story about Mr. Bureau, one that got at his methods and, I suppose, his heart.

The story took place in the early 1990s. There was a lot of syrup around. Mr. Bureau borrowed money from the banks and leveraged it out. He had barrels of syrup piled up at his warehouse, in the driveway at his house, and in his three-car garage. He had barrels stacked around his swimming pool.

Mr. Bureau visited Bruce in August and tried to sell him syrup, but Bruce said he had too much already. Bureau tried again in October. Bruce told him he could buy it more cheaply elsewhere, that he didn't need it.

"Around about November, December, the banks started to get really nervous. They thought Mr. Bureau was going to go bankrupt, and there was a lot of turmoil. The banks wanted his wife to sign over the homestead rights for security, but she refused to do it. They were married for thirty years, but they had a big blowout and she left. They never got divorced, but she went to Sherbrooke, and he's been single ever since then because of that."

In January Bruce began to run out of syrup. He drove to Quebec to talk to Mr. Bureau, and offered what he was paying other producers, knowing it was below what Mr. Bureau paid for his syrup, knowing he would be taking a loss. Mr. Bureau refused to sell.

"Then I needed several truckloads of syrup, so I called back. By now it was late January. Mr. Bureau had been carrying this syrup all year and paying interest on it. I told him I would take the syrup now, but he told me the price had gone up again because of costs. He's hanging by his fingernails, his wife had left him, and he had the gall to up the price on me. It ticked me off, and I didn't buy anything."

In Acworth Ken Bascom made calls looking for syrup, and Bruce made calls, but they couldn't find syrup in Quebec or anywhere else. "Two weeks later I called him again, and he upped the price again. I drove up there and we talked about it, and I tried to get him to come down. While I was standing there I could see them loading syrup to go out to competitors."

Bureau had raised his price four times. "So what did I do? I bought six truckloads. One month before the season was to start, and he ended up selling millions of dollars of inventory that he had all year at a very substantial profit."

It was as the man said. Syrup finds the money.

A few years later Bruce talked to Mr. Bureau about what happened that season. "He said to me, 'Speculating on any product like maple syrup, it's mostly in a person's mind.

You've either got the ability to hold on, or you don't. My wife didn't know how to handle the risk and was afraid.'

"I said to him, 'Aren't you afraid, Mr. Bureau?' He told me, 'If you're going to stay in this business and buy syrup and speculate on contracts, you've got to know when you're right and when you're not right. You've got to know how to play the game,' he said."

15

THE SUGAR CAMPS

OF ST. AURELIE

On MARCH 13 a new ten-day forecast called for even higher temperatures throughout the northern states and Canadian provinces. The forecast now predicted temperatures in the midseventies, with nights above freezing until at least March 22. Temperatures were already twenty degrees above normal. They were thirty-five degrees above normal in the Midwest. The Weather Channel was reporting sixty new high-temperature records nationwide, with dozens more to be broken. Bill Karins, weatherman for MSNBC, began his report on *Morning Joe* on March 13 with, "What a beautiful forecast. And it continues for a week!"

Beauty is in the eye of the beholder. The forecast for Acworth on March 13 called for a more subdued 35° to 55°. Often Kevin's readings were below the forecast because of their perch on Mount Kingsbury, but not on this day. At Bascom's it was 45° the morning of March 13 and reached 63° in the afternoon. March 13 also happened to be Town Meeting Day in New Hampshire, which had once been the day to begin tapping trees.

On March 13 Kevin had another big day at the evaporator, making 1428 gallons of syrup. His total reached 11,850 gallons, about half of last year's crop. He was well ahead of the 2011 production going by the calendar, but Kevin wasn't optimistic at all. "I'll be surprised if we make any on Monday," he said, which would be March 19. That would be his earliest finish ever, following his earliest start ever.

That morning, when Kevin was boiling, Bruce came out of the office once again, again pulling a hairnet over his head. Bruce tended to wear his like a bathing cap; Kevin wore his under his baseball hat. I tried for the beret look, but it was almost impossible to make the hairnet look anything less than comical. "I hate to admit this," Bruce said, "but the Federation is looking pretty smart right now. I would say this is going to be the worst crop in twenty or thirty years. And the syrup is all dark."

He said he was glad he didn't sell those loads of syrup to Maple Grove.

He had just finished a morning of phone calls. He talked to Guy Bolduc, of Bolduc Products in St. Victor, Quebec, in the Beauce. Bolduc ran a tier-two company and sold syrup to some of the big chains in the United States. "Guy wanted me to tell him about the syrup crop. I said to him, 'Do you want it straight, or do you think I'll give you the runaround?' He said to me, 'I think you'll give me both, Bruce.'" He laughed at this—Bruce often told me that buyers never tell the whole truth to each other. But Bruce heard some good news. "He said there's two feet of snow in St. Victor and St. Evariste. The Canadians are producing now. They made a lot of syrup in a few days. They can produce a year's crop in a week's time up there."

Robert Poirier also called from St. Zacharie, Quebec. Robert said the season had taken off in the St. Aurelie camps and along the Golden Road in Maine, just over the border. "They produced a lot of syrup last week. With the warm weather the roads are getting muddy and the big trucks will get stuck up there. Soon they won't be able to get in or out. Some of the producers want to sell now.

"Maine will make a lot, but I will have to pay the Federation price, or close to it. I've got sixty trailer loads there now. Fifty percent of my capital is already consumed." Sixty trailer truckloads represented about $7.5 million worth of syrup at the bulk price.

Bruce took another look at the chart before he left for lunch. "We'll be done by next Wednesday." His prediction was two days beyond Kevin's, for a finish on March 21.

I HAD BEEN to St. Zacharie to visit Robert Poirier nine months ago in June of 2011. At that time Robert was picking up syrup in Quebec and Maine and shipping it to New Hampshire.

St. Zacharie is eighty miles southeast of Quebec City and ten miles from the US border. The landscape around St. Zacharie is mostly forested, with far fewer fields than the prime agricultural regions further west and south of Montreal. The terrain is made up of long rolling hills and deep valleys. The primary roads are straight, and someone cresting over one hill can see miles ahead as the road sweeps down through a trough and maybe a village and then climbs up the next hill—the land resembles long sound waves with low frequencies. Heavily loaded timber trucks barrel down those hills like roller coasters, and speed limits seem only a suggestion. St. Zacharie has a touch of the desolation of the upper latitudes. The scant apple trees bloom in June, and the fruit never really ripens. "It's always winter here," one syrup producer told me.

Before the recession and collapse of the housing market a few years ago, the lumber industry was booming. Bruce often talked about the logging and lumber trucks backed up three deep all day long at the single traffic light in St. Zacharie. Since then the population of St. Zacharie had dropped from 2200 to 1900 because of logging but also because the jeans factory closed and the work moved to Asia. The building where the factory was housed is now rented by Bruce Bascom.

Robert Poirier came late in life to the maple syrup game, but he was a quick study and had the proper beginnings. Robert started working in the woods early. He was one of twenty-three children. His parents could multiply but not fully provide, so at the age of eight Robert and a brother went to live at the farm of an aunt and uncle. Robert talked about getting 10 cents a day for working in the hay fields. He quit school at fifteen, and at seventeen he was working full time as a logger, making two dollars a day cutting pulpwood in the timberlands of Maine.

Robert did logging around Mount Katahdin for ten years and later ran his own logging company. He might have still been in that business had not a tree fallen too close and a limb hit him in the head. He walked out of the woods with his face covered with blood and drove himself to the hospital. After he recovered Robert looked for other work, finding a part-time job as an assistant for someone who was buying maple syrup for Bruce Bascom. When Robert realized that the man was embezzling syrup, he told Bruce about it. Bruce fired the man and asked Robert to take his place.

Robert was about to find a true calling. He had taught himself to speak English and had a fine memory for the right details. When Bruce talked about Robert he would say that of the 150 syrup producers Robert dealt with in Maine and Quebec, he not only remembered their names but also the names of their children and grandchildren. Visiting the sugar camps and talking to the producers, the sucrier, he gradually assembled a large buying base. Robert's workdays went all by memory, regarding the places he would go and the numbers of barrels he would find there. In 2011, when he turned sixty-nine, Robert told me he would work until his memory gave out. Bruce felt replacing Robert would be impossible and hoped he would work another twenty years.

Bruce described Robert's temperament as hot and cold, which meant that he could get upset. Although Bruce was one to push up Robert's mental temperature. In 2010, on my first trip with Bruce into Quebec, we spent a day visiting important people in the maple syrup business, partly so Sam Bascom, Bruce's nephew, could meet them. We stopped at a Maple Grove facility, dropped in on Real Bureau, visited Guy Bolduc, toured a CDL evaporator factory, and stopped last of all at the warehouse in St. Zacharie. Robert met us first thing in the morning at a restaurant, and Bruce immediately needled Robert, telling him, with a smile, that he wanted Robert to "go slow" with his buying. Robert didn't say anything in response, but he grew quiet. A couple of times more that day Bruce mentioned that Robert should go slow.

The final time was when we were in the warehouse standing near the tall stacks of barrels. Robert had bought 1.7 million pounds of syrup by then, at a price in the neighborhood of $4.5 million. He told me when I rode with him that his goal was to buy 2.1 million pounds, or about 191,000 gallons. In the warehouse they talked about the producers who had sent syrup, but then once again Bruce said, as we all heard, "Robert needs to go slow." Robert went hot: "Bruce! You always tell me to go slow, but then you always tell me you don't have enough sirop!" Sirop, the French word— Robert pronounced it melodically as *sear-rope,* making a trill on the Rs.

In 2011 I returned to Quebec on my own, making two trips that June to talk with Robert and collect syrup with him. Robert's workday began early, at 4:30, when he rose to do paperwork, and he was usually at the warehouse by 6:30. I arrived at 7:30, thinking I was early. When I remarked about the length of Robert's workday he said, "It's good for Bruce."

Robert's feelings were tending toward the hot side again on this day. He had talked to Bruce and said to me, "I ask Bruce if he wants me to buy this sirop, and he says yes, but he keeps saying go slow. These people want their money. If I don't buy their sirop, someone else will. I told Bruce, I won't have to deal with this next year." But I had the feeling he would.

Robert used a ten-wheel delivery truck to gather syrup. We soon left for Maine, for the St. Aurelie camps. St Aurelie is actually a town in Quebec, and the border crossing is there, but the area of the camps takes the same name. They are along the Baker Pond Road in timberlands in Somerset County, Maine. As we sat at the border crossing, waiting for the guard to check my passport, Robert told me about when he worked here cutting pulpwood—not maples, they were sugaring in these woods then, but softwood, conifers. "In 1959, when I worked at this place, there were one hundred and fifty cars lined up on Monday mornings, with four to five hundred people waiting to cross the border and go work in the woods."

People have made maple syrup in these woods for more than a hundred years. They were making syrup then on the Quebec side too, but these lands were used by people who didn't have access to woods on the Quebec side and so ventured across the border. They established camps and then passed them, along with the leases from the timber companies for use of the land and trees, on to their families.

Baker Pond Road was well maintained but unpaved. On days when it rained they closed the road to keep the big trucks from breaking it up. "I never broke up the road," Robert said. Moose tracks were along the road. We passed trashed-up open sites with piles of logs and went by sugar camps, some with several buildings. There were pumphouses and the webs of mainlines and tubing. The sugarbushes were all well groomed, all with the soft green shine of maple leaves on a clean understory.

As we passed a sugarbush Robert said, "That's a small one, only twenty-five thousand taps." Of another he said, "That has eighty-thousand taps." I asked how many sugar camps were along this road. Robert said, "I can tell you," and began counting, whispering to himself.

"Thirty-five," he said.

Robert looks something like the actor Paul Newman, with light blue eyes and sculpted cheekbones, his gray hair swept back, a kind of sweet mystery about him, and some shyness. He smiled with his eyes. After we drove several miles and had taken a fork in the road, with no signs along the way that I could recognize, I said it must be easy to get lost here. Robert looked as though I just didn't know and told me more about working here as a teenager. He had four horses and took them into the woods, and he hired a feeder to take care of them. Other men used the horses too. They worked twelve-hour days cutting logs and hauling them to the road with the horses. They stayed out here for a week at a time and ate only the food they brought with them.

Robert told me that the sugarmaker we were about to see had been in the next bed when Robert was in the hospital after his accident in the woods, though Robert hadn't remembered. One day they met on Baker Pond Road and stopped to talk, and the sugarmaker, whose name is Claude Morissette, told him he had been in the hospital with him. He told Robert he had heard rumors that he didn't pay enough for syrup. There were many such rumors, Robert said; about eight years ago Bruce traveled to the St. Aurelie camps and a sugarmaker got mad at him about the price he paid for syrup.

We turned and drove through the woods to his place, and Robert said, "Claude has worked at this sugarbush for thirty-two years and built it up to forty thousand taps. He put all his profits from making sirop back into the business, and now he is making money for the first time. He made sirop with horses and buckets, then a tractor, and now tubing."

Claude was happy to see Robert. He showed us around the place, taking us to a tool shed where he kept two very large generators, which provided all their electrical power.

We went into the sugarhouse and looked at his big evaporator, six feet wide and sixteen feet long, and we lingered over
the map of his sugarbush, with the tubing lines stretching
out into three zones in patterns like leaves. Claude showed
us his cabin, a rustic but clean and comfortable-looking
place, and said his wife stayed there with him during the
syrup season. Claude was now putting on a fresh coat of
paint. Robert backed the truck up to the storehouse, and
with dollies they loaded on forty-eight barrels of syrup. The
barrels were heavy, of course, weighing 600 pounds each,
and Robert worked up a sweat.

We returned to the warehouse to unload the syrup. Robert
had a full-time man at the warehouse named Bruno Guay,
who went about unloading. A woman named Raymonde
Lariviere worked recording drum weights and data needed
for customs to cross the border. Robert also employed a
truck driver who made the trips to Acworth.

While they worked I looked at the barrels. The warehouse
was divided into two sections, and Robert kept Quebec or
Federation syrup on one side and Maine syrup on another.
Maine syrup was technically US syrup, and Robert inspected
that himself before shipping it to New Hampshire. Federation inspectors graded the Quebec syrup. I enjoyed looking
at the barrels and reading the names and places where the
syrup had been made. They conveyed the breadth of the territory Robert covered and the trust he gained. The largest
producer was in the village of Notre-Dame-du-Rosaire near
the St. Lawrence—he owned his land, Robert said, and had
165,000 taps. He sent 501 barrels: "Five hundred plus one.
He says it was a slow year." Another sugarmaker had 100,000
taps. One group of sixty-eight stainless-steel barrels from

the town of La Frontiere, also near the St. Lawrence, would be shipped to Europe. Robert's territory extended northward into the Gaspe Peninsula, an eight-hour drive away, a region, I was told, that had opened up to syrup production in the last twenty years with changes in the climate. And Robert's territory extended into Maine, to the St. Aurelie camps and those along the Golden Road, which ran from the border to Jackman, Maine. Due to Robert's efforts Bruce was the majority buyer in Somerset County, Maine.

When they finished unloading we got into the truck again and returned to the St. Aurelie camps. He made different turns this time and followed a road called the Dump Road, passing by camps, some with names, others with numbers, until we came to one with a sign that read, "Nadeau Sugar Camp." Near the road was a log structure, green and mossy. "That's an old sugarhouse," Robert said. Further along appeared an opening and a building that looked like a house except for the tanks alongside and the mainlines running into it.

It had gray walls and a blue roof, a tall section that was a tank room, and a long single-story section that was the sugarhouse and, at the end, the living quarters. A woman came out to greet us, slender, middle-aged, pretty with reddish hair. Her name was Suzanne Nadeau, and she seemed eager to talk. She showed us inside. The evaporator was dismantled, with the pans removed, and was now serving as a workbench—Suzanne was making droplines, or "chutes," when we arrived. They talked about the season, which for them was quite good. She showed us the calendar near the evaporator—they started boiling on March 17 and finished on April 28.

Suzanne said that her husband, Fernand, was in the woods with the tractor, but soon he came rumbling along and we went outside to load barrels. Fernand stayed on the tractor, using the bucket to lift the barrels with chains and a device that clamped on the upper rim of the barrels. Robert attached the chains to the barrels with a helper who followed from the warehouse. Suzanne and I watched, and she talked about their sugarbush.

Fernand grew up in Quebec, as had Suzanne. He made maple syrup with his father as a boy and then waited until retirement to buy a sugaring business. They lived in the United States for thirty years, in Connecticut, where Fernand worked in construction. Their two sons were born there. One lived in New Hampshire, worked in construction, and took time off to come here during the season. Another son lived in North Carolina, was in the military, and was serving a tour in Iraq. Financing the purchase of this business was difficult because they weren't buying the land, only the buildings and equipment and the rights to the trees. Fernand mortgaged just about everything they owned to buy this place.

The sugarbush was a mile square. All the sap ran directly into the sugarhouse. They had put pressure gauges on some of the lines, and these were so useful for checking leaks that they planned to attach them to all the mainlines. During the season Fernand, Suzanne, and a helper checked tubing on snowshoes. They lived here all the time during the sugar season, but this time of year they spent weekends at their lake house south of Montreal. They heated the place with wood that Fernand cut, using the tractor—what was it about a tractor, she asked, that once you had one, you wondered how you ever managed without one? Suzanne liked burning wood and the extravagant heat it supplied. They took fire-wood with them on their weekend trips and would give a load to Suzanne's sister this coming weekend.

I had heard about the Nadeau syrup before. In the Cooler Dave St. Aubin told me he thought the best-tasting syrup came from this region of Maine. He said that the owner of a pancake restaurant came to the Cooler to buy barrels of syrup for his restaurant. He selected eighteen barrels, all but one from this region and the majority from the Nadeau camp.

In the truck Robert told me that when he first met the Nadeaus they got mad at him because they heard he paid a low price for syrup. He won them over, he said, by giving them a barrel, telling them they could pay eighteen dollars for it or they could have it for free if they sold him their syrup. They may also have been swayed by the fact that Bruce bought the entire crop, including late-season dark commercial grade.

After lunch Robert and I headed out from the warehouse again, and he said, "You're really going to see something here." We stayed in Quebec and drove to a place in St. Zacharie, going a few miles along one of those straight roads until we came to a sign that read, "L'erablier Mario Maheux." The driveway was lined with pines and then turned into an opening, where I grasped what Robert meant. Before us was a bright yellow sugarhouse, a sizeable building with walls faced with logs. The trim was green, and the metal roof was green too. Next to the big building was a smaller garage on the same design, also banana yellow with green trim and filled with barrels of syrup. Robert backed up to the garage and began loading.

Soon up the road in a cloud of dust came Mario Maheux himself in his pickup truck. He jumped out of his truck. Mario was a carpenter, dressed in jeans, a sweatshirt, a hat, and he carried a pencil behind his ear as carpenters do. He came to the garage and spoke in quick French. "Ingles?" he said of this visitor. Robert had been buying syrup from Mario for ten years, but only in the last two years had he gotten seriously into sugarmaking. He had inherited this building from his father, who planned to use it as a sugarhouse bed and breakfast, but that didn't work out. Mario was now living in the sugarhouse, and for him, Robert said, it was the fulfillment of a dream. After they loaded twenty-eight barrels we went inside for a look.

Like other places that were both sugarhouse and home, this building was sectioned into two parts. But there was overlap here, that's the important thing: overlap between the living part and the working part, and that's where the beauty was. Downstairs at the entrance was a combination dining and living room, with nice furnishings—an oak table with eight chairs, a comfortable couch, an antique hutch, an upright piano in tune. There were rocking chairs and lots of windows. Just above this room on the second floor was a sitting room with leather couches, a television, a divan by the window, and . . . an open trunk full of women's hats. A woman's touch, from Mario's girlfriend, as Robert told me. Both of these rooms, downstairs and upstairs, were paneled in pine, even on the ceilings, which gave them a warm honeyed glow. Upstairs, leading off from the sitting room, was a balcony around an open space from which you could look down upon the evaporator and into the sugarhouse, as though like a theater.

The character of the sugarhouse part was totally in contrast to the two living rooms. The walls were a brilliant white, and that white ran up the inside of the balconies on the second floor. The evaporator itself was stainless steel and highly polished, which added to this brilliant hue. The stacks on the evaporator rose up through this whiteness and through the knotty pine ceiling. The effect was to channel light from downstairs through the upstairs. It was a cathedral effect, the most magnificent presentation of the core of a sugarhouse I had ever seen, and I could understand why Mario Maheux had come flying up the road to show it to us.

On the first floor away from the evaporator was a small kitchen with burnished aluminum appliances and a nook with stools for snacking. Near the evaporator were two barber chairs, another clever touch, for kicking back and watching the evaporator, in season or out.

THE NEXT MORNING Robert said he was going to "take me somewhere," which I took to mean somewhere good. He asked if I had boots, and I took my hiking boots from my car. When we drove off he said, "I'm going to show you a sugarhouse," with an expression that indicated he meant it.

Robert had talked to Bruce that morning again and had been reassured. "Things are good," Robert said. "Always good." He smiled as though to say they had their ups and downs. Bruce gave him permission to buy a new scale for $2500 and told Robert he could buy more syrup.

By now the St. Aurelie camps were feeling like familiar ground, and again I enjoyed the soft June glow of the sunlight coming through the treetops. We rode for eight, maybe ten miles before Robert followed a side road and parked by a pile of firewood. Nearby were two old-fashioned wooden gathering tanks on sled runners. "We're going up there," he said, pointing to an overgrown pathway. Soon the path turned muddy. There were lots of moose tracks in the mud. Strands of sagging tubing lines hung between some of trees.

Then, ahead up a rise, I saw a clearing and some structures. They were made of logs. One building was much larger than the others, and as we got closer I saw smokestacks jutting from the roof.

"Two old guys, they worked making sirop here," Robert said. They were brothers, Charles Edourd and Pierre Abbel Larochelle. "They made sirop here from the time they were ten years old, and their father made sirop before them. This place was worked for a hundred years."

We climbed up a path to a clearing, a small field with tall grass up to our waists. Along the clearing were some log buildings. The roofs were missing, the metal most likely salvaged. "One of these was a camp," Robert said. "The other was for horses. He came up here in the summer and cut hay for the horses."

The cabin hadn't been used in a long time. There was another newer cabin made of boards on the other side of the clearing. The old log cabin was for storage, and inside were some parts of sleds. In the other cabin for horses was a small hayloft and an entryway so low to the ground it was more like a burrow. The feeding bins were cribbed where the horses gnawed on them. A cracked leather harness hung from a nail.

"The men used only horses here, never any machines. They made those logs by hand, with a saw and an axe. They made all the logs for that sugarhouse too. And they made those smokestacks." The stairway going down into the sugarhouse had rotted out, so we walked around and climbed inside.

The big logs used to make the base of the sugarhouse were flattening from the weight of the building, helped along by the years of steam. There was a patchy layer of concrete on the floor and buckets lying about. Further evidence of the history Robert meant to convey to me lay just outside the doorway, where a cast-iron cauldron sat, turned over. "That was the way they did it long, long ago," he said.

"They made about seven or eight barrels a year, using buckets and, at the end, tubing in some places." Robert gave a little laugh. "The horses learned to duck under the tubing when they went through the woods to a place where they had buckets." The horses pulled those gathering tanks we saw at the road.

"The old men were able to move the barrels of sirop. They were heavy barrels, the old kind that weighed about a hundred and thirty pounds. They moved them out of the sugarhouse and on to the sled. The horses would pull the barrel, that must have weighed close to eight hundred pounds, all the way to the road. I would grade the sirop there." Robert started buying from them ten years ago, a few years after he started working for Bruce.

Now I knew, in the way Robert told this story, why he wanted Bruce not to tell him to go slow. He was a buyer, it was his calling, and that work connected him to these people in the deepest ways, to what they loved and the ritual that gave meaning to their lives. Of course he didn't want to go slow.

"The sirop was very dark," Robert said, "C grade, or D grade. They couldn't make light sirop on those old evaporators."

He smiled, remembering. "One time when I began to grade their sirop I asked them how the sirop was. 'A grade,' one said. I tested it, found it was C. I tested another barrel and it was C. Barrel after barrel, all C. When I got to the last one I said, 'Which one is A? I thought you said it would be A.' They said, 'You have to give us one!'"

We walked out along the trail with tracks worn by sleds and hooves. "The men lived in St. Prosper," he said, which was a village near St. Zacharie. "One drove an old Pontiac, another a beat-up pickup truck. One was married, the other wasn't. They fought all the time. One checked his watch every minute when he worked."

As we walked out he said, "I wish you could have seen them making sirop here." We stopped by the gathering tanks again, and I opened a lid. Robert pointed to the edge at the opening and said, "Look how it's worn, where he put his buckets." Like the threshold over a well-worn doorway.

We ate lunch, made a brief stop at the warehouse, and then Robert said to me, "I have a surprise for you." We left in his pickup truck and followed roads in St. Zacharie. We went over a hill with long view of the woods. Robert said, "All these maple trees, as far as you can see, all around here, they are all tapped."

I had asked Robert what he did during the sugar season when everyone was boiling, but he hadn't answered. Now he said, "We're going to my sugarhouse." We arrived at a place with a gated fence. "During the sugar season," Robert said, "I stay here all the time."

Here the sugarhouse and the camp were in separate buildings. Robert told me he bought the land in 1964. A hundred and fifty acres, for $2500. "With five hundred dollars down and a low interest," he said. "I cleaned the woods and planted maple trees. What used to be fields now have maple trees that are tapped." He has 4000 taps now.

We went into the sugarhouse and looked at the equipment. "I have lots of tanks here, in case I can't be here and the sap mounts up." Two of the tanks looked like silos.

The cabin was homey, with many family photographs on the wall. "My five-year-old granddaughter comes here when I make sirop. She just plays, doesn't work."

He said, "This is where I like to be." Again I perceived the profound connection he had to this culture. When I first came to Quebec to talk to sugarmakers I thought I would see the powerhouse in action, the 100 million pounds manifested in industrial-sized buildings, but what I saw most of all were family sugarhouses, each family having worked diligently over the years to make the dream of sugarmaking, their particular dream, come true.

We looked at some of the photos of Robert's family, of his four children and his nine grandchildren. One older photo was of a man riding an ox—Robert's father, he said. Other people were standing by: maybe they were brothers. His father was doing the work of sugaring, and the ox had been pulling a sled. Robert said he had started sugaring with his father when he was five or six.

LATER THAT AFTERNOON he graded the Nadeau syrup, the forty-eight barrels lined up and waiting. Robert first worked through a couple of barrels of commercial that were made on April 30, two days after the end date on the calendar at the Nadeau's sugarhouse. These would probably be cleaned and filtered at Bascom's and sold to process meats. He tasted the best of the Nadeau, which he thought was made on April 25. "It's smooth, like cream," he said. That was a good way to describe the feeling of syrup in the mouth.

Robert was nearing the end of the grading when a syrup producer came in who I will call Jacques. Jacques was a large man with a booming voice, wearing tinted glasses and with a bit of a beard. It didn't take long to see that Jacques was someone of great feeling and expression, and he reminded me of the actor Gerard Depardieu in that way. Jacques was upset about something, something to do with the Federation.

After Robert told me his name I remembered seeing it before. I was in Bruce's office once, early on, when he showed me an invoice from the Federation so I could see it as an example. Jacques's name was there, and what made it easy to remember was the receipt for $236,000 worth of syrup.

I have to say I was mesmerized by this man, his expressiveness and physical presence, and the melodic flow of his French, and I wanted badly to know what he was saying. Finally Robert turned to me and said, "He is owed two hundred thousand dollars by the Federation and they won't pay."

"What percentage did they give?" I asked.

"Seventy-five," Jacques said. He went on in French. As he talked, Robert kept making little comments, and Jacques would laugh. Robert was enjoying making Jacques laugh.

"You have lost weight," Robert said.

"It is hard eating two meals a day with the Federation," Jacques said, and they laughed at this.

After Jacques left and as I was about to leave for New Hampshire, Robert came out of his office with an ashen look on his face. He had talked to Bruce, who told him that he wasn't going to pay the Federation, that he was going to wait. That he was out of money. "I will have to stop all the pick-ups," Robert said. He seemed close to anger when he said, "I will talk to Bruce."

I wondered if Bruce was merely stressed with having to buy all that syrup, the many millions to spend.

"No," Robert said. "Bruce sleeps better when he has a problem. I tell him that. He has thick blood. Nothing worries him."

16

THE ROUTE OF

THE SUGARMAKERS

AFTER I RETURNED to New Hampshire I called Robert. He said he had a long talk with Bruce and everything worked out. There was a problem with Federation invoices, the problem was solved, and now he could buy syrup again.

I also had a long talk with Bruce. "The problem Robert doesn't see is that the other two-thirds of my supply is coming from the US all the time," he said. "Over the last thirty days we brought in four months' worth of syrup. You've only got so much money to buy with. Right now I can't buy more than sixteen to eighteen additional trailer loads."

Bruce went through the list of buyers in the United States who sent loads of syrup. Each cost about $120,000. A buyer in central New York, three trailer loads. Another buyer south of Buffalo, three loads, one left to go. Another in central New York, four loads. Another near Croghan, New York, west of the Adirondacks, seven loads. A buyer north of Croghan, two loads. A buyer from Swanton, Vermont, four loads. Another buyer from northwestern Vermont, three loads. The Vermont dairy farmer with 3000 cows, four loads. An Amish buyer from Ohio, five loads.

Everyone was buying US syrup first because it cost less due to the Federation pricing and the exchange rate—it now cost US$1.04 to buy a Canadian dollar. I was given a chart by another processor that showed that during the summer of 2011 a pound of Federation syrup at $2.81 actually cost $2.92—eight percent more—because of the exchange rate.

"Robert is highly successful at purchasing on the Canadian side, but I just don't need all the tonnage he can obtain," he said. "When I add up what I'm going to get in the US and what we're getting in Maine I start to reach a point where I have enough syrup. I don't want to carry additional syrup into the next year if I can help it. I want to go slow and extend my credit and buy syrup at the opportune time, which is now. I also want to start liquidating syrup in the fall and get the building empty so I don't have syrup sitting around through the year. I want to have an empty building for what's coming in next year."

Bruce said that the Federation surplus offered an advantage for processors like him. "There's been so much expansion on both sides of the border that the probabilities are overwhelming as to whether there is going to be adequate supply or too much supply. Why should you buy ahead when everybody knows there's a supply in the Federation? If someone gets caught short, they can always buy from the Federation. No one wants to pay their extra twenty-five cents per pound, but they will. With the Federation supply available, the tendency is for companies to go into the fall with a lean inventory.

"Things have been skewed since the strategic reserve came into existence. One is that processors have no incentive to carry any more than the absolute minimum into the next year. It used to be that you made all kinds of deals to get enough supply to carry an inventory. What happens now is that you run your inventory down and the Federation gets stuck with theirs. If they're stupid enough to do it, then you're going to take advantage of it. It's a fair world, right?"

Not that Bruce wasn't going to pay for all that Quebec syrup sitting in the warehouse in St. Zacharie. He was, he said—they were Robert's suppliers, Bruce bought from them before, so he extended his loyalty to them. But he would be paying the Federation price, with the boost due to the exchange rate, plus $1400 more to ship each trailer load to Acworth.

The costs rankled on him because they seemed out of touch with the markets in 2011, as they would again in 2012. "This year in Europe," Bruce said in 2011, "prices are going up five percent because of the exchange rate. Yet there's a bumper crop, there's a surplus, and there's almost a recession going on. It's a stupid time to increase prices."

He added, "You go up too much, a little more Log Cabin gets sold."

A FEW DAYS LATER, when I returned to Quebec, I gave Robert a call from St. Georges, the city closest to St. Zacharie. He said if I came to the warehouse that afternoon, I could "see someone taste some sirop."

That someone happened to be a woman named Pascale Boivin, who led one of the inspection teams from Centre

Acer, a company employed by the Federation of Quebec Maple Syrup Producers to test and grade syrup. There were eleven teams of graders testing the 2011 maple syrup crop in Quebec, all 101.9 million pounds of it.

The team was working in the room reserved for the Centre Acer inspectors.

When I arrived Ms. Boivin was sitting at a counter in front of a set of vials and some instruments. She was wearing a white coat, and her blond hair was tied up. Nearby, also wearing a white coat, was a young man, Alexandre Gregoire, recording data on a laptop. A third person was gathering samples from the warehouse, from the three long lines of barrels set aside for this day's work.

A fourth person was present, not in a white coat but in jeans and a plaid shirt, quietly sitting with his arms crossed like someone in a courtroom. His name was Cameron, and he was there to be a witness while his syrup and that of his two brothers was being graded—to make sure there was no funny business, I suppose.

"Bonjour," Pascale said when I took a chair beside her, and after a bit of talk she told me they were grading 250 barrels that day. She told me she tasted samples from 250 barrels of syrup every day. This seemed like a whole lot of sugar, and I asked how long she had been doing that. She conferred with Alexandre on pronunciation and said, "Nineteen ninety-four. I have been tasting since nineteen ninety-four. Seventeen years. Two hundred and fifty drums a day. I taste all the sirop. During the busy time."

I wondered if she disliked the taste of syrup, and that seemed an unfortunate occupational hazard. I asked, "Escu vous mange sirop?"

She thought for a moment. "In the winter, sometimes, when I am not tasting, I eat sirop on, how do you say, crepes."

She conferred with Alexandre again, who said, carefully, "She doesn't swallow."

"You spit it out," I said. Which she did, into a container on the floor.

The Centre Acer procedure seemed very detailed, though Pascale didn't think so. They tested for *brix*, or concentration of sugar (which was at sixty-six or sixty-seven percent, as elsewhere), and for *lumière*, or light transmittance, using a spectrograph. That determined the grade. It was basically the same procedure as at Bascom's, except for the more precise test for brix. After the two tests Pascale smelled the syrup, then tasted it, then spit.

"Soixante-huit," she said of the light transmittance of one of the Cameron samples. "Soixante-neuf," of another. Seventy-eight and seventy-nine, both A light grade. Alexandre keyed in the data for the appropriate barrels.

At one point I went out into the warehouse to look at the barrels they were grading. A worker named Bruno Guay was helping the woman who was taking the samples, opening the bungs with a wrench. I said to him, "There are two hundred and fifty barrels here?" "No," he said. "There are two hundred and fifty-three." He smiled at this and said some graders got upset when there were more than 250 barrels, but sometimes it just worked out that way. Bruno said the Centre Acer crew arrived at 8:00 that morning, started grading at 9:00, tasted 136 barrels in the morning and would taste 127 this afternoon. He smiled at this too—so much tasting.

They finished the Cameron syrup, and Monsieur Cameron quietly departed. They then moved to the final twenty-six barrels, which happened to be Robert Poirier's 2011 crop. The first, Pascale said, "quatre-vingts cinq," an eighty-five, an exceptional A light, though because it was the first barrel of the year, it had a bit of an off-flavor—first-run off-flavor, this was called. The next one tasted very good.

"Sirop good today," Boivin said.

Of course I had to ask. "Have you tasted bad syrup?"

"I have tasted a lot of bad sirop. In July, August, a lot of bad sirop."

It ferments, she said, or sometimes accumulates mold— "moisi." Or it can be buddy—"bourgeon."

They worked through Robert's barrels over the next hour and reached number 253. The feeling then in the room seemed to be joyous, as they stood and removed their white coats and began to relax. I went to where Alexandre was attaching labels to the barrels, pulling them from a portable printer. Every barrel of Federation syrup was labeled with a serial number, the brix, the lumière, the grade, and other identifying information. Data about the work of each grader was also on the labels. In this case, on the last barrel of Poirier syrup, the number for Pascale Boivin was 8922. We went right over to her. She was letting down her hair. We asked if that was a correct number—this hardly seemed possible. Pascale said no, it was not correct. The computer crashed twice this year and been replaced, and she actually graded—she conferred with Alexandre again:

"Ten thousand drums this year," she said.

"Au revoir." Before they departed, Bruno Guay was lining up another 250 drums.

THE NEXT DAY Robert told me I was going to see the most beautiful sugarhouse in St. Zacharie. He needed to stay at the warehouse to load a trailer for shipment to Acworth, but he said someone would take me there, a man named Jean-Claude Pare, who ran an *érablière* called Dole Pond Maple Products. He was a gregarious man, happy to practice his English and talk about the maple syrup industry, especially about that segment of French Canadians who sugared on the American side of the border.

There were forty-three of them in all, Jean-Claude told me. They averaged 30,000 taps each, and possessed about 1.3 million taps in all. Their output made Somerset County, Maine, the top-producing county in the United States. When we went to Jean-Claude's house we looked at the website of the Maine Maple Producers Association, where the group he belonged to was described as the "Bulk Syrup Suppliers that proudly operate sugarhouses in the State of Maine." They were members of the Maine Somerset County Sugarmakers Association, but Jean-Claude had also founded an organization of the French Canadians called the Alligash Group, which worked together to make certain they continued to get the E2 visas necessary to work on the US side of the border.

Jean-Claude had been making syrup in a camp near the Golden Road for twenty years. He started with very little money in 1991, working up his sugarbush, getting to 16,000 taps, and made his first good crop in 1995. Now Jean-Claude was at 37,000 taps. He and his wife worked together and hired a worker to check tubing. Finding the right people to check for leaks was difficult. "We must be 'minuteaux,' how do you say, fussy? To find the 'microfuite,' we call it, the little leaks."

The sugarhouse we went to was near the border, but on the Canadian side, and on government land. We traveled along some back roads, and Jean-Claude showed me some wooded land he bought—"It makes us proud here, to own land." He pulled off the road by a field and pointed to a long hill about a mile away. "See out there, you see the maples?" Then suddenly I could—a large monochromatic patch of maple green on the hillside.

The road into the woods was called "Route de Sucriers," the Road of the Sugarmakers. Jean-Claude said his own sugar camp was not very far away, on the other side of this hill in Maine. This side, however, which faced to the southeast, was warmer—by four degrees on average, Jean-Claude said. As a result, the sugarhouses here produced more syrup on average, three and a half pounds per tap, nearly a third of a gallon.

There were sugarhouses and camps all along the way. I waved to one man I saw in front of a cabin, who looked at me strangely—Jean-Claude told me you don't wave to someone around here unless you know them. We passed a sign that read, "Claude Giroux—Acericulteur." A maple culturist. It seemed to be the profession of choice in St. Zacharie.

"To buy sugarhouses in these areas is very expensive," Jean-Claude said. "Fifteen to twenty dollars per tap." So a 20,000-tap operation would be $300,000 to $400,000. "For private sugarbushes in Quebec it is much, much more. Fifty to sixty dollars per tap. It's crazy because the syrup cannot pay for it." That meant that in Quebec a 20,000-tap sugarbush on private land would cost up to $1.2 million. And that 165,000-tap operation that Robert talked about—up to $9.9 million at $60 per tap. Jean-Claude said that the camps had always been held closely and passed down within families, but now "strangers" were coming in to buy them.

At the end of the road we turned into a driveway where we came to the sugarhouse owned by a man named Vital Lariviere. Jean-Claude drove around to the south end of the building to a wall built to take advantage of sunlight, with fourteen door-sized windows—seven on the first floor and seven above. A very nice thing on a March day in Quebec, I imagined. The building, I am guessing, was thirty feet wide and eighty feet long. It was sided with natural pine, with small windows on the long sides of the building and, above, a red metal roof.

Off to the side was Lariviere's old sugarhouse. It was quite small and didn't take advantage of sunlight. Lariviere must have looked at the site of his new sugarhouse for many winters. Jean-Claude said, "He worked in there for years and thought about all the things he wanted in a sugarhouse. When he built this he put them all in."

No one was there, so we drove up to the sugarbush to look for Lariviere. We passed by a machine, a wood processor that he used to cut his firewood. By using only wood for heat instead of oil, Jean Claude said, Lariviere saved enough money to pay for his living expenses. As we followed the road we passed a stack of firewood that must have been a quarter-mile long, trailing down the road and out of sight. Along the edge of the woods were mainlines. We stopped at a pump-house, looked inside, and saw the pumps and a video camera trained on them.

Jean-Claude called Lariviere, who said that it was too hot to work in the woods, so he was lying by his pool but that we could go inside and have a look around. Jean-Claude drove back to the south end.

Through that entryway was a kitchen with a round wooden dining table with four chairs and, on the refrigerator, photos of Lariviere and his children, teenagers. Mounted on a wall was a row of video monitors, one for watching television and the others for watching pumps. Off the kitchen was a room for drying wet clothing. A beautifully tooled stairway led up to the bedrooms.

Beyond the kitchen was the sugarhouse, and the first impression was one of space, open space and lots of room. There was a tool bench, well organized, along one wall—he must have been thinking about that tool bench while working in that other cramped sugarhouse. The evaporator was large, six feet wide and eighteen feet long, but not fancy. The pans were removed, and some ash was still in the arch. The evaporator wasn't in the center of the room but instead off to the side. Above it was a box-shaped chimney, paneled in pine, wider and longer than the evaporator—the purpose must have been to channel as much steam as possible through the upper vents. On the outer paneling was affixed a garden hose, cleverly threaded through a bicycle wheel, with counterweights attached so that the hose could easily be pulled down and put to use.

"Vital is willing to try new things and experiment," Jean-Claude said.

The R.O. room was in a back corner, nothing special to look at, just another typical room with tubes and pipes and dials. Next to it a stairway led up to a balcony with tanks for holding sap, both raw and concentrated.

In most sugarhouses the evaporator sat center stage, but that was not the case at Vital's place. In the middle of this sugarhouse, sitting on a raised platform, was a large spa for hot water baths—what more could you ask for after working in the snowy woods, checking tubing on a winter day or after boiling sap for many hours? I remembered someone telling me that hot maple syrup fresh off the evaporator and a little whiskey was a very good drink, though that was my fantasy, not theirs. Based on this tool of enjoyment and other innovations, I now understood why Robert thought this was the most beautiful sugarhouse in St. Zacharie.

On our way out along the Route of the Sugarmakers Jean-Claude said, "Around here everyone talks about sirop. You go into the store and they talk about sirop d'erable, and at the restaurants they talk about sirop. Everybody does it, everybody talks about it here."

17

SEASONS OF CHANGE

BY SATURDAY, MARCH 17, the sap run was down to a quarter of the amount of a week ago and the sugar content down to a range of about 1.2 to 1.5 percent at the Bascom lots. Bruce was at the store that Saturday.

"Maple Grove is flat out in Quebec," he said. "They're protecting themselves against a poor crop. It's going to be a very poor crop."

A producer named Dave Richards came into the store. Richards ran the Grant Family Pond View sugarhouse in the town of Weare. He said to Bruce, "You got a rebuild kit on that pump?" Bruce looked across the room, put his tongue to his teeth, and headed for a shelf.

Richards said he was preparing for Maple Weekend, which was a week away. Because his sugarhouse was located between the cities of Manchester and Concord, Richards had good traffic. On Maple Weekend he served hot dogs, cakes, and donuts and gave away maple treats. "It will cost me about fifteen hundred dollars," he said.

"You'll double that in sales, though," Bruce said.

"We'll quadruple that. We won't have sap, but we'll simmer water." They would simmer because it was too expensive to do a full boil. "They'll be asking, 'Where's the syrup?' I'll say, 'It's outside, in the jugs.'"

When Richards left, Bruce got online and looked at the forecast for Jackman, Maine, the major town in Somerset County and the town closest to the sugar camps. Their forecast didn't look good either, with ten days of hot weather and nighttime temperatures above freezing. That was exceptionally unusual for northern Maine. They usually boiled until the end of April.

"This kind of weather is once in a hundred years," Bruce said.

WHENEVER I DROVE from Bascom's along Crane Brook Road I passed the Clark sugarhouse and the Clark farm across the road and up a steep hill. I had gotten to know Alvin Clark over the past couple of years and followed events at his sugarhouse. The Clarks were next-door neighbors to the Bascoms, though next door was a relative term because the Clarks are in Langdon and the Bascoms in Acworth, and the two sugarhouses were at least a mile apart. Back in the 1960s and 1970s, when tour buses brought people here from Massachusetts and Connecticut, they stopped at Bascom's and at Clark's. The close relationship went far back. Alvin Clark was a close friend of Ken Bascom. Alvin's father, Leroy Clark, was a friend with Glenn and Eric Bascom. Alvin owned journals from the late 1920s showing that after Glenn Bascom's wife died, he was a nightly visitor at the Clark household.

When I left Bascom's on the morning of March 17 and saw the door to the Clark sugarhouse open and Alvin's car there,

I had to stop in to see how Alvin and his son David were faring during the 2012 season.

"Hey!" Alvin said. He was wearing a funny-looking fur hat with long ear flaps that made him look a little like a Bassett hound. Alvin knew how silly he looked and was grinning. He was eighty. He had strong features—his face reminded me of hand-hewn beams. His eyes were a powder blue. He was sitting by the woodstove in the little kitchen where, during the sugar season and especially on Maple Weekend, they served coffee and donuts, chili, and hamburgers and also sold syrup and maple candy. Alvin had a fire going in the woodstove.

"That hat must be warm," I said.

He laughed. "Do you want to try some sugar on snow?"

"Of course I do."

This would be a first for me. I had heard a lot about sugar on snow and was fascinated by the antiquity of it, this way of eating maple syrup that originated with the Native Americans and was the featured product at sugar parties for centuries. Alvin cooked some syrup down to a sauce stage and then dropped spoons of the syrup on snow in a pan. It had congealed enough to lift away a piece with a toothpick. Such a delicious burst of flavor in the mouth, as the icy taffy softened and the sweet maple flavor released. It was very chewy, and I could see why they called this treat leather aprons, though actually I thought I understood only the leather part. I looked it up—Benjamin Franklin considered himself a "leather-apron man," as a mechanic or printer, celebrating his artisanal roots: "Keep Thy Trade," he wrote, "and Thy Trade will keep Thee." That worked here.

Alvin was giving his sugar on snow recipe a trial run in advance of Maple Weekend. "Though we'll probably be boiling water again," he said with a laugh. Actually the Clarks hadn't done so badly in 2012 and were having an average year. They too kept a production chart on the wall of the sugarhouse. It went back to 1959, the year Alvin took over the sugarhouse from his father and the year David was born. The chart lengthened over the years and was about six feet long now and four feet high, and visually almost like a work of art, with its red lines and contrasting black lines telling of the length of the seasons and amounts made. After we ate enough sugar on snow to satisfy—it didn't take long— we went over to look at the chart. David had started boiling on February 16, just before the first big run, and had boiled fifteen days since then. On March 12, when Kevin Bascom set a new record, David Clark had a big day too, making 107 gallons. On their evaporator, which was heated by wood, four-foot split cordwood that David cut during the off-season, and using sap reduced with an R.O. to an 8 percent concentration, the Clarks could produce 25 gallons of syrup per hour. As of March 17 they had made 937 gallons, well behind the 1400 gallons they made in 2011 but on course to have an average year.

Yet everyone knew that 2012 was not an average year, with its early start, snow drought, and pending forecast for North Carolina weather.

"I've never seen a winter like this one," Alvin said. Then he thought for moment. "Of course, 1981 was a dry winter. And there was that winter in the 1940s when we got five feet of snow when the apple blossoms were out. That was a strange winter."

We looked at 1981 on the chart, which read, "Biggest Production," at 1000 gallons. Alvin had started boiling on February 16 that year too. After a few sporadic boils and a pair of intense two-week runs the season ended on April 1.

And there was that 2010 season noted on the chart, when David first boiled on February 23 and when the early warm weather came. The boils were sporadic, it was 60° on March 19, and David's last boil was on March 31. Three days later, on April 3, the temperature was 85°.

ALVIN'S CHART AND sugarhouse had been the focus of many news stories. Most newspapers in the maple syrup regions ran a story every spring. Alvin's chart may have become the most famous production chart in the industry in 2004, when a story ran in the *Boston Globe* with the headline, "Warming Trend Blamed for Syrup Season Change."

The lead paragraph read, "The state's maple syrup producers say they can see the effects of global warming in their backyards: they are tapping their trees about a month earlier than they used to. . . . A giant chart on the wall of the Clark Sugar House in Acworth shows that the maple syrup season began changing about twenty years ago."

The story quoted Alvin, who said, "Most everybody's tapping a lot earlier than they used to." The story went on to say that the Clark chart might be a glimpse of the future. Scientists were predicting that New England's temperatures would rise by six to ten degrees by the year 2050. And then, the climax of the story, a statement by Barry Rock, a professor at the University of New Hampshire who did research on climate change. "I think the sugar maple industry is on its way out," he was quoted as saying.

ALVIN HAD TURNED EIGHTY last summer and threw a party for himself. Alvin kept his farm looking pretty with many flower gardens, and a big vegetable garden and raspberry patch. Perched on the hill above the sugarhouse and Crane Brook he had lovely views to the eastward and the small mountains—the place became spectacular when the leaves turned in the fall. He and David owned about 800 acres, and they used 200 of them as pasture for a herd of thirty bison. Because of this, because the herd was a commercial operation for meat—lean meat, they would point out—Alvin's yard had the look of a gardener's dream and a Sioux hunting camp, with buffalo skulls drying and aging on top of poles next to the lovely raspberry patch. They served buffalo burgers at the birthday party and buffalo chili at the sugarhouse. Anyone who wanted buffalo meat could drive up to the Clark's house and buy it or buy syrup, plenty of that too. There was a mounted buffalo head outside the door to the little room where they sold the meat and syrup. At Alvin's party they set up an organ, and a group from Alvin's church sang a hymn and a patriotic song. It was like being at a party from 50 years ago, or maybe 150.

The first time I talked with Alvin was in 2010. It was mid-March, and the sap run was all but over. When I rode on the sap trucks with George Hodskins and Greg Bascom I learned that some producers had called Bruce asking if they could buy sap, and I also learned that David Clark was going to retap several hundred of his trees so that he could boil on Maple Weekend. One producer told me this was risky for the tree's health, to wound the tree again that late in the season.

I wanted to get to know the Clarks because I heard their sugarhouse was beautiful inside. Once, when I attended the Langdon town meeting, I heard Alvin speak in support of the food program for the poor in Langdon, and I'd noticed how much respect he commanded. So in 2010, on one very warm afternoon after I left Bascom's I stopped at the Clark sugarhouse. The mood that day was gloomy. Alvin told me it was a poor season, and he said that David recently had surgery to remove a tumor from his skull. He was left with a lot of medical bills, and the syrup crop was meant to cover them. Usually sales of syrup helped fund the farm operation, but not this year.

I didn't stay long, and Alvin followed me outside. He said it would be better to talk after the season was over, that I should give him a call and come up to the farmhouse. In June I did that.

Alvin's wife had died four years ago, and he lived alone in the farmhouse, but David was not far away, living in a house at the bottom of the hill and near the sugarhouse. Alvin told me that when David was working construction—he worked on bridges—he came up to the farm every morning at 3:30, and Alvin made him coffee and a lunch. Alvin had been born in this house, and it was packed with keepsakes and photographs and articles about maple sugaring and the sugarhouse. There was a buffalo hide on one of his couches and a buffalo head in the dining room where we sat and talked.

He showed me a photo of his father boiling on a flat pan in the woods, and later that summer we went out and uncovered that arch; Alvin dug through the leaves and humus like a bear, saying, "This is history." His father and grandfather had made syrup. When I asked how many of the households sugared back then he said, "Everyone. Everyone made it." He told me he was one of the first to get into plastic tubing and that Ken Bascom, his friend, came over often to look at it. Alvin got up to 3000 buckets, and it was hard work going through the deep snow to get to them. With tubing they were able to move their sugarhouse from the woods down to the road.

Toward the end of that visit Alvin said he had been invited to attend the opening of an exhibit about climate change at the science museum in Concord. He said a copy of his chart would be part of the exhibit. He didn't think he would be able to attend, though. David had no interest in going. He didn't believe in climate change. "But I do," Alvin said.

"I'll take you," I answered. "We'll make a night of it. We'll go out to dinner. Kathy will come." I was bubbling with eagerness. Alvin said to call a man named Richard Polonsky, the organizer of the exhibit. Polonsky had made the copy of Alvin's chart, and he had brought a video crew to the sugarhouse last year. I called Polonsky—he was as pleased as I was that Alvin would be attending. There would be a show in the planetarium and also a talk by Barry Rock of the University of New Hampshire. Polonsky said if we arrived early, he could show us the exhibit.

We had a good time that night, Alvin, Kathy, and me. We stopped at a diner in Hillsborough, and we laughed a lot. We were a little late getting to the McAuliffe-Shepard Discovery Center, but there was enough time to see a part of the exhibit, which was titled, "Seasons of Change."

Richard Polonsky, along with some of the museum staff, came out to greet us. Alvin had dressed up, wearing a yellow shirt and brown tie and jacket, and a baseball cap with the insignia "Apollo 14" on the front. Someone asked him where he got the hat, but Alvin couldn't remember. He had made a donation, he said. Alvin made lots of small donations to many organizations.

We climbed the stairs to the second floor, and Richard took us to a space where syrup was displayed in a cabinet. Alvin's chart was mounted on a wall nearby, reproduced in color with the red and black lines and the handwritten figures. Next to the chart was a monitor with a looping video of Alvin, working at his sugarhouse and talking about the changes he witnessed over the years.

It began with a shot on a March day, with patchy snow on the ground and Crane Brook running: *"From 1911 on we've been making sugar on this farm."*

There was a shot of Alvin by the evaporator, standing under buckets hanging from the rafters: *"My father and his brothers sugared. I've been sugaring all my life."* A shot of maple trees and tubing: *"When springtime temperatures are right, the sugar comes down, up and down, and we catch it."*

Alvin inserting a spout and attaching tubing, sap flowing in: *"All over, the other producers feel more or less the same as I, that something is happening."*

Crane Brook, swollen with snowmelt: *"Years ago, I remember we'd get heavy ground-freezing. This year, the ground around here never froze."*

Outside the sugarhouse, Alvin at a giant maple, checking tubing: *"I remember when the maples looked really nice, back in the forties, the fifties. Today they don't look near as healthy."* Near the end, Alvin in his truck, driving along Crane Brook Road: *"I read a lot about the polar bears, in the Arctic losing their homes. The ice is melting, the glaciers are falling into the ocean. The sea is rising—maybe not very much. The weather has warmed. I just hope we can continue on in our lifestyle, as we have in the past, in future generations."*

Alvin stood shaking his head when the video finished; he couldn't believe his chart was in a museum. We went into the planetarium then, joined an audience, and watched the planets spin, stars come into view, constellations rise and fall, and we saw an image of the sky outdoors on that night.

During intermission Alvin and Kathy went to see the "Seasons of Change" exhibit, and I talked to Richard Polonsky. He had enjoyed getting to know Alvin, was happy to have him there, and, when we returned to the planetarium, would bring him up to speak. Richard said that years ago he been a farmer and a sugarmaker, and it made him appreciate the role of maple syrup in the culture of New England. He then told me a story, one that I supposed had motivated him in this endeavor. Richard did his sugarmaking on his father's land. His father was a veterinarian who owned the largest mink farm in the eastern United States, but he lost all of his animals after giving them food poisoned by PCBs (polychlorinated biphenyls), which have been shown to cause numerous health effects in animals, including damage to their reproductive systems. He had traced down the source, sued Monsanto, and won his case, but before the trial began he had a stroke. The money he won, a million dollars, was paid out within a few days, Richard said.

We returned to the planetarium where Barry Rock was ready to give his talk. Rock was in his midsixties and had been working for many years on studies of the environment and chemical evidence of climate change collected using satellite imagery. He was the lead author of an important report about climate change published in 2001, titled the *New England Regional Assessment,* part of a series of reports on climate in the United States sponsored by the US Global Change Research Program.

Polonsky opened the program by talking about "Seasons of Change," saying it was sponsored by the National Science Foundation and that it would travel to a series of museums over the next four years. He said he was pleased to have Alvin Clark present and asked him to come up front and say a few words.

Alvin at first did what New Englanders often do when they talk about themselves, which is to draw family lines. He said he was related to the Greens and the Fisks. Of climate change he said, "I could see this coming in the chart year after year, since 1959. And I could see the gradual change in the weather as I kept the figures on each day and poured the sap."

And then, "You're welcome to come to our sugarhouse. I'm not a bragger, I don't like to brag, but we've got some of the best syrup. I don't like to say that, but people who have had it, they know it."

Richard introduced Barry Rock by saying that he had been talking about climate change and how it can affect maple trees for a very long time.

Rock began by pointing out the irony of his speaking here tonight, in the Christa McAuliffe Planetarium, named after the first teacher in space, who died during the *Challenger* disaster in 1986. Rock was working for NASA on the space shuttle project then, but after the explosion of the *Challenger* his project collapsed. Independently he began using remote sensing technology to study the effect of air pollution on the trees of Camel's Hump Mountain in Vermont. He grew up in Vermont. After giving a lecture on remote sensing at a conference he was offered a position at the University of New Hampshire. When he arrived in New Hampshire Rock found, sitting on his desk, a stack of letters that had been forwarded from NASA.

"The letter on top," he said, "was from a high school teacher here in Concord named Phil Browne. He thought I was still in California. He wrote that his students were devastated by the loss of Christa and that they had a negative image of NASA and of science. He wanted to know if there was anything I might do to get students interested again." Rock thought it might be promising to study white pines, which are sensitive to pollution. He and Phil Browne founded a program called Forest Watch, in which New Hampshire students studied the health of pine trees.

He began his talk by describing his work using satellite imagery to study New England forests. He said some things that I was hearing for the first time. He began with, "I don't want to be an undertaker. I want to be a physician." Which seemed to mean bad news. He explained that New England is downwind to the rest of the country, that six major air currents flow over the region on their way to the Atlantic Ocean. The currents move not only weather but also airborne pollutants, including gases and metals. He said, "We may think in New England we live in a very pristine area, but that is not true. We get air from everywhere else. New England is the tailpipe of the nation."

Tailpipe?

Not only that, Barry Rock said, but those pollutants flow into New England in a turbulent zone of the atmosphere between 3000 and 5000 feet. The compound of ozone can be found in concentrations there, Rock said—not the good kind of ozone that protects us earthlings from ultraviolet radiation but the bad kind that is found in smog. Ozone damages the cells in the needles of white pines and inhibits their ability to produce chlorophyll. It reduces their ability to convert carbon dioxide into oxygen—from the human perspective carbon sequestration is one of the most important things that trees do, storing atmospheric carbon in the tree's wood. He explained that other chemicals in those air currents can damage maple trees, reducing their ability to photosynthesize, which then reduces the maple's ability to create carbohydrates, and this, in turn, reduces their essential ability to produce sugar. Which in turn reduces their ability to produce healthy leaves.

Referring to this layer between 3000 and 5000 feet where pollutants congregate, Rock said, "Not only are we in the tailpipe, we are in a sort of atmospheric sewer. These are terms that have become widely used by atmospheric scientists. Tailpipe. Sewer."

It is hard to describe how I felt then. Annoyed, sad, disappointed, angry—even at Barry Rock for telling me this while aware that he was the messenger, the physician, the man advocating health. But he was talking about the activity I like most and the reason I wanted to live in New Hampshire, to hike in the mountains and to breathe that highly oxygenated fresh air, air that helped my thinking, I was sure, and to solve problems, including writing problems—that now, it seemed, if Rock was correct, was a hazardous activity. The world was turned upside down. I might as well hike on Fifth Avenue or Boylston Street.

When I later read the *New England Regional Assessment* I came upon a case study titled "Hiker Health" about a research study at Harvard Medical School that examined the effects of ozone and fine particulates on the lung function of people hiking on Mount Washington. They found a diminished breathing capacity even with exposure to low levels of ozone. "Acute ozone exposure in humans is associated with decreased pulmonary function and can result in shortness of breath, coughing, and pain while inhaling." It was saddening, reading that. And infuriating. I could see the signs of the future up on the trails, near the huts: *"Caution. Mountain Air Has Been Found to Be Hazardous to Your Health. It Is Advised That You Wear Protective Respiratory Gear."*

Also in the *New England Regional Assessment* were those reports and predictions mentioned in the *Boston Globe* news story, that temperatures in New England would rise by 6 to 10 degrees Fahrenheit by the year 2090. The difference depended on levels of emissions. A minor increase of 1.8 degrees had already occurred in the New England region since 1899 and likely brought milder winters, earlier maple sap flows, earlier ice-out dates, and reduced snowfall. The report stated—or actually understated, I thought, in typical academic language—that the increases of 6 to 10 degrees projected for New England and the Northeast "must be viewed as serious."

The authors of the *New England Regional Assessment* were required to use at least two climate models in making their predictions. Rock and his team chose one called the "Canadian General Circulation Model" that projected a rise in average temperatures by nine to ten degrees by the year 2090 and a ten percent increase in rainfall. The other originated in Britain and was called the "Hadley Climate Model," which projected an increase of six degrees in average temperatures and a thirty percent increase in rainfall by 2090.

In the report Rock wrote that although there was a wide difference between 6 degrees and 10 degrees, the results of either would be extreme. Using Boston as an example, with its thirty-year annual average temperature of 51.3°, he projected two possible outcomes. With a rise of 6 degrees Boston's yearly annual average temperature would be equivalent to that of Richmond, Virginia, with its yearly average of 57.7° Fahrenheit. A rise of 10 degrees would give Boston the climate of Atlanta, Georgia, with its annual average temperature of 61.3°. Average the difference and you land in Charlotte, North Carolina. A very nice place, Charlotte, but you wouldn't want New Hampshire to live there.

Rock also coauthored the case study on maple syrup that was part of the *New England Regional Assessment*. The researchers looked at historical trends and stresses from changes in climate. They concluded that the industry is moving northward, that in the past some regions of Canada were unproductive because of deep snow cover and prolonged freezes. The development of tubing and warmer nighttime temperatures had resulted in a shift in syrup production as far north as the Gaspe Peninsula in Quebec.

In conclusion, Rock wrote, with some feeling, "Most disturbing are the results of ecological modeling efforts that show the changes in climate could potentially extirpate the sugar maple within New England. The maple industry is an important part of New England character, way-of-life, and economy that, because it is highly dependent upon prevailing climactic conditions, may be irreparably altered under a changing climate."

In 2009 the *Second Climate Change Assessment* was issued by the US Global Change Research Program, with some changes in projections for the Northeast region of the United States. According to this more recent report, the average annual temperature had increased by two degrees Fahrenheit since 1970. As for projections for the end of the century, radically different climate futures were possible, depending on the amount of increase of greenhouse gases. Under a scenario for higher emissions, winters in the northeastern United States would be much shorter, with fewer cold days and more rain; the length of the winter snow season would be cut in half across northern New York, Vermont, New Hampshire, and Maine, and reduced to a week or two in southern parts of the region; hot summer conditions would arrive three weeks earlier and last three weeks longer in the fall; and sea levels would rise more than the global average.

One prescient paragraph anticipated the effects of Hurricane Sandy in 2012: "Rising sea level is projected to increase the frequency and severity of damaging storm surges and flooding. Under a higher emissions scenario, what is now considered a once-in-a-century coastal flood in New York City is projected to occur at least twice as often by mid-century, and 10 times as often (or once per decade on average), by late this century. With a lower emissions scenario, today's 100-year flood is projected to occur once every 22 years on average by late this century."

As for agriculture and forestry, the *Second Climate Change Assessment* reported, "Large portions of the Northeast are likely to become unsuitable for growing popular varieties of apples, blueberries, and cranberries under a higher emissions scenario. Climate conditions suitable for maple/beech/birch forests are projected to shift dramatically northward, eventually leaving only a small portion of the Northeast with a maple sugar business. "

Barry Rock ended his report that night with a success story about his work in the Czech Republic that could be an allegory for what could happen in the United States with the right effort. He showed us work he had done with remote sensing in that country, where during the Communist regime pollution levels from burning soft coal were so high that the average life span of Czech citizens living in mountainous regions was only thirty-one years. Now, under democracy, that had changed. They converted to nuclear power and cleaned up the air, and the average life span had increased to normal ranges.

During a question-and-answer period someone asked whether there was a direct correlation between high temperatures and the chemical problems in the mountain air—in that place called the atmospheric sewer and that region called the tailpipe.

Rock said there had been a two-degree rise in average temperature over the last hundred years, which should be creating more ozone, but there was also a counterbalance in the Clean Air Act. "It has done a wonderful job removing a lot of the precursors that would end up generating a lot of ozone. In terms of ozone and white pine, there has been a dramatic improvement."

And, of course, it had to be the case—if the trees were healthier, then we earthlings had to be too, right?

We left the planetarium and walked out into the warm midsummer night. To our surprise, spread out over the parking lot, were amateur astronomers with their telescopes pointed up at the sky. Eyeballs to the universe. Saturn was visible that night out in the clear sky, just as it had been inside the planetarium. We wandered from telescope to telescope, taking in Saturn's rings, hundreds of millions of miles away.

IN THE CLARK SUGARHOUSE on March 17, 2012, over sugar on snow, Alvin told me he had received a letter from Richard Polonsky. Richard was having some medical problems, which he confided to Alvin. Alvin read part of the letter aloud to me:

> Thank you for being such a spokesman on climate change. I know you worried, because people in the maple syrup business are skeptical and you certainly do not want to convey that maple syrup could dry up in the future. It is really time for people in every business that depends upon the land to recognize that there is something affecting weather patterns that is bigger than Mother Nature. We need to slow down or just stop polluting the atmosphere with all the chemicals we spew from burning fuel oil. It is amazing to me that the more advanced countries of Europe are able to produce goods and services with one-half the energy of the US, and that Japan only uses two-thirds per capita of what we do. With only two percent of the world's population we consume 20 percent of its oil.

Alvin and I visited the "Seasons of Change" exhibit again when it stopped at the Montshire Museum in Norwich, Vermont. On the drive home Alvin said, "The scientists at UNH are supporting me on this climate change thing. It will be forty or fifty years until we know if they're right. I'll be gone by then."

I asked if he would give me his explanation for the maple sap flow.

"Sure," he said. "There has to be enough water, and the leaves have to look good in the fall. Good color and not falling off the trees early from drought as they did in some places this year when it got warm. When it starts to get above freezing, up into the forties in the daytime and below freezing at night, water starts moving up the cambium layer. The sugar is stored up in the branches, having been made by the leaves in the previous summer. The tree pulls the water up from the roots through the action of barometric pressure. When the trees are starting to flow they are absorbing heat, and you can see a ring around the trunk of the tree. The water is coming up from underground, because of the thaw, but also because the ground doesn't freeze more than three feet down.

"The sugar maple is a sensitive tree. They are just like humans, in that sap is like blood. They are very sensitive, and that's why they are in danger from climate change."

18

SUMMER IN MARCH

ON SUNDAY, MARCH 18, the temperature in Langdon rose above 80°. That evening before sunset my wife and I walked a pair of dogs for a friend. While the dogs played I stood in a field and felt the pleasant spring air. Nearby, flying bugs drifted in a warm pocket. Off in the field I saw a small cherry tree that had begun to bloom. Overhead a bat flew by, searching for insects, I assumed. Later, when we arrived home, we heard from the small pond in the woods the sound of the peepers, the chorus frogs, riotous and joyful.

When Bruce said that the weather of 2012 was "once in a hundred years," he wasn't quite right. A study of satellite data from 1979 to 2010, comparing standard and extreme deviations, determined that some of the temperatures in the United States in March 2012 occurred with a likely frequency of once in every 4779 years. Because the data in the study was only for a 31-year period, and during a time when the planet was warming, the researchers stated that if they had used a century of data, the extent of deviation from the norm would have been much greater. So Bruce could have said that the weather in March 2012 was once in every 5000 years. You could also say that it was the kind of weather predicted to occur at the end of this century.

These "Summer in March" conditions were a meteorological event, caused in part by an unusual position of the jet stream, which looped to the south in the western United States and curled far over the Great Lakes and Canada to the north. This caused a high-pressure area to stand in place over the midwestern and eastern United States, blocking cold air masses and holding in place warm air from the South. In the western states the southerly loop trapped a low-pressure area and drew cold temperatures from the north, bringing record snowfall to Oregon.

Though the Summer-in-March conditions were primarily a weather event, they were also likely an event driven by global warming. As the meteorologist Andrew Freedman wrote, "Although studies have not yet been conducted on the main factors that triggered this heat wave and whether global warming may have tilted the odds in favor of the event, scientific studies of previous heat events clearly show that global warming increases the odds of heat extremes, in much the same way as using steroids boosts the chances that a baseball player will hit more home runs in a given year." The lack of snow, which, when present, tends to reflect heat and cool the soil and air, had also contributed to the heat wave.

March 2012 was the warmest in the United States since record keeping began in 1895. The average temperature in March in 2012 was 51.1°, 8.6 degrees above the national average for March. There were more than 14,000 temperature records broken nationwide. Perhaps the most unusual

occurrences were the 21 temperature records in March occurring at night and the low temperature for the day that
broke previous daytime high-temperature records. The January to March period in 2012 was also the warmest in history dating back to 1880. And as it would turn out, 2012 was
the warmest year in history. Every state in the United States
experienced a record warm temperature in March.

Chicago broke daytime records nine days in a row, begin-
ning on March 14. All the record temperatures were in the
eighties: 82° on March 16, 82° on March 17, 85° on March 21.
The average high temperature in Chicago in August is 82°.
Thus the name, "Summer in March," given by meteorologist
Jeff Masters of the Weather Underground.

Record high temperatures were set in cities throughout
eastern Canada on March 21. The high temperature in St.
John's, New Brunswick, on March 21 of 25.4° Centigrade, or
78° Fahrenheit, set a record high for March and was also
higher than any previous recorded temperature in April.

On March 20 Burlington, Vermont, reached 80°, the earliest 80° day in that city's history and thirty-nine degrees
above the average temperature. On March 20 Concord, New
Hampshire, set a record at 81°, as did Caribou, Maine, at 73°,
breaking its record by twenty-three degrees. On March 21
the low nighttime temperature at Mount Washington, New
Hampshire, was 44°, which broke the previous daytime
record of 43°.

The heat wave of March 2012, the Summer in March, Jeff
Masters said, "was simply off-scale, and ranks as one of
North America's most extraordinary weather events in
recorded history."

On MARCH 16, in the midst of the heat wave, the American Forests blog published a short article titled "A Biological Clock" by Katrina Marland that began with an explanation of how our own biological clocks work, describing how tired we can become after pulling an all-nighter, then stated that scientists at the University of Edinburgh had identified the genes in plants that regulate their circadian rhythms. "They have found a set of 12 genes and one particular protein that work together to help the plant go dormant at night, saving its energy for growth, processing food and other actions that it can only perform during the day when the sun and other conditions are right." The genes help the plant to make adjustments and to change with the seasons. "The knowledge has possible applications in a number of fields, but perhaps most important is helping scientists understand—and possibly even predict—how plants respond to interruptions in their natural cycles. If you have experienced, as many of us have, particularly strange weather patterns lately—here in Washington, D.C. we've had 80-degree days in March and our blooms have been out for weeks—it's easy to see how significant knowledge like that could be."

Maple trees also seemed to be going through a disruption to their biological clocks. The buds began to swell during the March heat wave, and that spelled the end for some sugarmakers. Many of those who kept producing made buddy, off-flavored syrup.

Peter and Deb Rhoades boiled from March 8 to March 15, shutting down when the temperatures began to soar. Usually the Rhoades sent 80,000 gallons of sap to Bascom's, but in 2012 that amount was down to 21,000 gallons.

At Smith's Maple Crest Farm in Shrewsbury, Vermont, near Rutland in the central part of the state, Jeff Smith boiled from March 12 to March 20. On March 12 the temperature at Smith's farm was 80° outdoors and 100° inside the sugarhouse. After nine days of 80-degree temperatures Smith shut down and pulled his spouts.

A sugarmaker located in Londonderry, New Hampshire, on a south-facing mountainside, said he experienced temperatures in the nineties during March. The trees produced sap that was like jelly.

One sugarmaker in upstate New York near Lake Champlain went fourteen days without a freeze but kept producing sap with tubing and vacuum based on the pressure differential. He noticed that, during the warm spell when there were no freezes, the run slowed down at night and then picked up again at nine o'clock in the morning. On the warmest days, "the four-day hot season" as he called it, between March 17 and March 20, the thickened sap plugged up the reverse-osmosis machines. At one point the sap looked like cottage cheese, and they dumped it on the ground but kept their vacuum pumps running so that the tapholes wouldn't seal. Because it was so dry, he said, "we were drawing air through the tree fibers." After a rain the vacuum pressure went up again. They resumed boiling after the hot days passed, but the syrup was buddy from then on.

At a sugarhouse in Franklin County, Vermont, sap exposed to sunlight in the tubing lines reached temperatures above 100°.

They boiled at David Marvin's sugarhouse on March 19 but then decided to shut down, at least temporarily. Their sap was also like cottage cheese there, in northernmost Vermont, and they too dumped it on the ground. "We're going to wait and see," David said when I called, "because we've never faced this before." He added, "Our fellow in Quebec thinks the season is over, that the trees are tired."

IT WAS 50° AT BASCOM'S when Kevin took his reading on Monday morning, March 19. The view of the mountains in Vermont was spectacular that morning, with the clear skies and the sunlight striking them from the southeast. The snow on the ski slopes was patchy. The maple trees had that mauve color that seems to hang like a mist when the buds begin to swell. The workers went outside on their morning breaks, where they could see the valleys and take in the sun—it was a gorgeous day, this last day of winter. At the little pond below where they sat, the concupiscent frogs kicked and rippled the water's edges. The fields were greening up. The air was full of the scent of maple after Kevin began boiling.

The sap truck ground up the hill and rolled through the parking lot. Only George Hodskins was gathering sap now. The sap was still running fairly well at Cole's and Ryan's, two of the colder lots—George said that during a twenty-hour period the trees at Cole's had produced 4300 gallons of sap from the 5500 taps. The sap was "a little greasy," George said and would surely make darker syrup.

I went into the Cooler, usually the happening place this time of year. Day after day in 2011 the trucks had been lined up at the Cooler, twenty or forty or sometimes fifty trucks pulling up to the dock. Not so many this year.

Dave St. Aubin was finishing some paperwork for a dairy farmer from Westmoreland who brought in two barrels of syrup. Both were commercial grade. He was going to use the money to pay his bill at the store. He said the sap was running at his sugarbush, but he didn't think he would be boiling on Maple Weekend. "I don't know why they pushed the date so far back," he said. "So the people up north will have something, I guess."

After the farmer left, Dave said to me, "We've been selling more syrup than we've been taking in." He tallied his slips to make sure, and it was true—more barrels were going out than coming in, sold to those sugarmakers who had poor crops and needed syrup for their customers or for Maple Weekend.

In came another dairy farmer, one of those grizzled old fellows with a perpetual five o'clock shadow and a circumspect look who has put in crazy work hours over the course of his years, though this farmer was retired and "paying capital gains tax," he said with some disdain. He was from a town eighty miles to the north and was a maple syrup producer, but he hadn't made enough this year to meet his needs. He sold the syrup from his home—"Right from my kitchen," he said.

He told Dave St. Aubin, "I want the lightest syrup you have." Light syrup was at a premium now. Last year B grade was hard to find. Dave jumped on the forklift, and the farmer walked along behind. I walked with him, through the Middle Cooler and down the ramp into the New Cooler. Dave turned toward a mighty stack of black barrels, four high and four wide. The farmer looked around at the contents of the New Cooler and said, "I'd like to have the interest he pays. I heard he has a credit line of fifteen million dollars."

I responded with, "I heard peepers last night."

"Well, it's shut down, then," he said.

Dave lowered four barrels from the top of the stack. He opened each one and drew out a sample and put each in a clear container so the man could see it. The syrup, made at Bascom's, was as light as Chardonnay. Dave offered some to the farmer to taste, but he just shook his head. We walked back to the scales, following Dave, who filled out the paperwork and then loaded the barrels on the farmer's old truck. "They won't be going anywhere." Though actually they would, but slowly—each barrel had 660 pounds of syrup. The farmer left for the store.

Dave didn't like the pace of work. "It's too slow," he said. "Last year you never could have had just one guy out here."

In the store Bruce and the old farmer talked for a while, but when he left, Bruce turned to me and began talking about the price of syrup. "It might be two-sixty," he said. "And they may keep it at two sixty-five. David Marvin said he would have a price by Wednesday, but he's backing off."

This befuddled me, despite the explanations. If the price was $2.70 a pound last year with an exceptional crop, why would it be $2.65 or $2.60 this year with a poor crop? It seemed wishful thinking on Bruce's part.

"With this hot weather, the crop will be off dramatically."

"So there won't be enough supply?

"No, there should be enough." Bruce grabbed a piece of paper and drew out the figures—the United States at 20 million pounds, Canada at 90 million, 15 million in carryover from 2011. "So that's a hundred and twenty-five million, which will cover demand, but barely." Some people might hoard or hold on to specific grades, he said. The Federation would probably release supply strategically from their surplus. Bruce was considering his own strategies to get producers in New York to release supply—maybe he would buy lots of Canadian and spread it around.

His was an anxiety of nickels and dimes, multiplied by millions and compounded by supply. That 10 cent difference between $2.60 and $2.70 would mean a difference of a million dollars over the purchase of 10 million pounds of syrup.

Just before he left the store Bruce said, "I know what's going on out there today." The Cooler, he meant. "People are buying drums back." That must have added to his anxiety, to see syrup floating out the doors, back to producers.

Another customer came in. Ted Young, who had brought two helpers, was in his seventies and looked very fit, with well-muscled arms in a short-sleeve shirt. Ted said he had owned and run two feed and grain stores in southern New Hampshire "and retired on that." He sugared on Kearsarge Mountain, in Warner, but with the warm weather had already shut down.

Ted sugared with tubing on gravity, meaning he didn't use a vacuum, though now he was considering installing one.

"I believe there's something to this global warming," he said. "If you don't have vacuum, you're not going to make it."

Down below, in the sugarhouse, Kevin was boiling. A year ago, on March 19, Kevin had also boiled, but the temperature had been between 30° and 42° that day. On March 19 in 2011 only a week had passed since the ice storm. He was on his tenth boil then and would boil twenty times more, for another three and a half weeks.

The syrup Kevin was producing on this March 19 had that buddy smell. There were a few descriptions for the smell of buddy. Leafy was one. Dirty socks was another.

I told Kevin that I heard peepers in the pond last night. "That's usually the sign that it's over," he said.

And so it was, a day later.

Kevin's chart read,

3/19 Clear
50°–74°
342.18 B grade
16,117 Total

3/20 (Spring Begins)
50°–73°
683.55 B grade
341.45 Commercial
17,142 Total Gallons

19

Sugar on snow

A ROUND MARCH 19 the extreme southern loop of the jet stream that hung over the western United States broke off and formed a giant eddy that spun slowly eastward across the continent, shepherding a low-pressure area. By the end of the week the heat wave was over, and colder temperatures returned. In places like southern New Hampshire, a new sap run would have begun if the trees hadn't already started to bud.

Two years ago David Clark had retapped trees so as to have something to boil on Maple Weekend. In 2011 that wasn't necessary because the dates were moved ahead to the third weekend in March, and the Clarks had barely gotten underway—that weekend they boiled water because the trees shut down during a freeze. In 2012, at the Clark sugarhouse, there was no pretense of a boil, no simmering of water.

Their season also ended on March 19, their earliest finish ever. A look at their chart showed pauses in other seasons, for a week of cold or rain, but they had previously always started up again. From 1959 until 1998, when the Clarks stopped boiling on March 31, the season had always gone into April.

Not that 2012 hadn't been a decent year. David Clark made 987 gallons of syrup on nineteen boils. Not to mean that the spirit wasn't festive at the Clark sugarhouse that weekend; it was festive and magnanimous. They brought miniature donkeys down from the farm for kids to pet. The inside of the sugarhouse was warm and inviting. Jugs of new syrup were lined up by the counter, bison burgers were on the grill, and bags of maple cotton candy hung from clips like a row of balloons.

The evaporator was silent and cool, which seemed strange, but you got used to it. Last year, when they boiled water, David fed four-foot logs into the evaporator, and the fire roared while steam billowed through the roof. But that was last year. Now there was a long table, on top of which were baking pans, filled with snow.

And there was Alvin, wearing another funny hat—this was shaped like a buffalo head, with glass eyes and cute yellow horns. Alvin ladled thickened syrup on snow, making leather aprons. He had toothpicks on hand for anyone who wanted to lift a piece off from the snow. He had a bowl of dill pickles nearby to counter the sweetness, in the French-Canadian way.

I said to Alvin, "Where did you get that snow?"

"A gift from above," he said and laughed.

I persisted. "Alvin, where did you get the snow?"

"A gift from God," he said, with another laugh.

That was good enough for now. And when you thought about it, isn't that what snow is, a gift from above? In these places, for these people? For everyone, actually? Snow was water for the plants. Snow was for prosperity and celebration. Snow for fulfillment, and some of that was here, on Maple Weekend.

"We've had about a hundred people come in," Alvin said. "People from as far away as Connecticut."

Someone asked how the sugar on snow was made. "You cook the syrup longer, until it's two hundred and twenty-four degrees. Then you let it cool. If it's too hot, it will go right through the snow."

He offered some to us. As before, this taffy was fun to chew, with the sudden release of flavor and the quick dissolving. Alvin had made some small maple pecan pies, a specialty of his. He gave us two, and we sat down to eat while visitors crowded around the table. The little cloth horns were sticking up above their heads.

There sure was a lot to rest the eyes on in the Clark sugarhouse. The chart, of course, the famous chart with the stories of the seasons in red and black. A history in buckets—old wooden ones, new wooden ones, all sorts of metal ones, hanging from the rafters and the walls. Lanterns hanging, too, from the days when they lit the sugarhouse. Yokes for trained oxen, from when they had pulled the sleds. A collection of spouts, from the latest plastic spouts to ancient carved wooden ones as thick as broomsticks. And information, such as how much sap to make a gallon of syrup or photographs for identifying the Asian longhorned beetle. Framed photos, newspaper stories, paintings of sugarhouses. Old-fashioned painted metal syrup containers. A framed collection of fluted sugar molds for individual servings—the label on one was "Ruth Bascom's Old Sugar Tin Collection," after Bruce's mother.

On a high shelf were etched cups given to the Clarks for winning the Carlisle Award for the best syrup in New Hampshire. They had won it six times between 1976 and

2010. A photo rested nearby of Alvin at age five, dressed in a fur-collared coat and sitting by a flat pan over an open fire on a stone arch.

Alvin, true to his way, had given the place a homey touch. He put red and white carnations on the picnic tables and potted pansies on the windowsills near the restaurant booths.

As we sat in one of the booths with our pecan pies Alvin came over to talk, to tell us about a video featuring him and David, when a boy came up and asked, "Do you just put hot syrup on the snow?" Alvin put an arm around his shoulder, bent down and said, "You heat it up to two hundred and twenty-four degrees . . ."

MAPLE WEEKEND at Bascom's was a different kind of affair, though it was just as entertaining in its own way. The parking lot was empty when we arrived after leaving the Clark's, empty except for the big luxury tour bus sitting prominently in the lot, waiting for the special guests. Bascom's didn't open their doors on Maple Weekend but instead hosted customers who had been invited by Arnold Coombs. This year's group included someone who distributed syrup in the Southwest under a private label in Texas, a syrup broker from California, and a broker who sold syrup in Asia and Europe. The East Coast buyer for United Natural Foods had come, someone from Stonewall Kitchen in Maine, the owner of a group of grocery markets in New York City, and a syrup broker who worked out of Amsterdam.

We went to the store, hoping to find them, thinking we might hear Bruce's talk, but no one was there. We went to the Cooler, where Greg Minard was tending to someone who bought syrup, but he didn't know where Bruce and the group were. "It's slow here," Greg said, echoing Dave's comments of a few days ago. "You never could have done this with one person last year."

Because the New Building was a part of any tour, we went there and passed by the loaded pallets and thousands of boxes. There was Gold Coast, Coombs Family Farms, and a row of 200-pound tote bags about to go to Boar's Head.

We went to the door of the bottling room and looked through the window in the door. Everyone inside was wearing hairnets, including Bruce and Arnold Coombs. I hesitated going in because I felt like I didn't want to interrupt and because of a look I saw on Arnold's face. He seemed concerned. I wondered maybe if Bruce had been going on too long. We turned and left.

I was curious to know whether I was correct about the concern I saw, so I called Arnold on Monday. He had just come from a meeting where they had discussed Maple Weekend. Arnold said that Bruce had been preoccupied that day. He had been on the phone with David Marvin right up to when he was supposed to begin talking. "Bruce batted a thousand before," Arnold said, meaning in previous weekends. "He batted seven-fifty this time."

Arnold said that Bruce and Marvin had been talking about price but also about how to prevent a panic in the event of a shortage. I said that Bruce had been saying that the price of syrup would stay the same as last year or maybe be lower.

"That's Bruce's method," Arnold said. "He has to keep a game face on. In 2008 they said the price wouldn't go up, but

it did. The farmers will take a nickel more if someone is offering it, and generally they seem to be holding on to their
supply. But as of now, nobody knows. Some producers in the
north made it through last week and the high temperatures
in northern Maine and Quebec. In Franklin County they
didn't. The trees budded out up there.

"You talk to producers and they say, 'half a crop.' You ask,
'Is it half of a normal crop, or half of last year's crop, which
was a once-in-seventy-years crop?' We'll have a better handle on this when the Open House comes along." The annual
Bascom Open House, he meant, held at the end of April. A
big party for sugarmakers.

"As for last weekend and being in the new building,"
Arnold said, "it was impressive. Sometimes you have to show
them how viable it is to put another jug on the shelf."

During maple weekend last year I had headed down to
Massachusetts on Saturday and worked my way north, continuing on Sunday. We stopped first at the North Hadley
Sugar Shack, where people were waiting in line for seats in
the pancake restaurant while others gathered around the
evaporator, went out to look at the buckets hanging in the
woods, or rode on the horse-drawn wagon. We stopped in
Deerfield at the Williams Maple Farm, where the business
in pancakes was also brisk—and the boiling too: they hung
3000 buckets throughout the town and on trees at Deerfield
Academy. We stopped at the Davenport Maple Farm in Shel-
burne, where there also was a restaurant full of customers
and an evaporator running downstairs, and we talked to

Russell Davenport, a sugarmaker in his eighties and a friend of Ken Bascom's; he said he had nominated Ken to be a member of the Hall of Fame. In Vermont the snow was deeper, and we stopped at the Sprague Sugarhouse in Jacksonville, a handcrafted post-and-beam structure, and watched a cool dude, wearing shades, feeding the firebox with four-foot wood, and where we bought some of Mrs. Sprague's maple cream. And we drove to Brattleboro, to the Robb Family Farm on Ames Hill Road, across from their dairy, where they didn't use an R.O. because they didn't believe in using them, where they had just finished a good week at the evaporator, boiling all day on Thursday and making seventeen gallons.

On Sunday I stopped first at Alvin Clark's, and he told me they served 300 people the day before, probably because it was so cold. David was boiling water, and Alvin laughed at that idea. I talked to two people who had traveled from Cambridge, a researcher who grew up nearby in Keene and one of his students, a Chinese doctoral candidate, and the researcher said he brought the student there because this was the only thing you can buy in this country that isn't made in China, to which she smiled and said, "Thank you"—though his ideals were shaken when he learned that the Clarks use an R.O. I headed north and stopped at Hillside Maple in Cornish, where their production was drawn on the boards on the wall—12.5 gallons one day, 14 another. In Plainfield I stopped at the Taylor Brothers Sugarhouse, which had 5000 taps on tubing a few miles away and trucked their sap home. I finished at the Mount Cube Sugarhouse, owned by Peter Thomson, son of the former New Hampshire governor Meldrim Thomson, where they served rolled crepes that you dipped in hot maple syrup—maybe the best treat I saw on my tour. Thomson's sugarbush was steep and stood just below the Appalachian Trail. He said his father, who had sold his house on Long Island to get away from the crowds, had bought this farm on the agreement that the people who owned it would teach them how to sugar. "I've been sugaring for fifty-eight years," Thomson said. I felt like I covered a lot of ground that weekend while knowing I had visited less than one percent of the sugarhouses hosting visitors.

In 2012 I decided to stay close to home and went to the Clark sugarhouse on both days of Maple Weekend. Last year you had to go inside the sugarhouse to get warm. This year the forsythias were blooming and the daffodils were up. This Sunday was like a day in late April.

People did come, though, and they did enjoy themselves. Alvin was wearing his funny buffalo hat again, and fresh pans of snow were on the table. I heard someone ask Alvin where he found the snow.

"A gift from above," he said.

A group arrived, a family with some guests visiting from Japan, and the kids were all over that sugar on snow.

We watched from a picnic table, and at one point Alvin came to talk to us. He had a pan of sugar on snow in his hands. Kathy picked up a piece and said she liked eating the snow as much as the sugar. "It's clean snow, no animals have walked on it or anything," Alvin said, with a big laugh.

The sugarhouse had emptied out by midafternoon when a contingent of Bascoms walked in. Among them was Harvey Bascom, who was Glenn Bascom's son. He came with his wife, two daughters, and a son-in-law. Harvey had a birthday last week, turning ninety. They held a party for him at the church in Alstead, and a lot of people came out, Harvey told us when he sat at the picnic table with us. Alvin was extra-attentive to Harvey, making sure he had enough sugar on snow and a sample of syrup and enough coffee.

I said something to Harvey about how youthful he looked. He seemed a picture of health and happiness, clear eyed, with white hair and smooth skin.

"Not a wrinkle on his face," said his daughter Marcia. Harvey gave a little smile and twirled a piece of sugar on snow on a toothpick before popping it into his mouth. I had to wonder—could sugar on snow be the secret of long life? Or maybe it was the approach one took to eating it.

My first meeting with Harvey Bascom had been clumsy on my part. I had read a book written by Eric Bascom, the minister and Ken Bascom's brother, titled, *Up Where the Old House Burned Down*. When I met Harvey I suddenly recognized who he was and blurted out, "You're that boy! The one who went to live with a relative after your mother died, before the fire."

Harvey looked taken aback. "Well, I guess so," he said. With quickening embarrassment I remembered that he was a real person. Fortunately he forgot my error and now sat happily at the picnic table with some sugar on snow and hot coffee, enjoying his hour in a sugarhouse.

Harvey had owned the dairy farm that Bruce now leased out. His daughters lived in houses nearby. One of Bruce's sisters told me that Harvey's household was always a happy place where there was always a lot of food and a place people liked to visit. Harvey later told me that even a skunk used to visit for food, entering through the cat door, making his way to the kitchen, eating from the cat dish, and then making his way out again without much bother.

Glenn Bascom was sixteen years old when he came home
from Kimball Union Academy for Christmas break. He had
been attending that school to become a minister. Though
Glenn didn't know it, he was carrying the measles and soon
infected his entire family. The results were disastrous. His
mother first died, then his father, then a sister. Glenn was
the oldest, Eric the second oldest, and both were minors, so
the ownership of the farm was put into question and an uncle appointed as guardian. He wanted to sell the farm and
divide the proceeds among the remaining children, but
Glenn and Eric wanted to keep and manage it. There was
some contention, and another guardian was appointed,
Alvin Clark's grandfather, Edwin Clark. He helped the boys
run the farm and also get a mortgage.

Glenn didn't become a minister, though his brother Eric
did. Glenn married and had five children. Harvey was born
in 1922. When he was three years old his mother died of
pneumonia. As winter approached, Glenn placed his children with relatives and friends. Harvey stayed with the
Clarks for a while and then moved to Keene and lived with
an aunt. Because of this, there were, fortunately, no children
in the farmhouse that cold February night when it caught
fire. Glenn started throwing things out the window. Neighbors came running. They let the animals out of the barn and
threw the oats, their feed, into the snow.

For two weeks Glenn Bascom lived with the Clarks. Then
he moved into an uninhabited farmhouse nearby, the house
where Harvey now lived.

His brother Eric bought the farm up above on the hill not
long after. Glenn became a potato farmer and made some
syrup in the spring. As he grew older he worked for Ken
Bascom, tapping trees and gathering sap. Sometimes he

shared in the boiling—he did most of the boiling that year in 1958 when Ken Bascom was in the hospital with a fractured skull. Glenn was one of those old-timers who Bruce and his schoolmates tried to impress by gathering sap furiously after school. Glenn was a quiet man, very religious, a pacifist. He lived to be ninety-nine years old.

While we sat at the picnic table and sipped coffee and sampled some syrup, I talked to Harvey's daughter, Marcia Oster. She worked as a church organist. Marcia and her husband lived in a house they built on the site where the farm burned down. I said something about the sugar parties that were held at Bascom's and that this one at the Clark's today must have been something like those then. I asked if she remembered those parties and the sugar on snow.

"Oh yes," she said. "I used to work there, serving. It was so busy, lots of people there. The doughboys." She smiled.

"I wish it was still like that."

ON THE MONDAY AFTER Maple Weekend David Marvin came out with a price of $2.80 for Double-A light syrup.

"My concern was that the crop was up last year," David said. "I couldn't see why in a short crop we should stay the same or go down. Bruce will match that, as will others." He was right.

"It took a little nervous energy. It's a big decision. Don't think I take it lightly. If the others don't come up, the syrup will come to me." He laughed at that.

After this announcement Bruce said, "I was at two-seventy, two-seventy-five. He came out with a higher price and I had to raise mine to keep my suppliers. He forced the price up, and I had to capitulate.

"He's smart," Bruce said. "He bumped up the top grade, Double A. But Double A won't be one percent of what I buy. Dark Amber is at two-seventy."

Which meant that for Bruce, the price was not going up from last year. Not on the American side.

"There's been a hard freeze up north," he said. "They could make a lot of syrup yet. Robert Poirier says they will have two and a half pounds per tap in Maine, but they won't say so. They never have a good year up there."

Finally Bruce said, "I'm not too panicked. The more I can get out of Maine, the less panicked I'll be."

He was ready for it to arrive. "I've cleaned out a hole in my basement. I've got the biggest hole in a warehouse in the United States. Maine could produce a lot of syrup," he repeated.

Then he said, "I sound like an optimist."

20

MOST OF MAINE

IS DOWNSTAIRS

BRUCE SAID OTHER PEOPLE were panicking too early, but in April he was buying all the syrup he could find—or, rather, all the US syrup he could find. He told Robert to go into Maine and buy everything he could. Robert was at the gates at St. Aurelie every morning by 6:00 and left each night just before the gates closed, taking out two trailer loads a day. He was sending a trailer load to Acworth every day, his driver making the seven-hour trip in the early morning, unloading, and making the return trip that same day, sleeping in his truck along the way.

His refrain during these weeks was, "By June there will be no bulk syrup anywhere," with the variations being July, October, or three weeks.

Bruce spent between $3 and 4 million over a two-week period in April, making deposits to his agents in New York and Ohio—sending checks for $250,000 to one, $150,000 to another, $80,000 here, another $250,000 there.

I met one of these agents at the end of April, at the Vermont Maple Festival in Swanton, when I spent a day traveling around with Bruce. Being with Bruce Bascom at the maple festivals was by far the best way to take in those events. He schmoozed, chatted, cajoled like he did at the store, and he plainly enjoyed just taking in the sights, such as watching and talking about a line of evaporators, different models all steaming at once outdoors, each with an attendant, as we did that day at the CDL plant. After a while I left him and went inside for coffee, and I was standing in the store when I saw on the far side of the room an Amishman pacing in an aisle with a cell phone to his ear. An Amishman with a cell phone, and I thought, *hmm*. I recognized him as Erwin Gingerich, from Middletown, Ohio. I had seen Erwin's barrels in the coolers at Bascom's. His barrels kind of called attention to themselves—they were the oddest and most mismatched collection, with beer kegs, metal cylinders used for soft drinks, plastic forty-gallon drums, battered steel drums, just about anything you could put bulk syrup in. I had also seen Erwin a few months ago at the maple conference in Verona, New York. Bruce invited me, telling me I had to see Verona, that it was a huge event, and it was—1000 attendees, by Bruce's count. In a hotel lobby I stood by while Bruce and Gingerich talked. He was thirtyish, dressed in the standard Amish fashion—dark pants, blue shirt, black vest, a brim hat, wearing a beard—and his wife stood behind him, wearing a long skirt and a bonnet.

And there he was, pacing, and I wondered if I could talk to him. The Amish producers interested me, as their way applied to making maple syrup, and there were often many of them at these events, especially at the Vermont Maple Festival. I had talked to another Amishman, Henry Brennaman, a few times and visited him in Salisbury, Pennsylvania, spending an afternoon at his kitchen table. Henry sent a lot of syrup to Bruce, buying much of it from his Amish neighbors. He didn't have electricity at his home, or a car—he drove a team of horses, but his wife, Rhota, told me Henry was an erratic driver even of horses, that he got distracted too often. Best to get distracted behind the reins than behind the wheel, I thought. Henry said in general it was the way of the Amish not to accept technology, but there was always the question of how much, it seemed, and how to negotiate the edges. Henry ran his bottling machine with an air compressor that used diesel fuel, not electricity, and he kept a telephone in a box by his store; for this he had been reprimanded by his pastor, Bruce told me. Henry arranged for rides to events like the Vermont Maple Festival—transportation was a problem, always it seemed, unless by horse and wagon. They were separatists and didn't believe in accepting money from the government: Henry was a foreman for one of the Amish construction crews with a couple hundred men that would build a barn in a day and put all the money they made into a fund for health care. I had watched a video, on my laptop of course, at Henry's kitchen table, of Henry leading a construction crew and building a barn, of Henry sighting the uprights with a spirit level. Rhota watched too, she hadn't seen it yet. The Amish could seem peculiar to an outsider, and I knew that I could seem peculiar to them—to them, I was one of "the English." But despite the differences you had to contemplate their choices about technology, their role as citizens of the world—the carbon footprint of an Amish man, of an Amish family, was very small, like a squirrel track. There was something about their way of living, especially from the perspective of 2012, that seemed very right.

When Erwin Gingerich finished his call he joined two other Amish men standing nearby. His father and brother, I found out. I walked over and introduced myself and said I had seen his barrels, that I had even tasted from a bunch of them when Dave St. Aubin showed me what it was like to work as a grader. I hadn't been that sugared out since I was a kid after Halloween.

The first thing Gingerish said about the season was, "The earliest tappers got the syrup." He partnered with his father and two brothers. They sugared and bought syrup to sell to Bruce. They didn't tap until February 3 because they were busy. "We do construction the rest of the year," he said. "Buildings of all sizes, from the ground up."

Erwin said, "We buy from about two hundred producers. Some are very small, only about ten gallons. Others are larger—one who has fifty-two hundred taps only produced thirteen hundred gallons this year because he tapped too late."

He said the Ohio crop was uneven. "I can't say if we had a good year because of the variations, according to tapping." Because of that, Gingerich had sent only two trailer loads to Bascom's this year, compared to the five he sent in 2011. Part of the reason, Erwin thought, was that people were thinking they would wait and see how the market played out. Another of Bruce's agents, Michael Parker, who sugared on the New York side of Lake Champlain, managed to eke out an additional load by telling his producers about the revived season and the possible big crop in Quebec and Maine.

Bruce had come back inside the building and was headed our way.

"The biggest buyer in Ohio," he said as he passed by. Pleasure seemed to rise up through Erwin.

He offered to give me one of his business cards, but he didn't have any on hand, so we walked outside to his truck to find one. It was quite a large truck, one of those crew cab models with a backseat. He opened the back door, and there was Erwin's wife, with a long skirt and wearing a bonnet, crocheting something. Erwin found a card and handed it to me. I didn't mention the truck, and I didn't want him to think I was judging him. He was a businessman, a smaller version of Bruce. For me just then the more pressing question was what I had seen inside.

"You're Amish," I said. "And you have a cell phone."

"We're more advanced," Erwin answered. He seemed to consider telling me more but didn't get into it. Too much to explain, I thought.

I had to leave. Bruce and Sam and David were getting into the car along with Steve Anderson, a packer from Michigan. I trotted up the road. But then I heard Erwin call to me. He was running behind and came up to me. "If you ever get out to Ohio, I could show you a couple of sugarhouses," he said.

I wish I could say that I made it out there. I hoped to. I bet I would have enjoyed it—and learned something too.

EARLIER IN APRIL Bruce had been saying the US crop would be down by about 15 million pounds. "Fifteen million, that's three hundred and seventy-five fewer tractor loads than last year. Forty-five thousand less drums." His prediction was that the US crop would be 18 million pounds. "Mark my words. It will be within two million pounds of that."

The outlook was much better in Canada, especially in the Beauce region of Quebec. The heat wave was followed by a freeze, and then the sap ran hard. By the second week of April the word was that Quebec sugarmakers had produced a pound and a quarter to a pound and a half of syrup per tap. That wasn't much compared to the US output, only a little more than a pint, "but when you multiply a pound and a half times fifty million taps you've got seventy-five million pounds," Bruce said. In Maine, according to Robert, they surpassed two pounds per tap. Not only that, Robert said, but the color had changed, going from dark to light, which seemed backward. "They've gone from D to Double A," said Bruce.

At Bascom's the local trade continued slowly through April. Bruce continued to think people were holding on to see whether there was a shortage and a price spike. But he also believed that in the fall many producers would be buying from him. Dave St. Aubin said they already were. "Some days twenty trucks come in to buy syrup," he said.

Bruce was in the store one afternoon when a sugarmaker from Vermont came in, a man named Doug Rose. He owned the Green Mountain Sugarhouse in Ludlow, near the Okemo Ski Area. Bruce asked how his crop turned out.

Doug was in his sixties, a jovial, gray-bearded man. "Sixty-five percent of normal," he said. "My wife says it's fifty percent of a bumper crop and one hundred percent of a bad crop." He laughed at this.

Bruce told him that the US crop was probably half of last year's. But some places did well, he said, such as the southern regions that took advantage of early seasons. "Pennsylvania, southern New York, Ohio all did good," he said.

He was sending some of that syrup west. "Ohio shipped to New Hampshire, so we can ship it to Michigan." Michigan had one of the worst crops, and Wisconsin looked to be even worse. Bruce was shipping to Wisconsin too.

"In Vermont almost everybody's made enough for retail," which meant there wasn't a lot left for bulk sales. And the syrup from Vermont was dark. "Haven King called and said there is no light syrup anywhere." King was a buyer for Maple Grove. "And a lot of it is buddy." This was another big question about the season: there were reports of a lot of buddy syrup that couldn't be used for pancakes.

"This is a pretty bad season, one in ten."

"I don't think we'll have another bad season," Rose said.

"Bankers think this might be good. That it will slow down the irrational exuberance." The expansion, he meant.

"My season was heavily affected by the poor skiing this year," Rose said. His sugarhouse was located north of the ski area on Okemo Mountain, along a main travel route in Vermont. "Those cars stop by my place on their way to and from the mountain. Not much of that this year."

After Rose finished in the store I followed him outside. "I've known Bruce for thirty years," he said. "I knew him when he was doing Saltash. Lost his shirt on that. Then he came back and made it here." Doug raised a hand toward the spread of buildings.

"He's a workaholic, you know. He never takes a vacation. You would never see him on a boat somewhere."

"That's unlikely."

"No one knows more than Bruce about the maple syrup industry. If you gave him three weeks, just three weeks, he could tell you where every bit of syrup is in the whole country, everywhere."

IN EARLY APRIL Bruce again asked if I had seen the sugar machine lately. They were doing a test run, he said, and a consultant would be operating the machine. They had already made a batch that was hard as a rock, and they had to break it up and dig it out.

We went into the building and climbed to the third story, where a group of people were assembled: Joe James, of course, and Kevin Bascom and his son Greg. A technician had come from Maine for the day to monitor the gaskets. An electrician was there. And the consultant, Howard Phykitt, an expert in pharmaceutical manufacturing and in this machine. When Bruce arrived they opened up the top hatch and pulled it back. The rank smell of overheated syrup rose into the air and, when you got close, burned the nose.

Joe dug out a bunch of maple sugar and put it in paper cups. The sugar was like dough at first. "Wait until it's cooled," Phykitt said. He was looking pale, and the electrician worried that he was dehydrated and needed water, but Phykitt didn't seem to care—he was determined to make the machine work successfully. With this new batch of sugar, he said to Bruce, who was on the ladder looking inside, "Not a good first run, but a good second run." Phykitt said they should take some of this batch to David, who was in his office and didn't think the sugar machine was going to work.

When the sugar cooled and dried a little more it began to act like fresh brown sugar. "It's a good color," Phykitt said. "The same color as maple syrup." Bruce, along with everyone else in the room, was sampling the sugar, pulling off pieces and chewing.

"Lunch," the electrician said.

Bruce chewed some and turned thoughtful.

Kevin had gotten on the ladder and was looking inside. Bruce whispered to me, "Kevin has a mechanical mind. This is a big puzzle to him. He'll understand this machine throughout."

Joe took the sugar and put it into the refrigerator to see how it performed after more rapid cooling. Most importantly, Joe also was getting to know this new machine and taking notes. With the old machine he had done a lot of listening, and he had been trying to listen to this machine. One time some of the others saw him put his ear up against the machine. They laughed and told him he no longer needed to do that. But Joe intended to keep listening. He missed using his nose. "I can't smell it," he said. "It's all closed up."

Joe returned a few minutes later with pieces of maple sugar on a tray. They were almost like hard candy. Everybody started working on them. Bruce grabbed a piece the size of a hatchet head and broke off a piece with his teeth. He chewed and took on that thoughtful look again.

"Good," he said through a mouthful of sugar.

Outside he was liking what he saw. The day helped boost his optimism—the trees were greening and the scent of the dairy farm was drifting up the hill. Buoyed, maybe even on a sugar high, he said of the sugar machine, "Most people could not do this. You have to be fearless to do something like this."

BRUCE SCHEDULED HIS spring Open House for the weekend after the Vermont Maple Festival. It was meant to provide a final statement on the season.

Bascom's was the ideal place for a party, with its hilltop site, isolated location, and views that made you think big.

Sugarmakers came from Maine and Quebec, from New York and, in some years, even Ohio. Some brought and sold syrup before taking in the events of the day.

Leader had one of their big evaporators set up in the parking lot, throwing off steam, while folks gathered around to watch and ask questions. Bruce and David had scheduled a range of classes, and in parts of the warehouse, amid stacks of tubing and used equipment, experts talked about vacuum, reverse osmosis, sap hydraulics, the selling of sap, and the lighter topics such as making candy. Employees were moved over to the New Building to serve food, which, of course, was free to anyone who wanted it. Tables were spread out where pallets had been yesterday or in aisles among racks of packed syrup. Woodsmen wandered around everywhere.

I began the day with Alvin Clark while Steve Childs, a maple specialist from Cornell, talked about making maple confections and selling them at fairs. Childs covered cotton candy, maple candy, maple cream, maple marshmallows, maple nuts, maple cheesecake, maple ice cream, and we kept getting up for samples with each demonstration. By the time he finished I too was thinking of how I could sell all things maple or even open a café themed only for maple, as it was all so delicious and inspiring—and not a pancake to be seen.

Bruce was wandering about that day—he was the host, greeting the special arrivals and very important people. When Carole Rouleau appeared, dressed as though for a night out, with her companion, Silvie, who I had once seen at Bureau's inspecting syrup with her hair up in silver blond ringlets, Bruce practically bowed to them before he led them away to the New Cooler and showed them the tanks, the touch screen, the rotary fillers, the sugar machine, and the barrels in the basement.

Five guys had worked in the Cooler in 2011, and the trucks had been lined up twenty deep that morning. Bascom's paid out $230,000 during that Open House. This year they saw half as many trucks and fewer amounts of syrup on them, and only two guys worked. Greg had a chair set up this year. In the afternoon I saw Greg loading six barrels into a van. He exclaimed, "Selling! I don't remember selling last year!"

Joe was helping out in the Cooler, but basically he was just hanging around. Joe was back working on the old sugar machine again while a valve was being replaced on the new one. Joe said they had made thirteen test batches on the new machine. They had used 250 gallons per batch, $100,000 worth of syrup in all.

At lunchtime Bruce was with two other guests, Steve Jones of Maple Grove, and Haven King. I knew Steve Jones, having visited him at Maple Grove the year before and made an unusual connection—we had both been born in the same hospital on Cape Cod and delivered by the same doctor. Steve Jones had a Cape sense of humor. I asked if I could join them and, by way of lightening the situation, he said, "Sure, it's all bullshit anyway."

My visit to the Maple Grove plant and its relative vastness had put the Bascom operation into perspective. I had first stopped in at the gift shop and learned about the history, how Maple Grove started out as a candy operation begun by two women and had grown through successive generations. I saw on a video that each year Maple Grove made 40 million nips of maple syrup, 1.5-ounce containers used in restaurants, and I learned from Jones that they were blended syrup, that during the shortage of 2008 they had to switch over and then didn't go back to pure because of cost. Jones told me, as Bruce had, that the price of syrup was getting too high, that it had nearly doubled since 2007, when it was $10 a quart in the large supermarkets and was $18 now. A major cause for the hike was the shortage in 2008, when everyone had to raise prices. Then the Canadian dollar got stronger. The Canadian dollar had been worth about 70 cents only a few years ago. Jones also wondered, like Bruce, whether there was a market crisis ahead.

He took me on a tour of the factory, and if you could say that a packing line had some magic built into it, then you could say it about this one. Watching it move reminded me of the way I once felt when I saw a spectacular model train set in a toy store, running around the room on a shelf just out of reach. The machines were old, but they ran smoothly; Maple Grove had five mechanics working to maintain them, Jones said. They had two large rotary fillers, each capable of filling 250 jugs per minute—together the systems could fill 500 jugs per minute. We stood in our white coats with our goggles on and watched them stream by like an upbeat boogie-woogie. It was that magical.

Maple Grove was selling to Walmart and to BJ's—they had opened up the big club supermarkets. They were doing $80 million a year in sales, though not all was pure maple. Maple Grove sold blended and fruit syrups too, along with pancake mixes and salad dressings. At that time they were the largest purveyor of crystallized maple candy, with sales of $1 million a year. They seemed far out of reach in the race that Bruce seemed to be running. But that seemed to have changed in May 2012, when I sat down with Bruce, Steve Jones, and

Haven King. One major change was that Jones had retired from Maple Grove. He and Bruce were conferring on possibilities, perhaps a year from now, though they weren't saying much.

Jones said that Maple Grove was backing off on the candy business. "It brings in a million a year, but for B & G [the company that owns Maple Grove] that's a pittance in a six hundred–million dollar company." The candy cost a lot to make anyway, and there was little profit. Additionally, the market was falling off because they now shipped the candy to a warehouse in Pennsylvania and sold it from New Jersey. "People who own gift shops in Vermont don't want to deal with calling New Jersey and talking to someone who doesn't know anything about candy, and then having to pay for shipping. They used to deliver it from St. Johnsbury. No more."

Bruce jumped right on that. "Who's going to take over that supply? We have a packing plant in Brattleboro that's eventually going to move up here." They produced a thousand pounds of candy a day on machines that Arnold Coombs's grandmother had previously owned.

I talked to Haven King, who worked for Maple Grove for many years and was buying syrup now on a contract basis in semiretirement. He had been buying for twenty-eight years. He had worked on quality control at Maple Grove before volunteering to receive barrels. That led to working in the field, visiting producers, and buying syrup, a more enjoyable pursuit. Later, when Maple Grove moved to buying nearly all Canadian syrup and built a warehouse in St. Evariste, near Real Bureau, he helped design the facility.

Of the 2012 season Haven King said he had seen something never observed before—maple trees producing sap in 80° weather.

Bruce said that Haven had picked his pocket a few times. Bruce tried to hire him away at one point. Haven said, "You offered to pay me fifteen cents a pound," and Bruce replied. "You would have had good luck getting that the second year."

They talked about the season, of course. "Below average," was how Steve Jones put it. He thought the Canadians would produce 90 million pounds, and Bruce thought the same. Jones said there were 38 million pounds in the Federation surplus.

"Thirty-seven," Bruce said.

The crop in Somerset County was good, Bruce said. There were sixty to seventy trailer loads on the Golden Road and at St. Aurelie. "Most of it's downstairs," he said. Which was not literally true, only fifteen loads were there now, but figuratively true: much of it would be downstairs before summer ended.

As was Bruce's way, he cajoled and was going back and forth with Steve Jones—the games traders played.

Bruce said, "You do about twelve million pounds a year up there."

Steve said they would be doing fewer. Then he said, "So do you."

Haven added, "When you count the sugar."

"That's probably true," Bruce said.

Had I heard what I thought I'd heard? They were both doing 12 million pounds a year when it came to buying and processing pure maple syrup?

So that was it, then. Bruce had reached his goal. He was no longer in the second tier. Bruce was in the first tier now, an equal to Maple Grove. That is, if it wasn't all bullshit.

THE NEXT MORNING, when I ran into Bruce, he said with urgency, "Robert Poirier is here, have you seen him?" The most honored guest. We went looking and found Robert standing with his son-in-law in a tubing class.

First we had lunch. Bruce talked about supply, saying, "In the next three weeks there will be no syrup anywhere."

Robert looked about, at the piles of food on the table, the many people milling about, and said, "Bruce, you must have spent ten thousand dollars on this."

"Probably more than that," Bruce replied. "But people come here and they come back six months later. Last year they spent a hundred and twenty-five thousand dollars both days in the store."

Bruce said he had so much on his mind these days, he was getting forgetful. "I paid a hundred thousand dollars to one producer and didn't even remember I had done it."

Robert smiled and said it was true. He then asked Bruce if he wanted him to buy 600 drums from the producer named Landry, the one who had 167,000 taps, but Bruce didn't answer. He then got up to talk to someone and Robert said, "Bruce is too hard. Sometimes he says he wants to buy syrup, and then after it's bought he says he shouldn't have bought it."

Robert asked, "Why does Bruce expand so much?"

"I think he wants to prove he can do it better."

Robert smiled. "The first year with me, they had just the small cooler. We sent eight loads, four or five hundred drums. Second year, twelve loads. Third year, eighteen loads."

After lunch Bruce took Robert on a tour. I tagged along, and we were joined by Cindy Finck, who worked with Arnold Coombs in Brattleboro. Cindy grew up in the same town as Arnold and, as a teenager, worked for Bob Coombs. Now she had a sizeable job—Cindy was responsible for selling the maple sugar.

We went to the bottling room first of all, and Bruce showed Robert how the syrup could be dialed in according to grade and then pumped through the tanks and filters on the way to the bottling lines. "They are running forty quarts a minute," Bruce said. "They could run eighty quarts a minute and fill two trailer trucks in eight hours."

Bruce led Robert through the Middle Cooler and toward the sugar room. Cindy Finck trailed behind. She seemed surprised. "Arnold always told me the sugar plant was top secret," she said.

We climbed the stairs, and Bruce explained the process, the cooking with steam and the use of vacuum to draw off heat and liquid. Then the second stage downstairs, where the sugar cooled and dried. Finally the third stage on the bottom floor, where the sugar was screened and put into barrels.

"It takes about two and a half hours to make a batch," Bruce said.

Robert kept looking at the parts and ran his hands over the bolts and fastenings. Bruce explained that a valve on the second floor was faulty and would be replaced at a cost of $35,000. Robert shook his head. The machine would shut down for a couple of weeks.

Cindy said she didn't like hearing that the machine would be shut down. She had been talking to some companies about huge orders. Frito-Lay was considering buying 1.5 million pounds of maple sugar. General Mills was interested.

She said that during the economic downturn the interest in maple sugar did not drop. "Chocolatiers are on a run to use maple sugar," she said. She and Arnold were trying out recipes.

Bruce led us to the room with the silos, seven of them that each hold 8000 gallons, about $250,000 worth of syrup. They were holding tanks, Bruce said. They pumped the barrels into the silos, and the syrup went straight into the filtering presses and bottling units.

We went down into the New Cooler, where Bruce described the well-planned dimensions. He said there were eight bays on each side of the basement, sixteen in all, each set off by a support post. If a bay was packed correctly, it would hold 500,000 pounds of syrup, or twelve trailer loads. Even more precisely, each single row of barrels, four high and all the way back to the wall, represented a single trailer load.

"Eight million pounds altogether, in the whole cooler," Bruce said.

There was no response, just a thoughtful moment. Robert was smiling.

"I will be able to fill this cooler in five years. I don't have the money now."

But maybe the bank would help him out, he said. Maybe give him some more gas. So he could ride a little more, a little further.

EPILOGUE

IN JUNE OF 2012, in the early evening, I walked by the sugarhouse to Bruce's house, the stone house. The flower gardens, tended by Deb Rhoades, were in full bloom. The late-day sun was lighting up the tall grass, while swallows flew over the seed heads, chasing bugs. Bruce was waiting on the patio, taking in the scene. "Nice piece of real estate," he said.

I had come to talk about the season. It had been a season of contradictions, and at the center was the paradox of expansion: the Federation had set up the ideal scenario for expansion in the United States, which had brought new players and increased tap counts, which could potentially increase supply in a season other than this one, a supply that Bruce was happy to direct into his Coolers. But it was also a supply that could possibly weaken the Federation, which had stabilized the industry, and bring a surplus to the market that could cause a crash in prices, resulting in a fallout of new producers. And round it went, during this strangest of sugar seasons: expansion was good but expansion was perilous.

"There was a discussion at Leader at the director's meeting last week," Bruce said. "Everybody unanimously thinks this expansion is a bubble. They think it might be good for

261

another two years, another five years, but they think at some point there will be too much maple syrup and the barrel price will fall.

"The only reason it hasn't dropped is because of Federation support in Canada. But at some point, I keep saying this over and over, they won't be able to control it because the Americans will be making too much syrup. It's the same old song—eventually supply and demand comes into play, and you've got to sell the stuff. The biggest thing in the maple industry in the future is going to be sales and marketing, getting people to buy it. Always has been, always will be."

In what may have been a counterdevelopment, the exchange rate had made a dramatic shift over the last three weeks in favor of the US dollar, and Canadian syrup was now cheaper than US syrup. "But it's too late for me," Bruce said. "I've spent most of my capital." Bascom's had taken in forty-nine trailer loads in May, with six trailer loads in a day and a half in June. A couple had yet to arrive—loads pieced together by Michael Parker west of Lake Champlain and Erwin Gingerich in Ohio. Bruce now had 6 million pounds stored away.

I wanted to know if the bulk supply in the United States had all been purchased, as Bruce had predicted those many times.

"There are some people holding or speculating, but most are holding for their own markets. They need syrup for fall foliage or some for Christmas for their stores. But I would say that ninety-five percent of the bulk syrup in the United States is gone. There are no complete loads now anywhere in the United States."

Yet there would be plenty of supply available, thanks to the Canadians. "The real cold areas made a lot of syrup during that cold spell when we were done," Bruce said. "Everybody stopped here around March twenty, gave up the ghost and pulled the spouts, but up north a couple hundred miles they waited it out and made quite a lot of syrup.

"We had the worst sugaring season I've ever seen. We broke records in the middle of March and then we were done by March twenty. There have been years when we haven't made hardly any syrup until March twenty, but this year we were totally done. The season basically lasted ten days. I don't know anybody who has documented a sugar season that's as bad. It got up to seventy and eighty degrees for almost three weeks. In the middle of March the tadpoles were out in the pond in front of the sugarhouse. They don't usually come out until the fifteenth to the twentieth of April, but this time they were out on the twentieth of March. And then we had that real cold spell, and it did them all in."

The USDA report was issued a week after Bruce and I talked. The maple syrup crop in the United States in 2012 was 20,988,000 pounds, or 1,908,000 gallons. Bruce's prediction wasn't so far off after all, and perhaps it was only the expansion in the United States that caused him to under-estimate by a million pounds. The report from the Federation followed. The crop in Quebec was 96,110,000 pounds, made by 7400 producers.

I ALSO VISITED David Marvin in June, and we walked in the sugarbush at Butternut Mountain. Production at David's sugarhouse was consistent with that of northern Vermont. After shutting down during the hot weather, when they had dumped sap because it looked like cottage cheese, they be-gan producing again on April 4 after the weather turned cold. The syrup lightened and then darkened again. Butter-nut Mountain produced nearly 4000 gallons.

Technology had accommodated them, and what David suspected turned out to be true: "We learned things about how to adjust to temperature and that we can have sap runs on temperature differentials with high vacuum." But there were limitations. "Technology won't overcome warm nights in the middle of the season," he said. Warm nights caused the buds to develop, and when the buds swelled, the sap turned buddy. In David's experience in 2012, every barrel produced after March 19 had a buddy flavor.

"Everything?" I asked.

"Everything. There was a lot of buddy syrup, and now we have to decide what to do with that. In the future, when we have these warm periods, we will have to find markets for buddy syrup." One way to use it was to make sugar, as the buddy flavor disappeared during the process, but the dry sugar market could not absorb all the buddy syrup in 2012.

David also had concerns about expansion in the industry. "I've heard of an investor who wants to buy a three-million-dollar property in northern Vermont and have a hundred-thousand tap operation in which he will haul sap sixty miles over a mountain. That tells me the industry is expanding." Which meant that they needed more markets. "You can say you'll increase the markets, but the markets should be increased first."

Interest in sugaring hadn't diminished. "What is it that they say about farmers: when the going gets tough, the tough get growing? Capital is going into maple. Dairy farmers and others are investing. It's a bright spot."

David laughed at the irony that, from his perspective, "This was a perfect season. If it was another big year, there would have been too much syrup and a downward pressure on prices." He would have bought the total crops from all of his 375 producers, and they too were expanding.

Of course, David was expanding too. His new building was nearing completion. While we walked up the road in the sugarbush, by the Cherry Corner and by the boulder where there were brick fragments from an arch of a century ago, David said Bruce was no longer in the second tier, that he was at the level of Maple Grove.

"And we will soon be too," David said.

DURING THE SUMMER of 2012 events were taking place that made the maple syrup industry a world story. Those stories didn't break until the end of the year, with the arrests of suspects in Canada for the theft of 6 million pounds of syrup from a Federation warehouse in Saint-Louis-de-Blandford, north of Montreal. The Federation had been renting the warehouse to store surplus from the 2011 crop while they built a third facility of their own.

The discovery of the theft was made on July 30, when an auditor hired to examine the supply found empty barrels and barrels filled with water. The Federation reported the theft to the Sûreté du Québec, the provincial police, and a wide investigation followed, with interviews of nearly 300 people, tracing the syrup to companies in Quebec, New Brunswick, Ontario, and the United States.

The investigation led to a company named SK Export in Kedgwick, New Brunswick. A sugarmaker named Etienne St. Pierre had started the business in 2002 and focused his marketing plan on Quebec syrup, believing that the Federation

rules didn't apply to him in New Brunswick. He ran advertisements in Quebec, promising confidentiality. In the beginning he sold primarily to Maple Grove, later branching out
to other companies, including Bascom's. The Federation had
been battling with St. Pierre over the years, running undercover investigations and demanding that he pay damages,
but he had ignored them.

Most of the stories played upon the surprising fact that
there was such a thing as a global strategic reserve for
maple syrup. The word "cartel" was often used, with comparisons to OPEC, pointing out that a barrel of maple syrup was
worth more than a barrel of oil. The stories described sticky-
fingered thieves and hot syrup. A hilarious story aired on
The Daily Show with Jon Stewart, a comic sketch that likened
the Federation to a drug cartel and maple syrup to cocaine—
an innocent reporter tried maple syrup, despite his reservations, then followed a path of addiction and crime, stooping
even to sucking sap out of tapholes, so hopelessly caught up
in the pursuit of syrup that he missed getting the big story.

A story with some equally funny but true moments appeared in *Bloomberg Businessweek* under the title, "The
Great Canadian Maple Syrup Heist." This story, written by
Brendan Borrell, described the dispute between Etienne St.
Pierre and the Federation and how St. Pierre's salty assistant, Julienne Bosse, took a more confrontational approach
than merely ignoring demands: "She scribbled her response
on a subpoena and faxed it back to the Federation. 'F— you
gang of A-holes,' she wrote. 'Ha! Ha! Ha! . . . We will keep
buying maple syrup forever.'" In another communication, after the Federation used a wrong address for SK Export, she
corrected them by writing, "7348 Rue Funck You." When of-

ficers from the Sûreté du Québec arrived in September 2012 with a search warrant, Bosse "pretended to wipe her derriere with it, gave the police the bird, and locked the side door." This loyal employee grabbed the keys to the warehouse from St. Pierre and "tucked them into her ample bosom." All this, Borrell wrote, while also making chocolate maple leaves and "melt-in-your-mouth maple meringues for sale in the gift shop."

Later that day, after a visit to a judge, according to Borrell, police pried open the warehouse doors and found a million dollars worth of syrup. Everything was seized the following day, including St. Pierre's forklift and his list of suppliers and customers. He told police that many of the barrels came from a man named Richard Vallieres, "one of Quebec's most notorious 'barrel rollers,' an unauthorized middleman who ran afoul of the Federation in the past and paid thousands of dollars in fines." On December 18 Vallieres was arrested and charged with conspiring with five others to steal the syrup. In all, twenty-two suspects were charged, including St. Pierre.

The story went on to say a Quebec television station reported that "at least 70 truckloads of stolen syrup have already made it to three distributors in the U.S., including Bascom Maple Farms in New Hampshire, one of St. Pierre's clients and the largest maple supplier in the U.S. Bruce Bascom says he fully cooperated with the Sûreté du Québec and they have ended their inquiries, but he declined to answer whether the company had purchased any stolen syrup. Two Vermont companies that reportedly purchased the syrup, Maple Grove Farms and Highland Sugarworks, did not respond to requests for interviews."

Many other news stories reported the arrests, including the arrest of a man named Stephan Darveau, who sold syrup to Highland Sugarworks and to Bruce Bascom.

After reading the *Bloomberg Businessweek* story in January I went to talk with Bruce. He was about to leave for the maple conference in Verona, and Sam and David were waiting in the car, but Bruce talked for a little while. He said that during the summer the Sûreté du Québec came to speak with him, along with an official from Homeland Security, because the syrup crossed the international border. "I bought a lot of syrup from Darveau," Bruce said, "but I had no idea it was stolen syrup. Darveau said he didn't know, either." He said he also bought syrup from SK Export.

"Maple Grove had loads that they have to return or are contesting returning. Highland has some too. But we don't have any. It's been sold. All that syrup is in people's stomachs."

Regarding Bruce's statement about Maple Grove, on May 2, 2013, the *Montreal Gazette* reported that the Sûreté du Québec and Vermont police visited the Maple Grove factory with search warrants on October 19, 2012. Maple Grove allegedly purchased multiple truckloads of stolen syrup. According to the report the company representative confirmed that the firm had bought syrup from Richard Vallieres in the summer of 2012 at a price "substantially below normal rates" as set out by the Quebec Federation of Maple Syrup Producers. Maple Grove later issued a statement that they had "purchased the syrup in good faith and had no reason to believe that it was coming from Quebec or that it may have been stolen. The prices paid were consistent with normal commercial prices for maple syrup purchased from sources outside of Quebec."

I soon left for South America for a few months to teach at a university. Bruce later informed me by e-mail that when the authorities had come to talk with him, "I gave them a tour, and no Darveau syrup existed in my inventory at that time. Within a couple of weeks my law firm in Montreal received a note from the Quebec police thanking me for our cooperation and saying that, as far as they were concerned, all inquiries had ended."

Regarding the Darveau syrup, Bruce wrote that he purchased syrup from a Vermont corporation called ESD-LLC, owned by Stephan Darveau, of Sherbrooke, Quebec. Bruce had paid by wire to a Vermont bank, and the syrup was delivered. "I was told many times that the money received by ESD in Vermont was paid to an Ontario company, which in turn purchased the syrup from Ontario and New Brunswick producers and syrup dealers. I was rather far removed from the initial purchase, being the third or fourth hand to the first transaction."

In May 2013 Bruce received an e-mail from his lawyer in Montreal that there had been a determination that the stolen syrup had not been sold at a significantly lower price in the United States, and this meant those buyers could not be held criminally responsible. Investigations were ongoing. Trials were expected to take place in 2014.

I also called David Marvin after reading the *Bloomsberg Businessweek* story. Marvin was also about to leave for the Verona conference and would be giving the keynote speech. He was planning to talk about expansion and to make the recommendation that producers make the effort to promote pure maple syrup in the cause against artificial ("that way we all win"). He intended to talk about the Federation pricing scheme, which he thought unsustainable. He also wanted to say something about the stolen syrup and how, in his opinion, it may have affected prices on the market. He had seen bids that he thought were completely unprofitable, and now he thought he knew the basis for them. "In the past when you talked about black-market syrup, everyone was skeptical. With stolen, it's a whole different perspective."

David thought the discovery of the thefts could ultimately be a positive development, because government authorities would now be looking more closely.

When I called Steve Jones he agreed. Jones had been on the advisory board of the Federation when he was a vice president at Maple Grove. "This will weed those people out," he said. "It will make anyone nervous who is wanting to play in the black market. Now, with the thefts, the full force of the Quebec authorities has come into play. And the border patrol."

David Marvin was rankled by all the funny stories, saying, "We look like buffoons, with all the silly jokes. Cartel, sticky situation, hot syrup. I say to everyone, let me tell you about it. It's not a joke."

The story in *Bloomberg Businessweek* came to a climax with questions about the Federation and whether it would survive in the long term. It noted that in 2008 Quebec claimed eighty percent of world maple syrup production, but that in 2011 its share had dropped to seventy-one percent, "as U.S. states and Canadian provinces without quotas have risen to supply cheaper syrup." The story mentioned that Senator Charles Schumer had inserted a provision in the Farm Bill to provide grants to farmers to promote the indus-try—New York had 280 million tappable trees, three times

more than Quebec. Simon Trepanier, acting director of the
Federation, and others were watching closely. "'We are not
idiots,' he says, adding that in his mind climate change ultimately will tip the syrup scales in favor of his countrymen."

He may be right. A few months later, on May 9, 2013, the
level of carbon dioxide in the atmosphere crossed the
threshold of 400 parts per million throughout an entire day
for the very first time. The reading was taken at the NASA
observatory in Mauna Loa, Hawaii. This promised to be a
dangerous threshold, with warmer temperatures, greater
storms, higher sea levels, and global disruption on the not-
so-distant horizon. According to reports, 400 parts per million carbon dioxide in the atmosphere had not been
achieved since the Pliocene epoch, 3 million years ago, when
temperatures had been three to five degrees warmer and
sea levels sixty to eighty feet higher.

During the summer of 2013, when leaf cover in North
American forests extracted 10 billion tons of carbon from
the atmosphere, levels of carbon would fall below 400 parts
per million, but that would be the final time, some reports
stated.

That was, of course, unless governments took action to
reduce the use of coal and fossil fuels and promote the
development of clean technologies, but so far the world's
governments, especially the US government, in the country
most responsible for the rise in the level of atmospheric carbon, had refused to take necessary action. It seemed highly
unlikely they would, even though economic disruptions
promised to be far greater later on if they didn't.

Maybe the maple syrup industry can speak for the rest of
the country, to the rest of the country, for it is a bellwether,

this earliest of agricultural traditions, the first to be taught to settlers by Native Americans, this pursuit that relies on sensitive fluctuations in temperature, as the sun advances north and the trees freeze by night.

Postscript

THE WINTER OF 2013 was a cold winter, more like that of 2011. The crop report for maple syrup issued by the USDA in June 2013 listed production nationwide at 3.25 million gallons, 35,750,000 pounds, an increase of seventy percent over 2012. The state of Vermont produced forty percent of that crop.

Bruce Bascom said the US crop was the greatest in over seventy-five years. He thought the crop was underreported and was possibly as much as twenty-five percent greater.

The number of taps was up in every region except for Maine, which remained the same.

According to the USDA the average season in the northeastern region lasted about two weeks longer than it had in 2012.

ACKNOWLEDGMENTS

I FEEL LUCKY that the kind of writing I do puts me in touch with such admirable people and worthy endeavors. I know I will miss mentioning some of the names of the people who talked to me during these three years of research, and I apologize for that. I had many conversations in passing in many places, often with people who didn't know what I was up to. My thanks and gratitude to all of those who informed me along the way about sugarmaking, about the life of trees, about weather and climate and many facets of the business of making maple syrup.

I thank Bruce Bascom first, for his openness and willingness to talk, going all the way back to our first phone call about the Asian longhorned beetle, which didn't play a large role in this book but did open up the doorway to a conversation with Bruce about the maple syrup business. Bruce spent hundreds of hours with me, traveling and talking at the sugarhouse and in formal interviews. He also sent me to and advised me to talk with all the right people, under the belief that there is much more to the maple syrup industry than people realize.

Thank you also to Kevin Bascom for his explanations of the processes and for time in the woods. Thank you to David

Bascom for letting me ride along and for answering my questions.

I owe Peter and Deb Rhoades a special thank you for the many times you hosted us and talked with us about making syrup, for the time spent at your remarkable sugarhouse, and for those times spent in the woods, which was my secret reason for writing this book.

Thank you to David Marvin for the many walks in the woods and times at the sugarhouse and at the plant in Morrisville and for informing me and answering my many questions in person and by e-mail and phone. You are a dedicated and passionate spokesman for the cause of all things maple.

A special thanks to Alvin Clark, who became my friend in the course of this research, beginning with our trip to the opening of the "Seasons of Change" exhibit and during the many other things we did together, including, especially, times at your sugarhouse.

My thanks also to Dr. Timothy Perkins, director of the Proctor Maple Center, with whom I had several conversations, who hosted me at the Proctor Center, who sent documents, and who answered my many questions, and from whom I also learned a great deal via his public talks to sugarmakers. Though he doesn't appear directly in these pages, his contributions inform this book.

Thank you also to Mel Tyree for hosting me and for his conversations about the sap hydraulics and biomechanics of the maple tree.

I want to thank another person who does not appear as directly in these pages as he might have but who also thoroughly informs this book: Arnold Coombs, the sales manager at Bascom Maple Farms and someone who has spent a lifetime in the maple business. Thank you to Arnold for our many conversations.

A thank you to Robert Poirier for hosting me in Quebec and for our many talks and for taking me out into the woods—for conveying your passion for what you do. If certain wishes come true, then you will be able to read this book in your own language some day.

The following people were generous in offering information, advice, their stories and their time, or even just a few helpful words: Liz Bascom, Brad Bascom, Greg Bascom, Judy Snow, Nancy Fowler, Sam Bascom, David Bascom, Crystal Bascom, Lorna Bascom, Brooke Adams, Steve Anderson, Mike Bennett, Pascale Boivin, Henry Brennaman, Rhota Brennaman, Real Bureau, Guy Bolduc, Joseph Brent, Jeremy Bushway, Martha Carlson, Bill Clark, David Clark, Fraser Cooper-Ellis, Dan Crocker, Doug Edwards, Anton Elbers, Michael Farmer, Michael Farrell, Brian Tedrow, Cindy Finck, Nancy Fortin, Fernand Gagne, Maurice Gagne, Gary Gaudette, Erwin Gingerich, Serge Gauvin, Anne-Marie Granger-Godbout, Gordon Gowan, Alexandre Gregoire, Bruno Guay, J. Mark Harran, Kevin Harrison, Kathy Harrison, Clarisse Hart, Mark Hastings, Gwen Hinman, George Hodskins, Joseph James, Steve Jones, Haven King, Daniel Lalanne, Vital Lariviere, Nick Lemieux, Doris LeVasseur, Tari Lyndaker, Mario Maheaux, Michel Maheaux, Ira Marvin, Gary Merrill, Lorraine Merrill, Tim Merton, Greg Minard, Mark Mitchell, Claude Morrissette, Suzanne Nadeau, Fernand Nadeau, Frederic Nadeau, Takashi Oshio, Jean-Claude Pare, Michael Parker, Robyn Pearl, Gerald Pease, Mim Pendleton, George Putnam, Marty Rabtoy, Pat Richards, Doug Rose, Carole

Rouleau, Kevin Ruane, Joe Russo, Dave St. Aubin, Ben Shepard, Richard Sipitowsky, Randy Sprague, Gardner Stetson, Steve Taylor, Peter Thomson, Jeremy Thompson, Dan Weed, Jennifer Weimer, Marty Wendel, Steve Wilbur, Tim Wilmot, Michelle York, and Tom Zaffis.

Thank you to Professor Barry Rock of the University of New Hampshire for weighing in on some of the issues of climate change discussed in this book and for your longstanding work on this issue.

I want to thank Richard Polonsky for his role in creating "Seasons of Change" and for including Alvin Clark, for inviting me to attend, for answering my questions, and for permission to quote from his letter.

My thanks to Lorraine Merrill, commissioner of agriculture in New Hampshire, for her thoughts on the maple sugaring industry.

Thank you to Lawrence Elworth, agricultural counselor to the administrator of the US Environmental Protection Agency, for conversation and for articles, and also to Mike Moats for referring me to him.

Thanks to Alexis Hauk for alerting me in 2009 to the situation of the Asian longhorned beetle.

Thank you to Eric Bascom Jr. for providing his book, *Up Where the House Burned Down*, which gave me an understanding of the history of the Bascom family.

Thank you to Richard Todd for his advice and encouragement in the planning and structure of this book, as it made such a difference.

Thank you to my colleagues and students at Emerson College for their support and encouragement, and to Lee Pelton for the granting of time to work on this book.

Thank you to my students at Universidad Nacional de Colombia Sede Bogotá, for their support and encouragement; thank you also to Diana Rojas, codirector of the Centro de Estudios de Estadounidenses de Colombia. Additionally, I owe a debt of gratitude to the Fulbright Foundation for the award of a fellowship to teach in Colombia, which also allowed me time to write drafts of this book.

Many thanks to my agent, Regina Ryan, for getting behind this project and supporting it so wholeheartedly and for her guidance and advice.

A special note of thanks to Lissa Warren, my editor and more at Da Capo Press, for your interest, energy, enthusiasm, guidance, and support.

Importantly, thank you and thank you to Isha Contway and Liz Whynott, to you and yours. And, as always, my gratitude forever to Kathy Olsen, who was there and into this from the very first day, who listened to it all over and over, fell in love with the sugarhouses just like I did, read every draft, walked with me and supported this effort every step of the way, while together and apart.